THE LITERATURE
OF THE SECOND
SELF

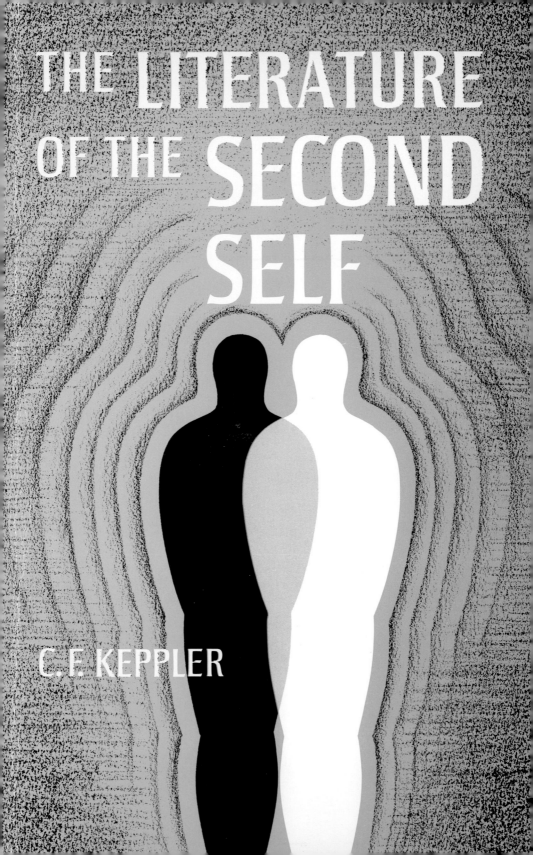

C. F. KEPPLER

THE LITERATURE OF THE
SECOND SELF

THE
LITERATURE o

THE SECOND SELF

C. F. Keppler

THE UNIVERSITY OF ARIZONA PRESS
Tucson, Arizona

About the Author . . .

CARL FRANCIS KEPPLER'S interest in the literary concept of the
second self first came to the fore in his doctoral dissertation at
the University of Michigan in 1956. Since then he has published
a novel entitled *The Other,* which centers in the unique relationship between the first self and the second self, embodying the theme
of which *The Literature of the Second Self* is a critical study.

A world traveler, author, and critic, Keppler published his first
story in 1928. In 1949 he joined the English Department of the
University of Arizona. He holds a B.A. from Princeton University,
an M.A. from the University of Arizona, and a Ph.D. from the
University of Michigan.

THE UNIVERSITY OF ARIZONA PRESS

Copyright © 1972
The Arizona Board of Regents
All Rights Reserved
Manufactured in the U.S.A.

I. S. B. N.-0-8165-0304-4(cl)
I. S. B. N.-0-8165-0351-6(p)
L. C. No. 71-163012

TO MY WIFE

Contents

Preface

When I first began work on this subject, many years ago, it was my plan to study the figure commonly known as the *Doppelgänger* or Double[1] as he appears in the work of certain nineteenth-century English writers of fiction, and to make use of him to establish a certain thesis about these writers. By painful degrees, as I worked, I came to realize that I did not really know what I meant by "Double," but had simply always assumed that I knew; that as a result I was sliding about haphazardly between notions that were far from identical with one another, and that the whole edifice of my argument was being erected on such a sandy and shifting foundation. Not only this, but in restudying the writings of others on the subject I could find nothing to serve as a guide or starting point. It appeared that all of us — all of us who had discussed or were attempting to discuss the matter — were placing the cart before the horse, were trying to use the Double of creative literature as an interpretive tool before knowing very much about who and what he is or how he functions, or before examining in a very comprehensive way the literature of the world in which he appears.

It was for this reason that I turned to the task represented by the present work: the humbler and more elementary, but it seemed to me more necessary, task of first getting as fully acquainted with the figure of the Double as a single work would make possible. In it I have avoided any attempt to use this figure in order to shed light on certain works of literature, but instead have used relevant works of literature, as broad a cross-section of this literature as possible, in order to shed light on the figure of the Double, in the hope of providing a groundwork that has not yet existed for more specialized studies. I have not set out with the purpose of proving any particular thesis about what the Double "means,"[2] but have tried to let my conclusions about his meaning emerge from the study of what he is, what he is like, and what he does. The task chiefly undertaken here is that of introducing the Double to readers who have doubtless encountered him before (he is so important a figure it would be almost impossible not to have done so) but are not quite sure where; readers who would like to know more about him and be able to recognize him when they meet him again; readers who would like to have some idea of the extraordinary extent and variety of the literature in which he appears: that which will be referred to in this study as "the literature of the second self."

Such an undertaking involves certain problems, and I should like to explain briefly how I have tried to deal with them. Outstanding among them is that of choice of material. Naturally this choice has had to be limited by my own limitations, and doubtless the better part of valor would have been to do as I originally planned, and to concentrate on that field with which I am most familiar. To have done so, however, would have been to defeat the purpose of piecing together as complete a picture of the Double as possible, of seeing him in his full variety; in no one author, or period, or literature, or language, are all aspects of him represented, and for a general introduction all aspects are necessary. Any such work that failed to consider, in however amateurish a fashion, such writers as E. T. A. Hoffmann and Hermann Hesse, or Victor Hugo, or above all Dostoyevsky, would be more a model of effrontery than of scholarly caution. On the other hand, to include all examples of creative literature in which the Double has played a part would be to reduce the introduction to no more than a list of titles.

What I have attempted to do is to strike a compromise, and to spread the net widely without spreading it too thinly. With the exception of the chapter on the Twin Brother, who is found mainly in the ancient literature of the East and Near East, I have confined myself to European and American literature since the end of the eighteenth century; in other words to the period since the beginning of the Romantic Movement, a period which has been particularly rich in the production of Doubles.

Wherever possible I have taken my illustrations from English and American sources, partly because I am more competent to deal with these than with the work of other authors, still more because so far as the Double is concerned it is just these examples that have received the least critical attention.[3] By the same token I have tended to avoid examples from the German *Romantik* (with the exception of Hoffmann, whom no treatment of the Double can afford to neglect), chiefly because such critical studies as have been made of the subject have concentrated mainly on these few writers. But otherwise, whenever it has seemed necessary to do so, I have not hesitated to venture, hopefully and vulnerably, both into literatures of which I have no specialist's knowledge and also into literatures, like the Russian, in which I have no familiarity with the language and am wholly dependent on translations by others.

Even limiting oneself to works written since the turn of the nineteenth century, however, one is still faced with an enormous number of examples, and I have made no effort to include them all. What I have undertaken is the analysis of a certain literary phenomenon, not a bibliography of the works that embody it. Frequently cases which, though excellent in themselves, merely repeat characteristics of those already covered have been omitted or simply touched on in passing, while, on the other hand, cases which are not very adequate examples have been included, at least briefly, for what they tell us by their very inadequacies. In general, in each chapter, I have worked from the less adequate examples to the more, letting the former prepare the way for the latter, and attempting to treat each of the works selected, especially the major ones, in such a way as to be understandable to the reader whether or not he is directly familiar with it. In no case, however, is the summary given merely a summary; primarily it is an explanation of how and why the work in question is illustrative of this or that point about the Double.

In order to give as much space as possible to these examples, I have for the most part omitted any consideration of critical commentary about them. Many of the works used are extremely famous, and often the criticism about a single one of them, such as *Faust,* constitutes a small literature in itself. In many cases, especially those outside English and American literature, my ignoring of critical commentary is due in large part to my ignorance of it; but even in the cases where I am better equipped, any attempt to take account of all relevant writings about the literature with which I am dealing would necessitate reducing the latter to a mere handful of works, and would make it impossible to rest this study of the Double on a broad rather than a narrow basis of illustrative material. In many cases I am aware that my interpretation is either at odds with, or partly or wholly in agreement with (it can hardly escape being one or the other), those offered by various other critics; I have cited certain examples of such discord or harmony, but cannot possibly cite all. Wherever a debt exists I have acknowledged it; beyond that I am not concerned with whether or not similar or dissimilar interpretations have been advanced before, but only with whether or not the particular interpretations that I have cited seem to me sound, and serve my purpose of illuminating the subject of the Double.

One type of critical commentary that I have omitted altogether, and this not simply to save space but because I believe it to be entirely irrelevant to the purpose of my study, is any evidence, pro or con, as to whether the authors of these works intended to incorporate Doubles in them. Let me make my position clear on this much-worried point. There are two main bodies of evidence that can be used for the study of any work of art. One is the artist's intention regarding it; the other is the work itself. The former is never known to us save at second or third hand, and even if it could be known with certainty it would still have no more necessary bearing on the content of the work than an artist's intention to produce an immortal masterpiece would have on the artistic merit of the result; it is a matter of biographical rather than of critical interest. The latter, the work itself, is direct and solid knowledge, always arguable as to interpretation but always available for such interpretation.[4] It is the latter evidence solely with which we shall be concerned.

Nevertheless, with all these limitations and exclusions, the body of material to be covered is still vast in scope, and raises the question of how most economically and effectively to deal with it. The historical approach is the one that has been used for the most part by other writers on the subject, but actually, except for so narrowly concentrated a study as that of Wilhelmine Krauss,[5] it is not so logical as it might seem. The Double has appeared with greatest frequency during the nineteenth and twentieth centuries, whether because during this period writers of creative literature have been influenced by psychologists or (as seems more probable) because both writers and psychologists have been giving expression to a greatly increased sense of the complexity of the human mind; but this is about the only historical generalization it is safe to make. Except for this, one of the strangest things about this strange figure is that he seems to have no history whatever. Even when we can hazard a guess about influences — Jean Paul's on Hoffmann, Hoffmann's on Poe, Hoffmann's and Poe's on Dostoyevsky — it is only a guess, and the influence, if it is there, is not very significant. The more one sees of the Double in literature the more it appears that he is the product not of tradition but of individual experience, and a new experience on the part of each writer who has made use of him.

The approach that I have followed, therefore, is not a history of the Double, which would force the material into a mold it does not fit, but in the older and broader sense of the word an "anatomy" of the Double: an attempt to get acquainted with him by seeing him from different angles, to analyze in a systematic way the wide variety of his aspects and moods and functions, and on the basis of this analysis to take up at last the question of why he seems to have come into being and so persistently to have remained there.

Because of the variety of material dealt with, all titles in both text and index have been italicized for simplicity, regardless of the length of works they represent. In the notes and bibliography the usual distinction has been observed.

Acknowledgments

The number of obligations that I should properly acknowledge, to the friends who have furnished words of advice, correction, and information, would be far too great to list in detail. I should like, however, to express my particular thanks to the English Department and the administration of the University of Arizona for granting me the various leaves of absence during which the research for and writing of this book have been done; to the staffs of the University of Arizona Library and the British Museum Reading Room for invaluable aid in tracking down source material; to the University of Arizona Press, through which publication has been effected; to Dr. Gerhard Adler of London for suggestions regarding the psychological background literature on the subject of the second self; and to Professor Jean Beck of the University of Arizona for his generous and patient assistance in the translation of several difficult German passages.

C. F. KEPPLER

1

The Nature of the Second Self

When the nymph Echo pined away of unrequited love, she left behind her more than a voice crying in the wilderness; she left both a moral and a mystery. It is the latter, the mystery, that will constitute the subject of this study. Partly there is the mystery of Echo's own case, of the voice which can now merely repeat in borrowed tone and words whatever is said to it, and which therefore becomes identical with the voice it echoes while still remaining the voice of its no-longer-existent owner. But far more famous as an example of this mystery is the sequel to Echo's story: that of the beautiful boy who in his vanity broke her heart, and paid for his vanity with the fact of his vanity, and in his enchantment with his own face faded away in his turn, not into a voice but into a flower. The face that enchanted him, as either boy or flower, was of course his own; yet gazing up out of the fountain's surface into the down-gazing face above it, desired as object by the other as subject, it was *not* his own; indeed the separateness between these faces is no less important to the legend of Narcissus than is their sameness. What we are to deal with, then, is the mystery of a contradiction, of simultaneous distinction and identity, of an inescapable two that are at the same time an indisputable one.

Today things like reflected sound waves or light waves are no longer the mysteries they were for us in our childhood, or for adults in the cultural childhood that produced such stories as that of Echo and Narcissus. Nevertheless in one form at least the mystery of simultaneous unity and duality has lived on, and remains as mysterious as ever. This is a figure which has appeared repeatedly throughout the creative literature of the world, best known by his German name *Doppelgänger,* or in English-speaking countries by the name "Double." His appearances have been sporadic, but they have been on the whole extraordinarily frequent, dating from beginnings so early that we must guess at their antiquity, and continuing up to the present day. Furthermore, while as an impossible blender of opposites he is of course a fantasy, his role has not (as is often supposed) been that of a crude spine-chiller like the specters of Gothic Romance; he is far too difficult and demanding a figure, demanding of both writer and reader, to be included for a cheap thrill.[1] He has played his part in some of the greatest works by some of the greatest authors, and almost never has this been a minor part, for there is something about him, for good or ill, that makes him tend to dominate whatever situation he is placed in. Strange he is bound to be: a figure of the shadowy unknown, retaining in his most benign aspects some of the uncanniness of shadow land. Yet he is neither a mere trick nor a mere convention; on the contrary, from the persistence of his appearances he would seem to be a product of very considerable importance to the writers of world literature; he would seem, in other words, to have his roots deeply fastened in the soil of human thought and experience.

Before we can examine these roots, however, we must know what this figure is, and the necessary first step is to decide what he is to be called. This may seem a trifling matter, but certainly part of the vagueness that has characterized such discussion of the figure as there has been is attributable to inadequate nomenclature. Neither the name *Doppelgänger,* coined by Jean Paul Richter in the late eighteenth century for his novel *Siebenkäs,*[2] nor its English rendering as "Double," is very suitable to describe the subject of this study. One difficulty is that both words inescapably suggest duplication, either physical or psychological or both. But physical duplication, as we shall see in a moment, is not necessarily a feature of the relationship we are setting out to examine; and psychological duplication, duplication in character, cannot possibly be a feature of it, since such duplication would result in no relationship at all, but merely an inert coexistence. An even more serious difficulty about these words is that they have been so loosely used by writers on the subject that they can mean virtually anything: in other words, they have no real meaning.[3]

The term "inner self," on the other hand, is too limited, suggesting a twofoldness which is purely internal.

The name that we shall adopt for this study has at least the virtue of being familiar to most readers without being misleading: the "second self." Like "Double" it suggests twofoldness without implying duplication; like "inner self" it suggests a deeper relationship but not one that is confined to a state of mind. Above all it enables us to make a most important distinction that the other terms, especially "Double," encourage us to overlook. Automatically, in being "second," the second self presupposes and is differentiated from the "first self."[4] For, as we shall see throughout, the two participants in the twofold relationship not only are distinct from each other but are distinct in a particular way. The first self is the one who tends to be in the foreground of the reader's attention, usually the one whose viewpoint the reader shares; he is the relatively naive self, naive at least in tending to suppose that he is the whole self, for he seldom has any conscious knowledge, until it is forced upon him, of any other self involved in his make-up. The second self is the intruder from the background of shadows, and however prominent he may become he always tends to remain half-shadowed; he is much more likely to have knowledge of his foreground counterpart than the latter of him, but the exact extent and source of his knowledge, like the exact nature of his motivation, are always left in comparative obscurity.

But to decide what our subject is to be called is not the same thing as deciding what he is, and this of course is the main problem that must be solved before any meaningful discussion can begin. What makes it particularly difficult is that we enter here not into the vacuum of the completely unknown, but into the chaos of the incompletely explored. However much they may disagree in other ways, the writings on the subject that have thus far appeared[5] all seem to start with a common assumption: that the second self is so well known to everyone that any preliminary definition can be dispensed with. Part of the difficulty, as I have explained, is the use of the unfortunate word "Double"; part of it is the lack of any clarification of this word. At one moment it seems to mean straight physical duplication, like the hocus-pocus counterfeits of Wu Ch'eng-en's story *Monkey;*[6] at another moment it is applied to relationships where no duplication or even resemblance is involved. It is used interchangeably for a case of biological twinship and for a case of psychopathic hallucination, with no apparent realization that the two are entirely different things.

Perhaps the main reason why this vital question of the nature of the second self has been left unsettled is that it not only seems so easy, but in a deceptive sense *is* easy; there is probably no one, whether or not he is a reader of creative literature, who does not know something about it. "An inevitable dualism bisects nature," says Emerson, "so that each thing is a half, and suggests another thing to make it whole."[7] Two kinds of such dualism are familiar to us all from our own experience. The simpler kind is the physical, visible dualism that we perceive in our own bodies or those of others; the extraordinary series of "pairs," all the way from the paired toes at the bottom to the paired cerebral hemispheres at the top, or throughout the whole rhythm of inhalation and exhalation, systole and diastole, that is the central manifestation of bodily life. But such perceptible twofoldness is not restricted to the individual body; the body itself has various sorts of "others" that echo and complement it. We need not go to *A Child's Garden of Verses* to learn about shadows, for each of us has a little shadow that goes in and out with him, and each of us has been struck with the persistence of this featureless twin that dogs his footsteps throughout life. Similarly each of us, and not just the fabled Narcissus, has a mirror image that appears before him in still water or other glassy surfaces, even more independent of him than the shadow (which is always attached to its original at some point) and a far more detailed likeness. Or the body may have a man-made duplicate, not mobile like the shadow or mirror image but in a way more impressive because more detached: the photograph, the portrait, the statue or bust, the waxen image. Finally there is the most famous of all types of physical dualism, where the twofoldness is not between body and reflection or body and object but between body and body, as in cases of identical twinship or those rarer and subtler cases where the linkage is not one of likeness but one of contrast.

This is one kind of dualism bisecting nature. But there is another kind also, perhaps less immediately recognizable but no less familiar. Our everyday habits of speech, often much more revealing than our conscious thoughts, are a constant indication of the fact. The average person, when under severe stress, often speaks of himself as being "broken up" with grief, "going to pieces" with nervousness. He must "take himself in hand," "pull himself together," "get a grip on himself." Or he may go further, and find that he has behaved in a way suggesting that he was "not himself," without questioning what self in that case he *was;* suggesting that he was temporarily "out of his mind," without deciding what wrong mind he was temporarily *in;* suggesting that he was "possessed," without realizing that one cannot be possessed unless there is also a possessor;

suggesting (the most significant phrase of all) that he was "beside himself."[8] Nor is it only in our expressions that we betray a sense of our
inward twofoldness. Faced with problems, each of us tends to commune
with himself by playing a double role: the rash and the cautious, or the
trusting and the cynical, or the seeker of advice and the experienced
counselor. The process of thought is always at least silently Socratic, the
self divided between the self that questions and the self that answers.[9]

For this, the psychological dualism, we have of course far more evidence than that of everyday habits of speech and thought. The new science
of psychology, whether as a field of academic research or as a branch of
applied medicine, has been in considerable measure a study of the twofold nature of the mind. The "animal magnetism" experimented with by
Mesmer in the late eighteenth century, though Mesmer seems to have
been unaware of the fact, constituted the beginning of therapeutic hypnotism in the Western world: the induced somnambulistic trance which
entrances that part of the mind ordinarily taken to be the whole mind,
and which through this entrancing sets free, awakens like the enchanted
princess, another part ordinarily hidden both to the outside world and to
the patient.[10] Later researches in hypnotism by such people as Janet,
Binet, Dessoir, and Prince yielded a wealth of material to support this
view. There were such remarkable cases as that of Morton Prince's "Miss
Beauchamp," whose subconscious personality, "Sally," was infuriated
by the fact that the physician could converse with Miss Beauchamp in
French, a language which the Sally-self had never bothered to learn,
though the conscious self spoke it fluently.[11]

Even more remarkable have been the findings of modern psychiatry
and psychoanalysis,[12] which have by now furnished an overwhelming
mass of detail to show that the waking individual ego-consciousness is no
more than a small and lonely outpost of light, whose knowledge of the
vast dark hinterland of psychic energy from which it has emerged is
fragmentary and inferential, and whose response to the pressures exerted
upon it by this hinterland is far greater than it has any idea. Often the
conscious mind tries to deny its unconscious through the mechanism of
"projection," attributing its own unconscious content (a murderous impulse, for example) to a real person in the world outside; at times it even
creates an external hallucination in the image of this content. Such evasion,
though dangerous, can be turned to therapeutic account, for it represents
at least the beginning of an acknowledgment of what is within; it represents,
however mistakenly interpreted at first, a confrontation of the denied
content, and so the possibility of a coming to terms with it.

These, the physical and the psychical, are the two kinds of dualism

which are familiar to everyone. And it is probably because of this familiarity that so little need has been felt to define the second self, or even
clearly to note that there is a difference between the second self which
can result from the former dualism and that which can result from the
latter: a difference, in other words, between the objective second self
and the subjective. The most serious omission, however, has been not so
much the failure to see the difference between them as the failure to see
that neither of them, alone, constitutes a true second self at all. This is
no longer a matter of mere nomenclature, nor is it an arbitrary decision;
it is a logical and necessary distinction. The objective counterpart of the
self and the subjective component of the self are both susceptible of
being explained, which means being explained *away,* as something other
than the second selves they appear to be. The legend of Narcissus has
been cited above as the most familiar of all examples, but it should be
remembered that only for Narcissus was the face in the fountain a
genuine second self; for us who translate this face into "nothing but"
reflected light waves it is not. The unconscious personality may be projected outward by its owner, but we who stand outside the situation know
that it is not another person at all; it is "nothing but" a cluster of rejected
or inadmissible mental states that have been excluded from full consciousness, but are no less a part of the same mind. This is not to say
that creative literature about such spurious second selves is necessarily
inferior in artistic merit. It is simply to point out that anything which can
be explained as something else can have no real existence of its own;
and that this is invariably true of both kinds of second self that are so
deceptively familiar to us all (deceptively, because they make the matter
seem so easy): the objective and the subjective. Each is a mistake, and
the literature that incorporates it depends for effectiveness on the fact
of this mistake, which may range all the way from the time-honored
mix-up of identical twins in Plautus' *Menaechmi* to the terrifying hallucination of Ivan in *The Brothers Karamazov:* a mistake always *understood*
to be a mistake, either throughout or ultimately, by the reader.[13]

I may seem to be laboring a very elementary point, but it is a point
of utmost importance to our purpose. Among other things it will enable
us to avoid spending time on vast quantities of writings ordinarily supposed to belong to the literature of the second self, but in the light of
this distinction seen not to be examples at all. Thus we can bypass all
cases of the purely objective "other," satisfactorily real in his possession
of an independent being, and linked to his counterpart by external ties
such as visible resemblance, but having no deeper kinship with the latter
in the realm of personality. The most common examples are such nonhuman duplicates as the shadow, the mirror image, the statue or bust,

the portrait, and the waxen copy. Only when such a mechanical reproduction becomes a living personality felt to be somehow continuous with
that of its original and entering into some important, counterbalancing
relationship with him, is it converted into a second self; otherwise it
remains simply an object. The fact that the hero or first self may feel it
to be more does not signify unless the reader shares his feeling.

Even to separate the reproduction from its original and give it an
independent mobility is not enough. Peter Schlemihl's famous shadow,
sold to the gray man for Fortunato's magic purse, shows a respect for
commercial bargains and a loyalty to its new owner, but remains just as
shadowy and inanimate as ever.[11] The mirror image which Hoffmann's
Erasmus Spikher surrenders to the wicked Giulietta is animated enough
to walk out of the mirror, but it also walks out of the story, and enters
into no significant relationship with the hapless Spikher.[15] The same rule
applies to the nonhuman counterparts of a more august sort, the supernatural visitants. Jupiter is not the second self of Amphitryon, in any of
the numerous versions of this story, but a philandering deity who assumes
the mortal's shape in order to seduce the mortal's wife. The angel who,
for more laudable purposes, appears in the form of Robert of Sicily and
forces the arrogant king to play the role of jester at the foot of his own
throne is no less an angel for his temporary disguise, and is totally separate
from Robert.[16] As for the human examples in this category, the most
common are those that have already been mentioned: the long-parted
pairs of twins like those of Shakespeare's *Comedy of Errors* and *Twelfth
Night,* who in the process of their reunion have produced some of the
most delightful complications in literature, but have nothing whatever to
do with the figure of the second self.

They have nothing to do with it because they depend wholly on an
external relationship, which in these cases as in most examples of the
objective "other" takes the form of visible duplication. Such duplication
may well be a feature of the relationship between the selves, but only
when it is accompanied by a deeper bond; when, as in Poe's *William
Wilson,*[17] the external sameness is made to serve as the symbol of a basic
internal continuity. But physical duplication by itself is never enough for,
nor is it necessary to, the literature of the second self. On the whole it is an
obvious and comparatively heavy-handed device, and the more important
treatments of the subject have tended either to convert it into something
more subtle, such as linkage suggested by contrast rather than resemblance,
or to dispense with it altogether.

In writings that incorporate the purely subjective "other" the situation is just the opposite. Instead of too little real union there is too little
real division; there are no separate selves at all. The most common

examples are those of what we call "split personality." In Holmes' novel *Elsie Venner*[18] we have the story of a girl whose mother, struck by a rattlesnake shortly before Elsie's birth, has transmitted to her along with her womanly nature a strong proportion of reptilian nature as well. Therefore Elsie, as her physician puts it, lives "a double being," her good part constantly at war with her evil part.[19] Nevertheless these parts are merely the opposing sides of a single young woman; there is at no time even the suggestion of external independent existence of the ophidian Elsie. When the "split" subject externalizes the split-off part of the psyche, as Stavrogin does with the spiteful being that haunts him through the suppressed chapters of *The Possessed,* he is merely deceiving himself with a product of his own diseased imagination; indeed Stavrogin realizes that this is the case.[20]

The "split personality" is almost always to some extent an "alternating personality," in which now one and now another of the combatant elements in the psyche appears on top. When this alternation becomes particularly violent and the supplantings temporarily complete, the results are often extremely dramatic, but they can still never yield a true second self. For one thing, they always take place within a single individual, however radically he may change as he shifts from one aspect of himself to the other. For another, genuine alternation means the total temporary eclipse of the displaced personality half, which is then no longer a self of any kind but at best only a memory. The werewolf who lives as man by day and as wolf by night is never more than one self at a time; indeed he is rarely more than one self at any time: either a good man at heart obliged for some reason to prowl as a wolf, or a wolf at heart who by magical powers can remain apparently a man while his wolf-self goes forth to perform his wolf-will. The possession of two coexistent bodies in such cases does not give us two selves, since while either the man-body or the wolf-body is active the other lies in a deathlike trance.

In the werewolf and similar figures we have the alternating personality in the form of popular superstition;[21] in that most famous of all supposed second-self stories, Stevenson's *The Strange Case of Dr. Jekyll and Mr. Hyde,*[22] we have the same phenomenon in the form of science fiction. There is never more than one mind, though it alters strikingly as it shifts from its Jekyll-state to its Hyde-state; there is never more than one body, though by means of the chemical mixture (a modern version of the old magic potion) it is altered no less strikingly. The mechanics of the situation make it impossible that Jekyll and Hyde should ever separate, let alone confront each other. To the extent that the Jekyll-nature reasserts itself through the Hyde-self's domination, or that Hyde clamors for release while Jekyll is in control, we have simply the internal contention of the split-personality halves, like those of Elsie Venner. At no time does Hyde achieve the independent existence, the objective reality, of the true second self.

As for cases of "possession," cases in which the new self that arises to supplant the normal one owes its existence to some force controlling the subject's will from without: these of course are all merely variations of the alternating personality. Usually the werewolf belongs in this category, as does such a creature as the dragon-lady of Morris' *Lady of the Land,* whose dragon-shape and dragon-behavior, imposed on her by Diana, take turns with her gentle loveliness.[23] A more familiar type of possession, that of hypnosis, has played its part in fiction as well as in psychology, but the division it brings about is, again, of a purely inward kind; the twofoldness is never complete. Thus when Svengali temporarily converts the tone-deaf Trilby into "la Svengali," the great singer, he does not, except in a figurative sense, create a second Trilby; there is never more than one Trilby-entity, and the "two Trilbys" of whom Gecko speaks in explaining the mystery are simply alternating states of the same mind, each wholly without knowledge of the other.[24]

One other literary creation that is sometimes referred to as a second self has even less claim to the title than either of the types (the objective and the subjective) that we have just considered; in fact it has no claim, since it is not related to the first self at all. This is the personified idea, the allegory. Admittedly the second self always *suggests* some aspect of the first self that has been suppressed or unrealized, but he is always, and first of all, imaginatively alive. When he is not — when for example he is like the evil image of John Lavington in Edith Wharton's *The Triumph of Night,*[25] which appears behind the kindly John Lavington's chair and fixes on the latter's victim a look of deadly menace — he is simply an abstraction, thin and bloodless as cardboard. Whatever one may think of the value of allegory in creative literature as a whole, it has no place in the literature of the second self.

But what then *is* the second self? The answer is given us by what has just been said about the two main spurious second selves that are so often taken for it: the fact that what each of them lacks is exactly what the other possesses. The objective second self possesses external reality, clearly independent of the first self, but lacks any sort of inward linkage or continuity with the latter; it is "second," but not "self." The subjective second self does share a basic psychical identity with the first self, but lacking external reality lacks any convincing simultaneous identity of its own; it is "self," but not "second." Therefore as the true second self is never either of these alone, so he is always, in some combination, and always at the same time, both together. This may seem a simple definition after all that has led up to it, but what it asks us to conceive of is far from simple. For such a combination is to the conscious mind a logical impossibility, a reconciliation of absolute irreconcilables. Unlike either its purely objective or its purely subjective side it is not to be met with in everyday life; it is a creature of the imagination, a particular kind of imaginative product which we call fantasy. This fact may give it a somewhat disreputable sound for some readers. But that fantasy is necessarily either a pastime of childhood or a symptom of mental disorder, or is necessarily a recoil from reality rather than at times the straining after a deeper penetration into reality than our factual experience can give us, I hope the reader of the following chapters will find cause to doubt.

This matter will be taken up in greater detail in the last chapter, when we shall have accumulated evidence to apply to it. Indeed all these preliminary statements about the second self will be subject to testing and amplification by the illustrative material that follows. But we cannot very well know what material *is* illustrative until we have some idea of what it is we propose to illustrate: the nature of the second self. And I have explained why, for the purposes of the present study, he will be given a definite meaning, that of an always contradictory being, a paradox of simultaneous outwardness and inwardness, of difference from and identity with the first self. The question may sometimes occur to us, as we read, whether if we knew all the facts we might decide he was all one thing or all the other, all physical duplicate or all hallucination; but the question must never be answered; we must always be forced to keep a foot in the camp of either possibility. It is this quality of paradox that makes the second self so difficult a figure to talk about, but that makes him also — at least has made him for many readers — so fascinating a one to encounter. He is always "there," a self in his own right, never translatable into a product of mental aberration; yet he is always "here" as well, his psyche intergrown by untraceable shared tendrils with that of his counterpart, and so never translatable into a purely external fellow being.[26]

As a result of this general twofoldness in the nature of the second self, there is a more specific twofoldness that always to some degree marks his relationship with the first self. On the one hand there is a certain closeness, a certain strange and special affinity between them. It is an affinity which, like whatever impulse causes the second self to intrude into the life of the first, can never be entirely accounted for by the facts of the case or by logical reasoning about them; naturally not, since facts or logic can deal only with the condition of separateness or that of identity, never with both at once. This affinity shows itself in various ways: by inexplicable emotional reactions to each other, usually antagonism but often attraction (perhaps always, at some level, both); by insistent preoccupation with each other that may be quite unwilled by either or even consciously willed against by both; by an intimate insight into each other's mind and soul, more often displayed by the second self but sometimes shared by both, and to both incomprehensible; by behavior to each other, or attitude toward each other, frequently as astonishing to them as it is to us. In all this we are more aware of reactions of the first self than of the second; not necessarily because they are more important to us, but simply because the fact of his being the first or foreground self makes them more readily accessible to us, while those of the second self, the background self, reach us only through the medium of the first. The second self is the shadowed self, surrounded by an aura of the uncanny that sometimes makes him seem to belong to a different order of reality from that of the world in which he moves, so that the first self may almost fancy his counterpart to be the product of his own mind, though at the same time he and we always know better. A part of this uncanniness is that the second self tends to be the possessor of secrets that the first self can never quite fathom, and thus in being the stranger is also the stronger, always tending to be in real control of the relationship.

On the other hand there is a quality, also unfailingly characteristic of the relationship between the first self and the second, which in a sense is just the reverse of affinity, though inextricably bound up with it. As I have already pointed out, the fact that the selves are sometimes physical duplicates does not mean that they are ever psychological duplicates. Not only must the second self be different from the first, but he must be different in a particular way, a way that is responsible for the dynamic tension that always exists between them. He is the self that has been left behind, or overlooked, or unrealized, or otherwise excluded from the first self's self-conception; he is the self that must be come to terms with. And therefore, despite all his special closeness to the first self, he is always in some form the opposite (livingly, not mathematically, the opposite) of the first self; indeed this oppositeness is the main link that unites them, for it is the complementary oppositeness of the two halves of the being whom they together comprise, a being sometimes suggesting the total human personality, sometimes a very narrow segment of it. Their oppositeness in nature tends to result in a certain (often profound) opposition in attitude, and it is this opposition that most frequently characterizes the special closeness between them. Even in the second self's more favorable manifestations, his attraction for the first self tends to be rooted in this fundamental opposition. Whatever their attitude toward each other may be — terror, hatred, revulsion, love, even at times a kind of worship — it is never that of taking each other for granted. There is bound to be emotional tension; there is very likely to be emotional if not physical eruption. There are no tepid relationships between the hemispheres of the soul.

Strongly contributing to this combined affinity and opposition in the relationship between the selves is the implicit suggestion that their relationship is not something that simply "happens" or is brought about by an understandable sequence of events; that the coming of the second self, *as* second self (for he may be physically present for a long while before asserting his true nature) into the life of the first is the result of some unknown force using but transcending all known ones, and choosing always the moment of the first self's greatest vulnerability to such coming. Since this quality of the relationship is a particularly important feature of what I shall call the Second Self in Time, I shall defer discussion of it until later in this study.

Another feature of the relationship which follows from what has already been said is that it is always not only an important one, but also a counterbalancing one. Other people, of course, may be involved in this relationship, but never in the same way or with anything approaching the same degree of intensity. Centrally, from the moment of encounter, first self and second self are preoccupied with each other, affect each other, exist for each other, whether for good or ill.[27]

So much for who and what the second self is. Let us now meet him in the living form given him by the creative literature in which he has appeared. To be sure, we cannot meet him as directly as we are accustomed to meeting (or supposing that we meet) one another, in the all-at-once, face-to-face fashion. As the second self has no history in the usual sense of the word, so also he has no face, or at least no single face that instead of being merely *his* is also *he;* and not to realize this is inevitably to take part for the whole. What we must do, therefore, is play a patient game, and become acquainted with him step by step through the different main aspects in which he allows himself to be seen. Naturally it must not be expected that all the examples dealt with will show in the same degree or proportions all the main characteristics that I have just described. Creative literature is not written to suit critical generalizations; it is the generalizations that have been inferred from the literature, and they do not always fit with mathematical precision. Even in speaking of "main aspects" I am guilty of simplification; actually there are as many aspects of the second self as there are appearances of him; and the result is that the same figure will on occasions have to be mentioned under more than one heading.

For all this, I believe we shall see that the general description of the second self offered above is a sound one, and that despite a certain overlapping of categories it is always to one group rather than another that any particular second self belongs. But simply noting and exemplifying the existence of such groups would be simply a mechanical job of classification. It is not any of these categories to which I am undertaking to introduce the reader, nor each of them individually, but rather everything that they add up to: the second self common to them all. Increasingly therefore we must try to find implicit in each aspect those aspects we have already studied, however widely they differ. Increasingly we must bear in mind that we are not walking down a straight line and passing these faces in review; we are finding our way around in a circle, looking at one face and then at another, but always looking in the same direction, inward toward the owner of them all, the strange creature who in being second necessarily partakes of being first, who in his oppositeness to his counterpart is always the same, who walks without yet is rooted within: the ancient paradox of the self beside the self.

2

The Second Self As Twin Brother

The attribute of a simultaneous duality and unity is not the only paradox we shall encounter in our study of the second self. Another is the fact that though he has no significant overall history in the sense of a pattern of development, he is certainly one of the oldest products of the human imagination, so venerable that he does not seem to originate in literature at all, but rather in accrued oral tradition, only later committed to written records.[1] And while this earliest version seems to have had little direct influence on the later forms he has taken, it will be well for us to become at least briefly acquainted with him before commencing our analysis of the more recent literature of the second self. For in the accounts of this remote ancestor, as is so often true of the imaginative products of early cultural stages, there is a simplicity of approach and design that can give us hints about man's ways of thinking, hints which in a later and more complex literature may become comparatively obscured.

The figures that are usually considered to be early forms of the second self we have already touched on in the preceding chapter, and we have seen why they are not. The shadow or "trailing soul" that plays so important a role among the taboos of the savage is for us, the readers or hearers about it, merely an objective phenomenon and the savage's apprehensions about it merely superstition; furthermore the savage's belief itself is only that it shares his life, not that it shares his personality in any way; it has no personality.[2] Of course the shadow, or the mirror image or any of the man-made copies, can *become* a second self, but only when an important process of conversion takes place, as it does not in any of the primitive superstitions I have studied: the conversion of such a physical extension of the self into an independent being that still retains its participation in the self it shares with its counterpart. As for the werewolf, the vampire, the "sending" of any sort,[3] the golem or mechanical man, and all the other members of that vast nightmare-brood: these are in the main simply alternating or possessed personalities, sometimes one state of mind which moves between two different shapes, sometimes two states of mind which displace each other within the same shape, but never more than a single self.[4]

The only figure out of such early imaginings which does qualify as a second self is that of the Twin Brother. Of course everyone today knows how twins come into being, and in this way they are as explainable to us as the shadow or the mirror image. But we must beware of supposing that to describe a process of origination is the same thing as to explain the thing that has originated; and in fact the phenomenon of twinship — the strange mutual attraction of twins even in antipathy, their frequent inseparability and incapacity to act save in conjunction with each other, their profound effect upon each other's lives — is quite as much a mystery in our scientific day as it has ever been. Furthermore we must understand that the Twin Brother in his early stages (the Twin Brother as an imaginative product, whom I shall distinguish by capitalization from the merely biological twin brother) is not always literally a twin, or even literally a brother, or even a blood relative at all. The term "Twin Brother" as we shall use it is not so much one that describes a circumstance as one that expresses an attitude, since in fable what counts is less the fact than the feeling about the fact. And in the fable of the Twin Brother the feeling is always one of a strange and special closeness between the Twins, each constituting one of a pair or dual unit, the inseparable and also inescapable half of a single whole.[5]

But what lies behind this feeling and the widespread preoccupation with the subject of it? We will not find our answer in such splendid heroic pairs as those most famous of Twins, the Dioscuri. All Twin fables that have come down to us from the past have undergone many centuries of shaping and refining. To get an idea of what the beginnings were really like we must turn to presumable analogues among primitive peoples of our own and recent times. Such analogues are not hard to come on; the Twin

Brother is found in virtually every corner of the earth, from the Kaffirs of South Africa to the Navajos of the Arizona desert, from the Chiriguanos of Bolivia to the Ainus of Northern Japan. And these examples indicate that the Twin Brother did not begin his career as a figure either splendid or heroic. To the contrary, the more primitive the tribal mentality the more likely is the birth of twins to be considered an unqualified catastrophe, and the more likely are both twins, often along with their mother, to be strangled at birth. The motives usually given are, first, that to bring forth twins is to degrade the human being to the status of animal that produces by litter, such as a dog or rat; second, that one man cannot be the father of two children at once and so one of them must be the fruit of an adulterous union.

But it is the conclusion of Rendel Harris, whose researches have shed so much light on the subject of Twins, that such reasons are merely masks for the real reason, which is neither disgust nor moral disapproval but the Great Fear, the fear of the uncanny.[6] The mistaken belief that one man cannot be the father of both twins seems genuine enough, but the inference drawn is not that the other father is some fellow tribesman or even fellow human, for such a culprit would not have the numinous power to produce something so strange. The father of one twin, therefore, must be a spirit — and to the primitive mind a spirit is seldom benignant but just the reverse — that has chosen this way, the way of the Twin Brother, to infiltrate with its evil influence into the communal life of the tribe.[7]

The theory of the Great Fear is given support by the fact that the slaying of both twins occurs only at or near the bottom of the cultural scale; in other words it seems to be a flailing out in blind terror at the general source of danger. Among primitives of somewhat higher intelligence it is recognized that since only one twin is of spirit ancestry only one merits slaying (or in some cases isolation or exile). And where the attitude toward the spirit world becomes more complex and the possibility enters that there are good spirits as well as bad, both twins begin to be looked on with favor, for instance as promoters of fertility. And yet such favor is not unmixed with fear. The Twin Brother may no longer be so dangerous a figure, but he is no less uncanny than ever.[8]

Nor does he ever cease to be uncanny, as moving backward in time but forward in cultural development we come to the Twin fables of the ancient civilizations. The Açvins, the great Twin horsemen of the Indian Rig-Veda;[9] Castor and Pollux, the Dioscuri of the Greeks;[10] Shu and the lion-headed Tefnut, or Horus and Set, of the Egyptians;[11] Jacob and Esau of the Hebrews;[12] Romulus and Remus, the founders of Rome:[13]

about all such figures there is much the same aura of strangeness as surrounds the Twins of primitive superstition, and a strong suggestion of the same reason for it: the underlying sense that twin birth cannot be a natural occurrence, that it signifies disturbance of the normal order of things, that it represents, in the person of one of the twins, the intrusion of the spirit world into human affairs.

Granted, there is one way in which the stories of the Twin Brother do not present the figure of the second self in as satisfactory a fashion as the literature of later times. They are all largely objective stories, told from outside, seldom enabling us to share the viewpoint of either Twin, seldom even telling us what such viewpoints are. Thus what we are so very much interested in, the emotional reactions which the Twins evoke from each other, we have little or no means of knowing about directly. In particular what we miss is the thoughts and feelings of the first self, so important to us because it is through these that we ordinarily come to know the second self.

This situation is no doubt partly due to the fact that such early products have little of the interest in psychological detail that we find in the conscious literary art of later centuries; they concentrate more upon event than upon the inner workings of the mind. In addition there may well be another and deeper reason, rooted in the nature of the Twin fable itself. It is a relatively easy thing to say that one Twin is of spirit origin; it is a very different thing to answer the question (and a peculiarly nice question when the answer is literally a matter of life or death) of which Twin one is talking about. From almost the beginning this difficulty seems to have been present, and it never seems to have been resolved with entire success. And with changing concepts of the role of spirit the difficulty, of course, is compounded, especially when two such concepts — e.g., the older, wild troll-like spirit embodied in Esau and the newer Jehovah-spirit which favors Jacob — appear in the same story at the same time. Perhaps most confusing of all is the tendency, in the more advanced and sophisticated Twin stories, to enhance the prestige of the heroes by making them both of at least semi-divine origin, as in the case of the Dioscuri, a name which means literally "boys of Zeus."[14]

Yet the Twins are never simply two names for the same person. Even when they do much the same thing, and in conjunction with each other, they are not interchangeable. Thus, though the Dioscuri work together in winning battles for the chosen side or saving sailors at sea, they differ from each other in their special skills, Castor being the tamer of horses, Pollux the boxer. And despite their title "Boys of Zeus" it is Pollux, not Castor, who at least in the early Greek cults is the truly god-begotten one. The same thing is true of Amphion as against Zethos, Herakles as against Iphikles, Romulus as against Remus.[15] Even when it is impossible to say that one is more "divine" than the other, it is usually not too hard to make the distinction between the more recognizably human or normal one, in personality if not in parentage, and the one who either in the facts of his origination or in his own character or appearance is comparatively the "stranger," the alien intruder from the Great Dark.[16]

The difference between the two — and it becomes clearer the more fully their story is developed — tends to be of the kind I have already described, not a mere random difference but an oppositeness, therefore forming a linkage as well, since the idea of the one implies the idea of the other to complement it, and this continues to be true even when a supposedly final parting takes place.

For in certain cases the Twins do part. Sometimes it is more or less peacefully to go opposite ways, one to the East and one to the West, yet each remaining as implicit in the other as do the opposite directions in which they have gone.[17] Sometimes the parting is violent, as when the twin supposedly of spirit origin is put to death, for example by the Ibo people of Nigeria, who slay (or at least in fairly recent times did slay) the second-born of the pair. But the Ibo do not consider that this slaying puts an end to the relationship; the survivor, or first-born, is thereafter given the remarkable name of *In'meabo,* meaning "two people," or the one who is two.[18] Among the Ngombe tribes of the Upper Congo, twins are considered a blessing rather than a curse; and so closely identified are they, and so sensitive is their relationship to each other, that the death of one twin from whatever cause is always attributed to his having been slain by his fellow twin.[19]

Hence the Twin Brother, alone so far as I know among the figures of this ancient and primitive material, is genuinely an example of the second self, and the sole ancestor of the second self of creative literature. He is a product of the apparently age-old tendency of the human imagination to think of many of its subjects as a basic oneness divided into a simultaneous twoness, while still retaining the oneness and using it as a cohesive force to counterbalance the divisive force. He is unmistakably outside, but just as inescapably inside; his reality is always that of one in a pair. And as the Twin of spirit origin he always tends to be the uncanny one, the at least potentially disturbing one, the alien intruder.

Such a distinction is most obvious, as we should expect it to be, in the many stories in which the Twins are not right and left hands working toward a common goal, but enemies working against each other, and the more inimical they become the more clearly identifiable they are as first and second selves. Of the Ainu demigods, Shi-acha the elder, the "rough one" or "wild uncle," is both the uncanny and the evil member of the pair, constantly making trouble for and harassing Mo-acha, the gentle "uncle of peace."[20] In North American Huron tradition Tawiskara and his Twin Juskeha, like Esau and Jacob on the other side of the earth, quarrel even within the womb, and once born quarrel on a universal scale, Tawiskara becoming the maker of all evil, Juskeha the maker of good.[21] And in the famous Twin myth that underlies the most famous of dualistic theologies, the dark, ill-favored, envious Ahriman, born of the doubt (realm of shadows) in the mind of his father Zervan, succeeds in coming first to birth, and thus achieves a nine-thousand-year supremacy over Ormuzd, the luminous child of faith, whose day has not yet dawned.[22]

Admittedly the clarity of distinction in these stories owes something to the fact that the Twins are less people than ideas, but even in cases where the enmity is personal rather than universal we still have no real doubt about which Twin is which. Jacob is the favored of God, but he is not the son of spirit; it is he who becomes the "true son" of the human Rebekah and Isaac. Esau from birth is strange, wild and shaggy as the animals he hunts, red in color as is so often the Twin of spirit ancestry,[23] impetuous, unpredictable, dangerous, though in his case the danger is counteracted by a combination of human cunning and divine favoritism. He is, mutatis mutandis, the "wild uncle," the stormy Tawiskara, the resentful Ahriman, above all the stranger, the outsider, whom his own mother does not hesitate to rob of the paternal blessing. Jacob, on the other hand, is the smooth, the peaceful, the reasonable man, the man whom we can understand.[24] The same contrast, though the characters are very different, is to be found between the earlier brothers Cain and Abel, who though not literal twins are no less two of a pair, inseparable even by the murder of Abel, which makes Cain *In'meabo,* the one who is two, the one who carries with him in the Lord's curse the self that he has slain.

These, of course, are familiar stories to all who have been brought up in the Judaeo-Christian tradition, and I should like to take for my main example of the conflict between Twins a somewhat less familiar story, and one of the most extraordinary of all. This is the legend of Parsvanatha, the Lord Parsva, the Jaina Tirthankara or "Maker of the River-Crossing," which is to say the crossing from the cycle of reincarnation, in which man is trapped by his own fear and desire, to the ultimate peace of nirvana.[25] But the river-crossing is not achieved at once; it comes only after a whole series of earlier existences in which the career of the hero is intimately bound up with that of his elder brother. This brother not only hates his Twin, but pursues his hatred through one lifetime after another and through all the countless ages in between (so closely associated are the two in the scheme of things that they are always reincarnated at the same time). The hatred begins when the evil Twin, then Kamatha, seduces the wife of his virtuous brother Marubhuti (the future Parsva) and, being exiled by his father for the crime, retires into the wilderness; when his wronged brother follows in a spirit of forgiveness Kamatha slays him, and in time also dies. Marubhuti is reincarnated as a mad elephant, but tractable to the voice of reason and religion, and therefore in his animal simplicity better fitted than Marubhuti himself had been for the saintly career that with his conversion he now begins. Kamatha, however, is reincarnated as a poisonous serpent, and when the reformed elephant comes to the river bank to drink, the serpent strikes — as he is to strike again and again in various forms, subhuman and human and superhuman, through the ages of reincarnation that follow. The forms are many and the ages are countless but the pattern is always the same; the wild impetuous Cain, eaten by unbearable envy, strikes down his gentle Twin and becomes a fugitive and a vagabond in the universe. But in the Old Testament the results of the crime are immediate and final; in the Jain myth the results have barely begun. Down the corridors of Time the two Twins move, largely unaware of each other but in parallel courses; and at each crossing of their paths the dark brother, for all the torments that his last sin of aggression has caused him in the interim, repeats it.

The effect of this persecution, however, is neither the destruction of the good Twin nor the permanent damnation of the evil one. The *In'meabo,* always Kamatha in his various successive forms, and always possessed by a savage fury toward his brother that makes him at each meeting attack and slay the latter (once, as a lion, tearing him to pieces and devouring him), nevertheless manages during his series of reincarnations to perform certain meritorious acts and at length to assume human form again, as the testy old Mahipala, grandfather (though still also Twin) of the young Lord Parsva. Finally, when Parsva has taken leave of his parents to enter upon the meditations that will give him release from his karma or life-wheel, he is attacked once more by his Twin, now the minor god Samvara, who with black face and wielding blackness itself as a weapon rushes upon Parsva, who in turn, wholly absorbed in meditation, remains unmoved. Samvara, the Kamatha of long ago, is defeated, but unlike Kamatha, unlike the poisonous serpent and the many other forms in which he has lived and hated and slain, he is also bewildered, at the sight of this unresisting Twin who has always fallen before him only to rise again, and who now as Tirthankara, emancipated though still embodied, brings peace wherever he goes. Reluctantly Samvara visits one of the great halls where Parsva is teaching, and listens; and suddenly the hatred of numberless centuries is melted, and he falls with a cry at the feet of his brother, and is reconciled with him.

Not all stories of Twins end in reconciliation; it needs the Oriental mind, with its insistence on finding a place for evil as well as good in the scheme of things, with its effort to bridge that division between opposites which it holds to be of the essence of the world's illusion and bondage, to incline to such an issue. The figure of Jesus, with his self-effacement and bottomless capacity for forgiveness, is reminiscent of Marubhuti-Parsva, but the story of Jesus envisages no such peaceful solution as that which we find in the Jain myth. In other ways, too, the story of Jesus as it comes to us through the New Testament is very different from that of the Tirthankara; the only character who can be thought of as Jesus' persecutor is the apostle-betrayer Judas, and Judas does not slay Jesus with his own hand; what is more to the point, Judas is neither Jesus' brother nor his Twin, nor in any sense his counterpart. Yet the New Testament is not our only source of information on the subject, and when we broaden our consideration to take in less official documents as well, we find the question to be a far more complicated one than it at first appears.

Thus in the Apocryphal *Acts of Thomas,* an early Syriac account of the apostolate of Saint Thomas, Thomas and Jesus consistently behave toward each other as Twins, and Thomas is several times addressed as Jesus' Twin Brother;[26] indeed the name "Thomas" means simply "Twin." And there are stranger things as well. Throughout the *Acta Thomae* Thomas is referred to as "Judas Thomas." We know from both Matthew and Mark[27] that Jesus, considered as the son of Mary and Joseph, had four brothers, one of whom was named Judas or Jude; and this may be either the author of the Epistle of Jude, or the Judas, "not Iscariot," mentioned by John as one of the apostles,[28] or both. If so, the reference to Thomas as Judas Thomas may be a telescoping of two ideas: the brother of Jesus mentioned in the first two Gospels, and the meaning of "Twin" inherent in the name of Thomas. Nevertheless, for most people since the beginning of the Christian era, the name "Judas" has signified only one person: Judas Iscariot, the keeper of the funds, the taker of the thirty pieces of silver, the giver of the deadly kiss. As a result,[29] in a number of medieval legends the gaps between Judas the brother of Jesus, Judas Thomas the Twin of Jesus, and Judas Iscariot the betrayer of Jesus are bridged, and the last of these is represented as Jesus' elder brother.[30]

Nor does the process of telescoping end here; it goes on into a still stranger and more intricate nexus, still more strongly prevalent in medieval thought, and of still greater relevancy (as we shall see) to the subject of the second self. At first glance it would appear that in such a relationship Judas would be the human brother and Jesus the brother of spirit origin. But Jesus is the Son of Man as well as the Son of God; furthermore we have already seen that spirit origin in the Twin fable does not necessarily mean spirit in the good sense of the word; it is much more likely to hark back, as it does in the case of Esau, to the primitive concept of spirit as animalistic, both alien and evil. At all events it is certainly Judas and not Jesus who is the uncanny Twin, the shadowed Twin, and the nature of the shadow is specified by Jesus himself: "Have I not chosen you twelve, and one of you is a devil?"[31] He might mean the word in a figurative sense, but the Arabic Apocrypha, *Evangelium Infantiae Salvatoris,* makes the diabolical in Judas more than merely human depravity; at the moment when Jesus is born, Judas is possessed by, made one with, Satan.[32] And in Gnostic tradition this idea is carried still further. According to the Gnostics there are two sons of God, the younger of whom is Jesus, the elder of whom, from the beginning Jesus' dark counterpart and adversary, is called Satanaël. This is not the Satan of Job, who walks with the angels before the face of the Lord. This is the gloomy and awful figure of Antichrist, the former Lucifer whose morning-star splendor has been dimmed by the fires of Hell, the essence of active evil that came into being with the birth of the God of Mercy as His antithetical Twin, the mystery of iniquity that stands at the left hand of the sun of justice.[33]

In the medieval Jesus and the Jaina Kamatha-Samvara, the second self as Twin Brother is distinguished from the first self in the clearest and most obvious way, by absolute oppositeness and opposition between the evil of the former and the good of the latter. But the second-self Twin is not always evil. In Amerindian versions he sometimes not only cooperates with his Twin but saves the other's life:[34] a motif that we shall find to be of great importance to our study of the second self of creative literature. And in one of the oldest of all Twin stories, and at the same time one of the most profound and beautiful, he exerts his beneficial effect not by saving or restoring the first self's life, but by, so to speak, infecting the first self with the idea of death, confronting him with the fact of death and forcing him to struggle with the enormity of it.

This is the ancient Akkadian *Epic of Gilgamesh,*[35] the story of King Gilgamesh, king of the city of Uruk (biblical Erech, modern Warkah) in ancient Babylonia, and of his comrade Enkidu. I call them Twins, though the fragmentary state in which the poem has come down to us makes the literal relationship between them, as well as many other important matters, impossible to know with certainty. The partial destruction of the first column of text, for example, leaves the origin of Gilgamesh in doubt. When the goddess Aruru is called on to create Enkidu it is on the grounds that she has already created Gilgamesh; later, however, Gilgamesh addresses Ninsun as his mother. Ninsun, in the Assyrian version, later adopts Enkidu, who is "not my womb's issue"; and subsequently Gilgamesh and Enkidu are referred to as "the two brothers."[36] But these difficulties are of no importance. I have already explained that the Twins of myth and legend are not necessarily biological twins, or even blood relatives at all. Gilgamesh and Enkidu are unmistakably Twins in the sense of being members of a pair, the two counterbalancing halves of a self-contained whole, quite as much as are the literal brothers Marubhuti-Parsva and Kamatha-Samvara. Enkidu is created both strikingly like and yet unlike Gilgamesh. Shorter and stronger of bone, wilder and shaggier, he is so created for the specific purpose of serving as counterpart and counterbalance to his elder "brother," and the story of their relationship displays all the main features of the typical Twin fable.

It is a relationship, as I say, largely of cooperation and affection. But this is not the way it begins. Gilgamesh, mighty king of Uruk, has been guilty of shameless mistreatment of his people, leaving not the maid to her mother nor the son to his father. In order to check this arrogance Enkidu is brought into being, not in the city but out on the wild steppe, a wild man, shaggy with hair over his whole body, herding with the wild beasts and jostling with them at the water holes. Drawn away from such companions by a friendly harlot lass he goes to ramparted Uruk, where Gilgamesh has already been warned of his coming by the dreams of the star and the ax, both signifying a "stout comrade who rescues a friend."[37] On Enkidu's arrival the nobles rejoice: "For Gilgamesh, the godlike,/ His equal has come forth."[38] The two meet at the entrance of the market-of-the-land, Gilgamesh apparently proposing to indulge there in one of his customary orgies.[39] But this time he does not. In the gateway he is met by Enkidu, who bars the way with his foot. They grapple like maddened bulls, the wall shakes, the door post is shattered. Who technically wins the wrestling match need not concern us;[40] what is of importance is the wholly unprecedented effect which this encounter with his "equal" has upon Gilgamesh. He turns away, his fury abated, his intention abandoned; and the purpose of the gods is achieved.

Nor is the effect only a temporary one. For what follows this initial test of strength between the Twins is not further conflict but the deepest of friendship and the closest of comradeship. Together, after Enkidu's pleadings of caution have been overruled by his elder, they invade the Cedar Forest and slay the monster Huwawa (or Humbaba). Together they cut down the Bull of Heaven, sent against them at the request of Ishtar, who is furious because her advances have been rejected by Gilgamesh. The slaying of the Bull, however, compounds their offense; it is decreed by the gods that one of them must die, and Enkidu is chosen. In this story there is no last-minute saving or bringing back to life. The Twins are separated by death, but once more they are *not* separated; once more the surviving Twin becomes *In'meabo,* the one who is two. But the way in which Enkidu lives on in Gilgamesh is almost wholly philosophical rather than miraculous. In his grief at the loss of Enkidu, Gilgamesh is led apparently for the first time to confront the fact, far more monstrous than Huwawa, of the inevitability of death. Seven days and seven nights he sits beside the corpse, until he sees a worm drop from its nose; and he puts into words at last the awful question: "When I die, shall I not be like Enkidu?"[41]

This question, which has burned itself into his mind, takes him down into the great adventure of the Underworld, the meeting with Utnapishtim the Faraway, the seizing from the sea bottom of the plant of rejuvenation, and the careless loss of it to the serpent. But Enkidu does not drop out of the story; his death is the motivation for this vain effort to conquer death, and the poem ends with the raising of Enkidu's ghost through a hole in the earth, and a sad last colloquy between the dead Twin and the living one.[42]

Here again, though there is far more depth and feeling than in the usual Twin story, we are told little directly about mental processes, and are handicapped (it is always a handicap for our purposes) by the fact that we are not given the viewpoint of either hero. As to who is the first self and who the second, we can draw no conclusions on the score of immortality, since in this case both Twins are plainly mortal. The fact that Enkidu is the younger — like Jacob, Ormuzd, Abel, and others — and the comparatively cautious and reasonable one, might seem to suggest that he is the first self, but the evidence on the other side is far stronger.

Gilgamesh is described in the poem as two-thirds divine, though according to his legendary parentage he is only one-half so.[43] Enkidu is conceived by and within the goddess Aruru, the double of the god Anu, the essence of the god Ninurta, and the offspring of either Ninurta or (presumably) some other divinity.[44] In other words, as is so often the case in these more sophisticated products, both Twins are demigods. But as to which is the descendant of the original spirit-force from the Outer Dark there can be no doubt. Gilgamesh, demigod or not, is the familiar type, the powerful ruler who is abusing his power, the city man and trained warrior; in all these ways the foreground self. It is Enkidu who is the one of miraculous birth, the uncanny creature from the unknown wilderness, the shaggy wild animal-like one (cf. Esau) whose very appearance petrifies the hunter with fear; he enters Uruk and the life of Gilgamesh as an alien intruder of unexpected strength, a strength that not only changes Gilgamesh's mind as the result of their initial encounter, but changes it in a much deeper and more lasting way, colors it and awakens it and develops it, and affects Gilgamesh's whole character and destiny.

These are the two main kinds of Twin-Brother story sufficiently developed to give us Twins clearly distinguishable from each other: stories in which the second self is the evil enemy of the first and seeks the latter's destruction; and stories in which the second self, though at first perhaps appearing as an enemy, is in fact the friend of the first and seeks to promote the latter's welfare, or even to bring about his salvation. Though too many generalizations cannot be ventured as yet, we may say that regularly it is the second self who initiates the action in the relationship between them, and the first self who registers the effect of this action. In other words, we tend to be interested in what is *done by* the second self, and in what *happens to* (or within) the first self: a difference which, in view of our tendency to identify ourselves with the first self, is what we should expect.

And on the basis of the examples we have just considered, it would appear that a great deal in these Twin-Brother stories happens to the first self; that the effect exerted upon him (and often the effect exerted by this interaction upon the second self as well) is a profound and permanent one. While it would be blasphemous, of course, to suggest that Judas-Satan could have any effect on the character of Jesus, it is the betrayal by the former that leads directly to the latter's crucifixion. In the Jain story the character of the first self is affected by the persecutions inflicted on him by the second, and thus the good Marubhuti is gradually shaped into the saint who achieves emancipation as Tirthan-kara. In the *Epic of Gilgamesh,* Gilgamesh does not achieve spiritual emancipation; man seldom does; he achieves only the human lot of being fruitfully disturbed, but he achieves it no less by growth, by the inward shaping which results from his interaction with his other self. At the beginning he is arrogant and brutal, a shallow and self-centered, unreflecting creature. The dreams that presage the coming of Enkidu first awaken in him the yearning for the true comrade, to whom he is drawn as to a woman; his encounter with Enkidu in the gateway of the Market-of-the-Land puts an end to his overbearing temper and makes him capable of friendship. Whether or not it is the influence of Enkidu that causes Gilgamesh to reject Ishtar the fragmentary state of the story makes it impossible for us to know, but there can be no doubt about the effect upon Gilgamesh of Enkidu's death. Not only is he racked with grief by his loss; he is appalled by its larger meaning; he is outraged at the thought of death, at the indignity of death, at the empty mockery it makes of life. And like so many other heroes he descends into the darkness of an underworld that is both in the depths of the earth and in the depths of his own being, across the bitter waters and down to their very bottom to grasp the thorny plant which, like all sea-bottom treasures of myth and legend and fairy tale the world over, is the secret of renewed life, life-in-death; he grasps it for a moment, but cannot hold it. At the close of the poem, unlike the resurrected Jesus or the emancipated Tirthankara, he is a wretched man, but an almost unrecognizably deeper man — more thoughtful, more human, more sympathetic in his sorrow — than before the coming of his Twin and second self.

3

The Second Self As Pursuer

As we move from the material of communal tradition into creative literature proper, we find that the tendency characteristic of the Twin-Brother fable, to a hazing over of distinction between the selves, disappears entirely. It does so because the interest in external events is now accompanied by at least an equal interest in mental processes. Of these the thoughts of the first self are always more readily accessible to us than those of the second, which are never completely known to us and may never be known at all. Even when the first self is not the narrator or the speaker, he is always the self in the foreground, the one with whom we tend to identify ourselves, and whose judgment of values we tend at least initially to accept. The second self is always comparatively in the background, the mysterious alien intruder, the modern version of the uncanny Twin (child of the Woodpecker, child of the Thunder, child of the Great Dark) but more consistent in his uncanniness and therefore capable of fuller development as the counterpart, the complementary opposite, of the first self.

Such oppositeness, as I have pointed out, always involves opposition, rising from the fact of the second self's intrusion and continuing largely at his initiative and under his control. The opposition may be one of malevolence on the second self's part, such as we have seen in the stories of Judas and Kamatha-Samvara; or it may be one of a misunderstood and resisted benevolence, such as the value which Enkidu, seen first as a rival in strength and impediment to self-indulgence, brings to Gilgamesh. Of the two kinds, it is the former opposition, resulting from genuine hatred, that is the more obviously dramatic and has had the wider appeal for readers. And so the second self most often encountered in creative literature is akin to the most primitive concept of the Twin Brother in that he is the evil second self, whose malevolence, however, is not directed against the tribe as a whole but concentrated upon the person of his first-self counterpart. This is necessarily true, since in any relationship between the selves the interest of the one is always centrally focused upon the other. It is implicit in the phrase, "evil second self," that what he wants above all is to visit evil upon the first self.

But there are different ways of doing this, or attempting to do it; with the result that the evil aspect of the second self subdivides into three main aspects of its own. Of these the most familiar is the most undisguised and pugnacious, the one we have already encountered in the dark Twins Ahriman and Kamatha-Samvara and the Apocryphal-Gnostic Judas: the second self as Pursuer. The pursuit need not be a literal chasing; it may for strategic purposes sometimes let the first self appear to do the pursuing, but such stratagems are never more than temporary, and always the general movement is the same — a pushing forward of the first self, whether by a gradual crowding or a headlong driving, toward the precipice of catastrophe. Often the first self goes over, but this is not necessarily to say that the second self is left to enjoy his triumph any more than the first self is "saved" when, overeager or miscalculating, the second self goes over in his victim's place. As we have seen in our survey of the Twins, the relationship between the selves is too sensitively intimate a one to be brought to an end by their physical separation; and in general the destruction of the one entails, either figuratively or literally, the destruction of the other as well. Sometimes, though rarely, neither is destroyed, and the selves come to some sort of amity or understanding, in which case the second self ceases to be the Pursuer and enters one of the other categories.

I have called the second self of creative literature the modern version of the uncanny Twin, and since our instinctive reaction to the uncanny is still one of fear this parallel is especially strong in the case of that most obviously fearful second self, the Pursuer. The uncanny Twin, it will be recalled, is the Twin of half-spirit parentage, spirit originally in animal form (in the broad sense of any subhuman creature, including birds and reptiles). The result is that the uncanny Twin often himself retains certain animal characteristics, such as the shagginess of Esau and Enkidu. And it is interesting that in the recent and modern literature to which we now turn, the second self as Pursuer not only sometimes is animalistic, but sometimes is literally an animal. An excellent example is found in Poe's story, *The Black Cat.*[1] At first glance it may seem odd to think of this cat as a pursuer when it is the one victimized; by the same token it may seem that if either party to the relationship is to be considered the uncanny self it should be the narrator, who is morally much more of a monster than the "monster" he walls up within the tomb. But this is to interpret both "pursuit" and "sympathy" in too narrow a sense. In pursuit for our purposes, what is important is not the movement of the pursuer but the movement of the pursued, and so it is quite possible to pursue the latter — to move him in the right (meaning for him the wrong) direction — while seeming to do just the reverse. In sympathy what is important is not moral approval but a sharing of feelings, an understanding that is emotional rather than intellectual; and in this story it is the narrator, sodden and sadistic though he is, who claims our sympathy in this broader sense; the cat for all its suffering and justification remains the inscrutable figure, the shadowed figure, and, increasingly as we read the story over, a figure far more sinister than its morally abandoned master.

Actually the master does not begin as an abandoned person. He is tender-hearted to a fault, and especially fond of animals, above all his cat. Where this cat has originated we are never told, so that we cannot call it literally an intruder. But the description of it should be noted. It is large and beautiful, black in every hair of its body, and "sagacious to an astonishing degree"; so intelligent that the narrator's wife frequently alludes to the old superstition that black cats are witches in disguise. "Not that she was ever *serious* upon this point — and I mention the matter at all for no better reason than that it happens, just now, to be remembered." Such a gesture of digression in a story in which not a word is wasted only underscores the idea in our minds: that of a dark and dangerous uncanniness which has with whatever appearance of innocence penetrated into the world of light. The suggestion of shadowy origin is heightened by the cat's name, that of the King of Shadows, Pluto.

But it is not only in his more than catlike intelligence that Pluto is humanized. The master's special attachment to the cat is matched by the cat's special attachment to the master; they have become almost insepa-rable companions, would be entirely so if the cat could have its way. And it is significant that while the degeneration which now occurs in the narrator's character is never explained, the sentence which introduces

it begins, as though accidentally, with just the factor that we might expect
to work in the opposite direction, the close and affectionate relationship
between this man and his favorite pet. "Our friendship lasted, in this
manner, for several years, during which my general temperament and
character . . . experienced a radical alteration for the worse."[2] Rapidly
the narrator goes downhill, becoming irritable and even brutal, to his
other pets, to his long-suffering wife, to all but Pluto. But at length the
night comes when he seizes Pluto too roughly, and the cat bites his hand.
The bite is of no consequence in itself, but its effect on the narrator is the
turning point of the story. The words in which he describes this effect
are for our purposes even more important than the deed which follows.

The fury of a demon instantly possessed me. I knew myself no longer. My
original soul seemed, at once, to take its flight from my body; and a more
than fiendish malevolence, gin-nurtured, thrilled every fibre of my frame.[3]

I have spoken of the necessary wish of the evil second self to inflict
evil on the first self, and to do so in full degree means more than merely
to inflict injury from without; it means somehow to transmit to the victim
the evil of the victimizer, thus working mainly from within. Such a
process, it is strongly suggested, has been going on from the beginning
of their friendship, but all this has been only preparation for the moment
when the cat-teeth at last penetrate the human skin, and a more than
fiendish malevolence floods in, seizing control of the will. The fact of
psychic possession alone, as we have seen, is never enough to give us a
true second self. There must be something more, and in this case it is the
Black Cat, which at the same time that it asserts its supremacy within the
narrator remains outside him, objectively "there," and serving the essential
function of target for the malevolence with which it has infected its
counterpart. It is this simultaneous subjective power over the narrator's
will and objective helplessness before it that seals the first self's damnation.
With a penknife the latter cores out one of Pluto's eyes from its socket.
By this deed he is lost, and he knows it, and the compulsive hanging of
the cat that follows is almost an anticlimax.

In the latter part of the story another cat appears — or *does* it
really appear? For it is suddenly perceived by the narrator on top of the
very hogshead of gin at which he has been staring, and on which up to this
instant he has seen nothing. When he approaches it, however, he is able
to touch it with his hand, and hears it purr loudly in response. This device,
of suggesting the coincident subjectivity and objectivity of the second self
by simultaneously planting the suspicion that he is hallucinatory in nature

and presenting evidence to counteract such a suspicion, is one that we shall meet with repeatedly in the literature of the second self. But still this second cat remains strange, even though tangible and audible, for except for a white splotch on the breast it is the exact replica of the earlier Pluto, even to the fact that it has lost one of its eyes.

With matchless skill Poe walks the line between natural and supernatural; for on the one hand nothing happens that cannot be explained by natural causes, and even such things as the way in which the white splotch gradually assumes the shape of the gallows *could* be attributed to the narrator's state of mind and nerves; while on the other hand there are strong suggestions that the second cat is the first returned as avenging revenant. In any event, it pursues in the same manner as before, under the guise of affection, the affection becoming steadily more insistent and intolerable as the narrator's welcome of the "new Pluto" turns more and more into hatred and fear. Again the choice of words and images, with their emphasis upon a growing closeness, almost as though the cat were attempting to devour its master, or to crush him into the same body with itself, is important.

Whenever I sat, it would crouch beneath my chair, or spring upon my knees, covering me with its loathsome caresses. If I arose to walk it would get between my feet and thus nearly throw me down, or, fastening its long and sharp claws in my dress, clamber, in this manner, to my breast.[4]

* * *

Alas! neither by day nor by night knew I the blessing of Rest any more! During the former the creature left me no moment alone, and in the latter I started hourly from dreams of unutterable fear to find the hot breath of *the thing* upon my face, and its vast weight, — an incarnate nightmare that I had no power to shake off — incumbent eternally upon my *heart!*[5]

But this weight upon the heart is no mere allegorical burden of conscience. The cat is as physically real as its master, and in fact uses this physical reality to bring about the latter's ruin. Tripping over the animal on his way down the cellar steps the narrator snatches up an ax to slay it; when his wife interferes he is driven "into a rage more than demoniacal" (again, "beside himself") and buries the ax in her brain. He conceals the corpse within the walls of the cellar, plastering over the surface to make it match the surrounding area. The cat has apparently fled in fear, and for all his guilt the narrator sleeps soundly again. So well has he covered up the traces of his crime that the police who come to search his house can find nothing, until in bravado the narrator raps on the wall just outside the spot where the corpse is hidden. Instantly from within comes a sound: a sobbing cry that rises to a scream and swells into a howl "half of horror and half of triumph, such as might have arisen only out of hell, conjointly from the throats of the damned in their agony and of the demons that exult in their damnation." The wall is torn away, the corpse is disclosed, and sitting on the latter's head, staring at its victim with solitary eye of fire, is the Black Cat.

Outstanding among the qualities of Pluto, for our purposes, is that *sine qua non* of any second self, the paradox of simultaneous separateness from the first self and identity with him. Along with this paradox goes the peculiar closeness which always characterizes the relationship between the selves, an almost exclusive preoccupation with each other so that within the framework of this story neither can be thought of as an independent unit. Yet it is a relationship which, for all its initial amity, is from the start a basically uneasy one, full of potential tension and explosion. It is a relationship in which, as always, the dark, uncanny member is the stronger of the two, the controller of events only more obviously in the latter part of the story than in the earlier. It is a relationship which, finally, goes beyond anything explainable by the given facts or by logic. In part there are the inexplicable emotional reactions that the two selves arouse in each other; those of the first self — the unmotivated special tenderness, the inadequately motivated change to a special viciousness — being, as always, the more readily observable.

Of the cat's reactions we know much less. If we consider only its later behavior we have, of course, the motive of revenge, but if we consider the larger picture suggested by the story as a whole, of the cat's deliberately evoking both the tenderness and the viciousness, we have an unmotivated malignancy that goes back further than we can trace it, and is the primal source of all specific motivations. In part there is the inexplicable insight, this as always more prominent in the second self than in the first, which enables the cat-self to know the soul of the man-self and exactly what strategy is needed to destroy that soul, or more accurately to swallow it into its own black bestiality. Increasingly throughout the story the image of devouring, the devouring of man by cat (its clambering up his clothes, its vast weight upon his breast, its hot breath upon his face), is hinted at. Strongly contributing to this hint is the imagery of color and the use of color contrast to suggest the complementary oppositeness that is a main feature of any relationship between the selves. The narrator is "white," a man of good instincts and intentions, but with a core of blackness that in the course of his relationship with the cat spreads outward through his whole being; the cat is black in more than its fur, unknown and mysterious and malignant; its sole spot of white does not alleviate but intensifies its blackness, gradually assuming the form of the gallows to which, from a beginning and with a purpose that are never defined, it has pursued its human other-self.

Another type of nonhuman second self, also particularly suitable to the role of Pursuer, is the monster. Thus the "Horla," in Guy de Maupassant's famous story,[6] drinks water and milk like an animal but is not an animal, crouches on the narrator's breast like the Black Cat but is not a cat, smells the odor of a rose and flips the pages of a book like a man but is not a man, feeds on the life of its victim but is not a vampire. It is the Horla, a new and terrible being, whose emergence means that the reign of man is over.

Generally the malignant monster, the vampire for example, has little or nothing in common with the second self. It tends to be entirely impersonal in its choice of victim, who is merely a means to an end; it comes from without, and despite the temporary closeness of association, remains without, a clearly separate being. The Horla, however, is quite another matter. The relationship between it and its victim is from the first intensely and exclusively personal. Without at all knowing why, on that fine day when his spirits are so buoyant, the narrator salutes the Brazilian three-decker coming up the Seine, and at that instant, accepting the invitation, the unseen Horla that has come with the ship from across the earth fastens upon his life, becomes his inseparable companion. This is a little different from the traditional "invitation" that gives entrance to the witch. It is not an accident; it is an impulse that the narrator can never explain, as though some force within him, outside the range of his conscious mind, had responded in kinship to a force without. The relationship that follows, like that between the narrator and the Black Cat, is one of increasing closeness, very much as though the invisible pursuer were attempting to consolidate their two forms into one. At first it is only such things as footsteps sensed, not heard, just behind the narrator's own, the feet of the alien intruder placing themselves exactly where his own have been only an instant before. But by degrees the Horla moves inside, affects the working of its victim's senses, the things he sees, turns the words in his mouth into their opposites, communicates with him not through whisperings in the ear but through thoughts in the brain.

He has come, the — the — what does He call himself — the — I fancy that he is shouting out his name to me and I do not know him — the — yes — he is shouting it out — I am listening — I cannot — repeat — it — Horla — I have heard — the Horla — it is He — the Horla — He has come![7]

*   *   *

He is within me, He is becoming my soul, I shall kill him![8]

But killing the Horla by ordinary means, tricking it into remaining in a barred and locked room and then setting fire to the house, gives only the temporary illusion of success. For how does the narrator know that so strange a monster, with its special fineness of bodily structure that makes it transparent to the human eye, can be destroyed by so crude an agent as fire? And how can he expect to destroy by purely outside means a creature by now as much inside him as outside, as much he as not-he? "Then — then — I suppose I must kill *myself!*"

The animal and the monster, though nonhuman and difficult to humanize, are both very much alive; it is the irrepressible vitality of the examples we have just considered that gives them their main fictional strength. Still another type of nonhuman figure derives much of its effectiveness from the fact that it is inanimate save when brought to life for fictional purposes: the portrait, photograph, statue, waxen copy, or mirror image. I have already mentioned these things, and pointed out that even when animated they usually remain objective duplicates solely and have no subjective relationship with the selves of the people they represent. Such duplicates are the shadow of Chamisso's *Wonderful Story of Peter Schlemihl* and the mirror image of Hoffmann's *Story of the Lost Mirror Image*. But contrasted with these stories are two others, in which the phenomena of intercepted and reflected light rays, animated and most inhumanly humanized, do become second selves, each in the role of Pursuer, and a grim and blood-chilling Pursuer indeed.

One is the shadow of Hans Christian Andersen's story, *The Shadow.*[9] He is an ordinary enough shadow at first, until like Peter Schlemihl his owner, the clever young scholar who is visiting the tropics, loses him. It is very vexing, but soon a new shadow commences growing out from the scholar's feet, and with this he returns to his home in the North, forgetting the old shadow. But the latter has not forgotten. After many years the scholar receives a visit from a man he does not recognize, a strikingly thin man but plainly one of wealth and distinction. The caller reveals that he is the lost shadow, though no longer altogether a shadow, for he has become a body, entered the life of the world, and been immensely successful — chiefly by means of blackmailing people on whom, while he was still a shadow, his intangibility and elasticity gave him the chance to spy.

Very wealthy now, he has returned to buy his freedom, but the scholar generously gives it for nothing, and treats the other as a complete equal. By degrees, however, inequality of status returns, though of exactly the opposite sort to the inequality that once existed between them. The old shadow puts on flesh, while the scholar becomes so thin that friends tell him he is beginning to look like a shadow. At length he is prevailed on, for the good of his health, to go on a trip as the guest of his former shadow, and to serve (since the latter has none of his own) as his shadow's shadow. At the watering place that they visit, the shadow wins the love of a beautiful princess, and when she asks him questions he cannot answer he tells her these are things he has known so long that his very shadow can answer for him, and so it proves, for the shadow's shadow is the learned scholar, and the princess is enchanted at the thought of how wise a man must be to have so wise a shadow.

The scholar has served his purpose, but he is not sent home. When he accompanies the shadow to the land ruled by the princess, where she is to marry the shadow, the shadow proposes to the scholar that the latter's shadow-status be made permanent, and that once a year, when his new master sits in the sunshine, he must lie at his master's feet, "as shadows do." The scholar in outrage threatens to tell the truth, but no one will believe him; he is merely, as his heartless counterpart puts it, a poor shadow gone mad; and as an act of charity the princess, on her wedding night, has him put to death.

To some extent the shadow of this story has a practical motive, but actually the use he makes of his former master is only a means to the end of torturing the latter, humiliating him, and driving him at last to the hopeless resistance that finishes him off. From the moment the shadow reenters the life of the scholar it is clear that the real motive is not calculation but a malice so profound and icily controlled that it seems almost gentle. For this will to destroy the first self, in any relationship in which the second self as Pursuer is involved, practical motives are only the occasion, never the cause. The real motive is always the destructive will itself.

Such a fundamental, unmotivated animosity is found also in the second of the two stories about "animated inanimate duplicates," this one not about a shadow but about a mirror image, which, like the mirror image of Erasmus Spikher in Hoffmann's story, is voluntarily given up by its owner, much to the owner's subsequent regret. But Spikher's regret, like Peter Schlemihl's at having given up his shadow, is merely that of having made himself a social pariah; in this story the regret is of a much more active nature, being caused not by the fact that the mirror image has gone away but by the fact that, like the shadow of the poor scholar, it will not stay away.

The story in question is the early film scenario by Hans Heinz Ewers, *The Student of Prague*.[10] The student-hero is the dashing but dissipated young swordsman, Baldwin, who has squandered his inheritance in a merry life that has left him desperately short of funds. Sitting gloomily before the great mirror in his ancestral hall he is visited by a strange old man named Scapinelli, who asks the young hero to give him anything out of the room that he desires. Baldwin, supposing himself to possess nothing of value, agrees, whereupon Scapinelli walks off with Baldwin's image from the mirror. So far the course of events is very like that of the stories of Schlemihl and Spikher. Now, however, comes the change, for the *Spiegel-Ich,* once set free from dependence on its master, fastens itself upon the latter in a very different way, becomes the dogger of the latter's footsteps, the haunter of his thoughts, the thwarter of all his hopes and undertakings. Baldwin, having broken off relations with the dancer Lydu-schka, falls in love with a young countess, Margot, and wins her love in return. He engages to fight a duel with the countess' betrothed, firmly resolving to do the latter no harm; but before he even reaches the appointed place he sees his mirror image, no longer confined to mirrors, pass with a blood-stained sword in its hand; and to his horror learns that "he," in the person of his second self, has already slain his opponent. Such action is made possible, of course, by that intimate insight into the first self's mind, that ability to anticipate all his moves, that is character-istic of the second self in all his aspects. When Baldwin and Margot are again together they catch sight of themselves in a mirror; that is, they catch sight of Margot's reflection, but of Baldwin's, though he is standing beside her, there is no sign. Suddenly the missing image appears, not in the mirror but in the doorway of the room, grinning in mockery. When Baldwin attempts to flee he is constantly pursued by his tormentor. He gets a ride in a wagon, successfully covers his tracks, goes to reward the driver, and finds himself facing the *Spiegel-Ich.* Finally, having returned home and sunk once more into deep despair, he decides to take his own life. But at this instant the pursuing mirror image enters. In his fury Baldwin fires at it, and it vanishes, to reappear in the mirror. Baldwin laughs in triumph, but suddenly feels pain in his own breast, and in another instant falls dead.

In neither Ewers' story nor Andersen's is there any particular subtlety of character development, nor is the relationship between the selves explored in any depth. Nevertheless there is sufficient humanization and individualization of the duplicate in both cases to make possible its con-version into a second self, and all the main features of the second self as Pursuer are present: the closeness of relationship with the first self; the inexplicable insight into his mind; the contrast in character that at the same time constitutes a linkage (the icy cruelty of the shadow that is the "other side" of the scholar's mild benevolence, the vicious sadism of the reflection that complements the well-meaning impulsiveness of Baldwin);

the implacable malignancy, like that of the Black Cat or the invisible Horla, needing no motive but itself.

But the nonhuman figure of any sort always suffers from certain shortcomings when cast in the role of second self. The main difficulty is the impossibility of going very far with the process of giving him a genuinely developed character that can be counterbalanced to and made continuous with that of the first self, of probing for this purpose into the stuff of his soul, without either badly damaging verisimilitude or ruining the very originality of the effect that was aimed at in the choice of such a figure. It is in human rather than in merely humanized form that the second self, in all its categories, has been most memorably presented.

Naturally this is not to say that any human pursuer closely associated with his victim is necessarily the latter's second self. In Hawthorne's *The Scarlet Letter*,[11] old Roger Chillingworth fastens himself like a leech (and in the older sense of the word, used by Hawthorne, he *is* a leech) upon the Reverend Arthur Dimmesdale, the man who has made him a cuckold. But for all the closeness between the two men, it is not the sort that we are dealing with in this study. To the contrary, this closeness, wholly engineered by Chillingworth for the motive of revenge, has the effect not of drawing them together but of all the more sharply separating them. The essential irony of Chillingworth's vengeance is that his torture of Dimmesdale pushes the latter into self-renunciation and redemption, while it pushes Chillingworth himself into the arms of the Fiend, from whom by the end of the story he is not entirely to be distinguished.[12]

In other words, what we have to do with in *The Scarlet Letter* is a twoness with no real suggestion of oneness, and therefore only a pursuer, not a pursuing second self. In Dostoyevsky's novella, *The Double*,[13] we swing to the opposite extreme: a pursuer who possesses all the subjective continuity with his victim that Roger Chillingworth lacks, but little or none of the latter's objective convincingness. This imbalance is true from the beginning, when the pathetic little clerk, Mr. Golyadkin, who has been seen under embarrassing circumstances by his superior, pretends to himself that he is *not* himself, hotly argues the point within his own mind. "It really isn't me, it *isn't* me, and that's all there is to it." In the next chapter he visits his physician, Dr. Rutenspitz, and here we learn that Mr. Golyadkin is already suffering from systemized delusions of persecution, and that his physician is seriously concerned by his behavior. There follows the climactic "rejection by society" brought about by his ridiculous effort to force his way into a ball to which he has not been invited. It is only then that, alone in the night and almost beside himself with shame, he finds all at once that he is literally "beside himself," for out of the darkness appears his Double.

Now it is true that in all the stories we have considered so far in this chapter, Poe's and de Maupassant's especially, there is a certain suggestion that what happens to the hero is the result of his own disturbed mental condition. Such a suggestion is inevitable in view of the twofoldness of the second self's nature; since he is continuous with the first self's mind, he is bound to seem at times like a product of that mind. Indeed, it is not unusual for the first self too to have a strong sense of unreality about the second self, or at least the sense of a very different kind of reality from that of everyday. But this suggestion must always be accompanied by the simultaneous conviction, on the part of both the first self and the reader, of the second self's objective existence; and in *The Double* it is just such conviction that, for the reader and to some extent for poor Golyadkin himself, is systematically destroyed by the course which the story follows. The fact that other characters besides Golyadkin see and even speak with the newcomer, "Golyadkin junior," does little good, for by this time we are so well aware of the original Golyadkin's mental disorder, as well as of the other characters' awareness of it, that we cannot be sure either that the latter are not choosing to humor him or that the conversations in question ever take place at all. This is not because he is disturbed by the appearance and personality of Golyadkin junior; the first self is bound to be disturbed by such things, and deeply disturbed. The trouble is that in this story the disturbance of the first self *precedes* his encounter with the second, and it is disturbance so pronounced that we can have little faith in the dependability of his experiences. The result is rather an imaginative psychopathological case history, or (as Dmitri Chizevsky suggests[14]) a fictional study of the nature of existence, than a story about the second self.

Without doubt one of the works which influenced Dostoyevsky in planning *The Double* was E. T. A. Hoffmann's *The Devil's Elixirs*.[15] Like Mr. Golyadkin, Brother Medardus in this novel is a man of overwrought and at times of confused mind, so that there is in this account of his life, written by himself after his return to the monastery, some question as to how much has been literal event and how much imaginary. But the difference between the two stories is far greater than the resemblance, and it is this difference that places the Russian story largely outside, and the German one unmistakably inside, the realm of second-self literature. Mr. Golyadkin is introduced to us as a man of unbalanced mind, so that we tend to ascribe the extraordinary adventures that follow to the state of mind in which he begins them. Brother Medardus, on the other hand, introduces himself to us as an entirely rational youth who *becomes* temporarily unbalanced in the course of still more extraordinary adventures, so that we tend to ascribe the unbalance to the adventures, and even when the question of the literal accuracy of his narrative does arise, it is a genuinely open question as it is not in the case of Golyadkin.

This endlessly complicated novel centers in the corruption of Brother Medardus, as the result of being entrusted with the supervision of his monastery's relics, including a bottle said to contain one of the elixirs prepared by Satan for the temptation of Saint Anthony. From this moment, though he keeps the bottle locked in its chest, pride begins to make inroads into the breast of Medardus. One day a young count visits the monastery and is shown its chamber of relics by Medardus. The count is not named here, but there can be no doubt — from the fact that it is he who insists upon seeing the bottle and tasting the contents — that this is the same Count Victor who later reappears as Medardus' second self, converted into a monster of iniquity by his sampling of the forbidden liquor. Though Medardus, who in his usual piety and humility is the opposite of the cynical, arrogant count, refuses the latter's urging that he too try the elixir, the very smell from the uncorked bottle is enough to revive his sinful pride; he falls sinfully in love with a girl who is making confession to him; and he is saved from the further sin of fleeing from the monastery only by the prior, who, seeing the young man's disturbed condition, sends him on a mission to Rome.

The first adventure of Medardus' travels reintroduces the count, and apparently eliminates the latter from the story. In a forest, approaching a ravine, Medardus sees a young man asleep on a ledge and gradually sliding over the rim. Awakened by Medardus' shouts of warning, the young man loses his balance and hurtles downward out of sight. At this moment a groom appears, and mistakes Medardus for the young man who has just fallen, Count Victor, who has been planning to disguise himself as a Capuchin monk in order to carry out some design in the nearby castle. Tempted by his chance to embark upon a new life, Medardus enters the castle and commences an affair with the young Baroness Euphemia. We have here one of those bizarre jugglings of identity and pseudo-identity of which the German Romantics were so fond. For most of the household Medardus is simply himself, but for the groom and Euphemia he is Victor, disguised as the person he really is: Medardus. Thus Medardus is playing the part of a Victor who is supposedly playing the part of Medardus, so that the latter's real identity (like that of Rosalind in *As You Like It*) is serving to conceal his identity.

But in this case the disguise-within-disguise is no mere trick; it is the beginning of that delirium of self-abandonment — the abandonment of the Medardus-self to the Victor-self — that has been prepared for by the visit of the count to the monastery and the uncorking of the elixir of sin.

This infection of Medardus' soul continues now at a vastly accelerated pace. No sooner does he enter the castle than he finds himself embarked on the same series of crimes that Victor would have perpetrated had Medardus not come along: blasphemy, adultery, attempted rape, and a double murder. As Medardus rushes from the castle with a crowd at his heels, he laughs and shouts defiance at his pursuers in a terrible voice, so terrible that it stops them in their tracks — and then all at once he sees before him the blood-stained figure of his second self, and realizes that it is the latter from whom the terrible voice has come.

It is from here on that the real pursuit of Medardus begins, not by the inhabitants of the castle but by the supposedly dead Victor, who has not been killed but has been driven hopelessly insane by his fall, and who now even manages to get hold of the Capuchin garb which Medardus has discarded in his flight, and becomes convinced that he is the renegade monk Medardus. In this pursuit, dream and fantasy and fact constantly interpenetrate one another, but are not interchangeable with one another. Asleep in his room in a gamekeeper's house Medardus dreams that a dark figure enters by the door: a figure which to his horror he recognizes as himself, clad in his discarded Capuchin robes. The figure challenges him to climb up to the roof with it, where they will wrestle, "and the one who pushes the other over will become king and be able to drink blood." Suddenly Medardus awakens, to find just such a figure indeed in his room, but standing at his table with its back to him. The figure drinks up the remainder of the Devil's elixir and rushes out.

In the town where he next stops Medardus encounters the beautiful Aurelia, the girl whom he has attempted to ravish in the castle. Recognized by her as the man who murdered her brother, he is thrown into prison to await trial. From beneath the floor he hears a soft knocking, a voice calling his name, a voice that almost seems to be his own. The next night the same thing happens; there are sounds of scratching, rattling, scraping; a hole opens in the floor under his feet, and an arm appears with a knife in its hand: the same knife with which Medardus has already murdered the brother of his beloved. Medardus seizes the knife, and now a naked man forces his body waist-high through the hole, and Medardus once more recognizes — himself.

But Victor does more than furnish the knife. He confesses publicly to being Medardus, and the real Medardus is therefore freed, wins the hand of Aurelia, and is about to be married to her. Standing with her at the window, he sees his second self being drawn to the scaffold in a cart, and his eyes meet those of the madman below, who cries aloud the same summons he has cried before, but only in Medardus' dreams: "Bridegroom! Bridegroom! Come on to the roof! Up there we will fight with each other, and the one who pushes the other over will become king, and be able to drink blood!"[16]

Aurelia tries to tear him from the window, and Medardus, possessed suddenly like the owner of the Black Cat by "the demons of hell," slays her (he supposes) with the fatal knife, rushes downstairs, frees the prisoner, and runs off with him into the woods. Here, in an almost archetypal form of the second self as Pursuer, Victor springs upon Medardus' back and rides him like an incubus, giggling and howling as they stumble along.

> Hee, hee, hee! Hee, hee, hee! Little Brother! I . . . am . . . al-ways . . . with you, will . . . not . . . not . . . leave . . . you. Must . . . must . . . carry . . . me. Have . . . come . . . from . . . the . . . gallows. Wanted . . . to . . . break . . . me . . . on . . . on . . . the . . . wheel. Hee, hee![17]

When at last Medardus falls unconscious from exhaustion, Victor once more exchanges clothes with him, restoring him to the outward appearance of Brother Medardus, and to the long process of atonement for having allowed himself to be infected by his sin-maddened second self. But Victor does not drop out of the story. He returns to perform in fact the murder of Aurelia, the murder which Medardus has supposed that he himself committed; and he returns once more to visit his other-self Medardus just before the latter's death. What the issue of this visit is, whether expulsion of the Pursuer or some sort of final reconciliation between the two, we are not explicitly told, but at last the mad mocking laughs and cackles of the Victor-self die away, and Brother Medardus dies in peace.

Thus *The Devil's Elixirs,* far more than *The Double,* preserves the necessary balance between separateness and sameness. At the same time the hypersensitive temperament of Brother Medardus, and the reader's increasing involvement in the workings of his exacerbated mind, cause this balance at least to tilt toward the side of subjectivity.[18] In Melville's *Billy Budd*[19] we have a tilting toward subjectivity of a very different sort, caused not by emphasis on the inner workings of the first self but by just the reverse situation. In this story Melville is dealing less with the two sides of one fragment of the human personality (as Hoffmann does) than with the two moral poles of the human soul; really what he is presenting is, in a realistic and relatively modern setting, the ancient struggle between Light and Dark that we have seen embodied in the stories of Ormuzd and Ahriman, Marubhuti-Parsva and Kamatha-Samvara, Jesus and the Gnostic Judas. Such an effort always involves the danger, not of making the second self a mere product of the first self's mind, but of making both selves too clearly products of the writer's mind — allegorical abstractions rather than living characters. In *Billy Budd,* Melville avoids this danger, but a certain allegorical flavor is nevertheless present.

It is seen, for example, in the name of the first self. Billy Budd is twenty-one, physically and mentally mature, a "normal" young man in the best sense of the word. But in his innocence Billy is a child: "Baby Budd" as he is called, the unopened bud into which no worm of evil seems yet to have found its way. Impressed from the English merchantman *Rights of Man* into service on the outward-bound warship H.M.S. *Indomitable,* which in a time of mutiny and war must safeguard its indomitability by disregarding any rights of man, Billy retains all the sunniness of temper, all the unpretentious charm of person, all the unalloyed decency and good-will, that have made him the "Handsome Sailor" of the merchant ship and soon win him no less popularity among his new and more hard-bitten comrades.

There is one exception to the general rule, and this is a man as out of the ordinary in his own way as Billy: John Claggart, the master-at-arms, "a sort of chief of police charged among other matters with the duty of preserving order on the populous lower gun-decks." This duty he carries out by a system of espionage, an underground secret activity as different as possible from Billy's doings in the foretop. At almost every point the two are carefully contrasted. True, they have in common the fact that both are of mysterious and presumably distinguished origin, but even here they are opposites: Billy, though a foundling, shows in his whole person the traces of a noble descent, noble in both senses of the word; while Claggart, though evidently a man of education and breeding, appears to have been guilty of some dark, unnamed transgression that has forced him to flee the society to which he once belonged. But it is not only Claggart's past that is dark; like Ahriman, like Kamatha-Samvara, he is in all respects the dark being who contrasts with, complements, and menaces the light. Billy is fair, with yellow hair, welkin-blue eyes, and skin in which the rose still shows through the rich tan. Claggart is dark, with silken jet-black curls, inscrutable violet eyes that in emotion become muddy purple, and a pallid skin tinged with amber. Where Billy is frank and open Claggart is enclosed within a wall of reserve, most dangerous when he smiles or speaks pleasantly. Whereas Billy believes the best of everyone, Claggart believes the worst, and with special readiness when hatred inclines him to do so.

This sequence that is invariably true of the evil second self's attitude toward the first, of hatred coming before any rational cause for hatred, Melville is at particular pains to make clear. The hatred of evil for good is not to be explained by anything else but is itself an explanation: "the mania of an evil nature, not engendered by vicious training or corrupting books or licentious living, but born with him and innate, in short, 'a depravity according to nature'."[20] Claggart comes to misjudge Billy, and to assume an antipathy in the young sailor corresponding to his own. But this misjudgment does not signify a lack of capacity on his part to understand Billy; to the contrary he is (with the exception of Captain Vere, who does not enter into the relationship I am discussing) perhaps the only man on board possessed of such capacity, and strangely enough it is just from this capacity to understand that the misjudgment in specific matters stems. What he understands, not only through intellect but as Melville puts it "magnetically," is that here is a nature free from that malice which runs in Claggart's blood like a serpent's poison, a nature enjoying all the wholesomeness and peace of soul that Claggart has lost. Claggart's reaction is a monomaniacal hatred, but not a simple, unmixed hatred. For Claggart has the capacity not only to understand the phenomenon of goodness but also to appreciate it, and sometimes in a far deeper way than the merely aesthetic.

When Claggart's unobserved glance happened to light on belted Billy rolling along the upper gun-deck in the leisure of the second dog-watch, exchanging passing broadsides of fun with other young promenaders in the crowd, that glance would follow the cheerful sea-Hyperion with a settled meditative and melancholy expression, his eyes strangely suffused with incipient feverish tears. Then would Claggart look like the man of sorrows. Yes, and sometimes the melancholy expression would have in it a touch of soft yearning, as if Claggart could even have loved Billy but for fate and ban. But this was an evanescence, and quickly repented of, as it were, by an immitigable look, pinching and shrivelling the visage into the momentary semblance of a wrinkled walnut.[21]

The irrational opposition between the selves, as we have seen in the chapter on the Twin Brother, always contains, and sometimes, as we shall see, is completely outweighed by, an equally irrational attraction; and it is never quite possible to say where the one begins and the other ends, for like the psyches that experience them they resemble two trees growing out of a single root complex.

Of this opposition-attraction the second self is almost always more aware than the first self, whose comparative "normality" tends to make him accept such dark strange things only with reluctance. But in this case we have a first self so "normal" that he rejects their possibility completely, at least through the greater part of the narrative. Such innocence makes goodness incapable of combating evil in any active way. Yet at the same time Billy's is not the absolute innocence that would make his goodness invulnerable to evil. As a spark of Billy's brightness lies in Claggart's soul, so a tinge of Claggart's darkness lies in Billy's.

We are given a hint of this tinge very early in the story, when we learn that all is not quite so harmonious within Billy as we should expect from his outward appearance and general behavior; for under strong emotion his ordinarily easy and musical voice is liable to hesitate, to stutter, even to close off completely.

Not that a stutter, which might be thought of simply as the inarticulateness of good as contrasted with the glibness of evil, is itself a tinge in the soul. But as the story proceeds we find that this vocal defect is intimately associated with other and deeper-lying defects. When Billy sees a culprit on board being publicly scourged, what he feels is not the pity we expect but horror: a child's horror at the thought that such violence and public disgrace might somehow come to be visited upon *him*. Later, when an afterguardsman, acting as agent provocateur for Claggart, approaches him at night and asks him to join in a (purely fictitious) mutinous plot, we learn that Billy has a temper, and that his tendency to be horrified at the sight of violence is accompanied (as perhaps is always the case) by a tendency to respond to provocation with violence of his own.

And thus it is that Claggart's pursuit of Billy finds the latter vulnerable at last, fatally vulnerable in the climactic scene before Captain Vere where Claggart, his violet eyes blurring to their muddy purple, accuses the young sailor of treachery, and Billy, rendered voiceless by outrage, answers with a blow to Claggart's forehead, a blow that proves to be as thoroughly lethal as a bullet in the brain. This at least is the way Billy puts it: he bore no malice toward his accuser, and could he have answered with words he would have struck no blow. But a blow is never an answer; it is a retaliation; and the will to retaliate, no matter how well we may understand it, is always an ill will. As the spark of Billy within Claggart has burned briefly almost in a flame of love, so the stain of Claggart within Billy now spreads for an instant through his whole soul and bursts forth in one furious gesture that brings down both his pursuer and himself: the former in immediate death, the latter in execution at the end of a yardarm.

Thus, while in *The Devil's Elixirs* we have a first self whose mind is so readily influenced by his counterpart that we sometimes have trouble distinguishing between fact and fancy, in *Billy Budd* we have a first self who, far from tending to imagine too much, misses even what is plainly there to be seen, with the result that the author is forced to point it out for us in his own person. That is what I mean by saying that though in each case we have a major example of the literature of the second self, the former tilts slightly toward the psychopathic case history, the latter slightly toward the allegory. In the remaining two examples to be considered in this chapter there is no such tilting.

The first is a work by that other and somewhat later great sea-novelist, Joseph Conrad. In this story, *Victory*,[22] we find no less vicious and relentless a pursuing second self than Melville's Claggart, but we find a first self who, though a man of goodwill, is no unopened bud of innocence. Axel Heyst is the anglicized son of a Swedish aristocrat-philosopher, and the influence of his father's thought has had much to do with the shaping of his own character. The essence of the elder Heyst's philosophy is a "contemptuous, inflexible negation of all effort." "Of the stratagems of life," he has written, "the most cruel is the consolation of love — the most subtle, too; for the desire is the bed of dreams." "Look on — make no sound": these have been his last words of counsel to his son.[23]

But Axel Heyst has another father as well: the old Adam that speaks to him with the oldest voice in the world, urging involvement in the flesh and blood of life. The tragedy of Heyst is that he has never been able wholeheartedly to accept either of these paternal claims on his allegiance, because he has never been able wholeheartedly to reject either. He is repulsed by the fatuous vulgarity of "the world," yet irrationally lonely in his attempt to renounce it.

Like other sensitive men who can neither give themselves to the world nor turn their backs on it, Heyst is subject to that sin which is so peculiarly its own punishment, despair, and in a heavy mood he emerges briefly from the island hermitage to which he has retired and puts up at a hotel in Sourabaya. Unable to sleep, he attends a performance of "Zangiacomo's Ladies' Orchestra," and here is once again entrapped, at first by pity for, and then by increasingly sympathetic interest in, one of the "ladies," a girl whom Heyst comes to call "Lena," who is being subjected to both the brutality of Signiora Zangiacomo and the ardent advances of the hotelkeeper Schomberg. Heyst intervenes, spirits her away from her persecutors, and takes her back with him to his isolation at Samburan.

But isolation is possible only when one's indifference to the world is met by reciprocal indifference on the world's part, and Heyst has left behind him a Schomberg seething with resentment. At just this moment — the sort of moment when the second self always tends to appear — there comes to Sourabaya a strange trio. The leader is a tall, cadaverous walking skeleton with sunken eyes, who calls himself "plain Mr. Jones." His "secretary" is a feline cutthroat named Ricardo, and they bring with them an apelike retainer, Pedro. Taken in by Schomberg's stories of a store of wealth which Heyst has accumulated in Samburan, the three pursue Heyst to his retreat, arrive in the last stages of exhaustion, and are put up by him in a bungalow near the one in which he is living with Lena. Heyst is defenseless, partly because he is unarmed but more because he abhors the very idea of violence; and little by little the three strengthen their power over him. But a rift develops in their own ranks; Mr. Jones, infuriated by Ricardo's advances to Lena, shoots at his secretary and kills the girl, and a general carnage follows. Wang, Heyst's servant, kills Pedro; Mr. Jones kills Ricardo and then drowns himself; while Heyst, setting fire to his bungalow, is burned to ashes along with the corpse of Lena.

The pursuing trio constitutes a threefold unit of evil, corresponding to the threefold unit of good which they find on the island: Heyst, Lena, and Wang. But the central conflict is the one that we witness between the leaders of these two groups, Heyst and Mr. Jones: the sympathetic reasonable man with whom we tend to identify ourselves, and the alien intruder, who comes out of the unknown sea to invade the hero's island sanctuary. In all respects the two are as carefully contrasted as Billy Budd and Claggart. Heyst is a robust man with broad chest and shoulders, bronze-blond hair, tanned skin, and cool blue eyes. Mr. Jones is so thin as to be almost spectral, with little physical stamina; his hair is dark, his face pale, his dark eyes so sunken that they seem often mere patches of shadow. While Heyst is thoroughly masculine, "normal," in appearance and tastes, Mr. Jones is effeminate, with long eyelashes and thin, beautifully penciled eyebrows, and an absolute horror of women. And again the physical contrast is merely an external sign of the deeper inward one. Heyst is a sensitive man who recoils from the vulgarity of the world, but also a decent man, whose fellow-feeling for the unfortunate again and again draws him into the world, causes him to assume responsibility for others, and makes him vulnerable to the pursuit by Mr. Jones. Mr. Jones is a rapacious, cold-blooded desperado, "vicious, unconquerable, and deadly," a killer whose only interest in the unfortunate is the degree to which he can take advantage of them for his own ends.

And yet once more the diametrical oppositeness between them proves itself a linkage. Heyst is different from the savage Ricardo, but this is a difference largely of their being irrelevant to each other. The difference between Heyst and Mr. Jones is the very reverse of irrelevancy.[24] It is rooted in a basic sameness, and at the core of this sameness is a quality that might be called in traditional terms the intellectual sin of pride, leading to an attempted intellectual repudiation of the emotional and instinctual claims of life. In both men it is the same attempt, stemming from the same characteristics: unusual mental acumen, distrust of the feelings, self-centeredness, hypersensitiveness, fastidiousness. But the attempt takes them in exactly opposite directions. In Heyst the very sensitiveness that makes him recoil from life gives him the capacity for sympathy that keeps getting him involved in life, with consequent disillusionment and renewed withdrawal. In Mr. Jones the sensitiveness is of a purely selfish kind; he becomes involved in human life not through any tug of sympathy with it but only through the desire to exploit it. In Heyst's temperament there is the resultant tendency to despair, which makes him aware of and responsive to other people's despair. In Mr. Jones the tendency is to that shallow and restless form of despair which we call boredom, and which stirs him to further adventures in his own kind of involvement. Heyst's fastidiousness makes him shrink from competition, makes violence impossible for him, makes him avoid common women but find irresistibly appealing all that is *un*-common in Lena. Mr. Jones' fastidiousness leads him to be a sort of connoisseur in seeking out the competition that will be worthy of him. He practices his violence with complete indifference and the most elegant of manners. He avoids not only common women but all women, for in the realm of sex the fastidiousness that makes Heyst seek out only the purest and best makes Mr. Jones recoil with disgust from heterosexuality into what is obviously a homosexual relationship with Ricardo.

And joined with these features in the relationship between Heyst and Mr. Jones is that invariable mark of shared identity which we have seen in all instances thus far explained: that mysterious sense of closeness unlike anything which either of them experiences with anyone else. "You and the governor ought to understand each other," Ricardo tells Heyst, and Ricardo is more right than he suspects. They *do* understand each other, despite Mr. Jones' mistake about Heyst's hoarded wealth and Heyst's consequent puzzlement about Mr. Jones' motive; it is an understanding that goes far deeper than such specific matters as these, for behind it lies the inevitable seeing by each in the other of denied or unrealized facets of his own nature.

In neither case is this seeing conscious, but in the typical fashion of the second self Mr. Jones comes closer to such consciousness, and taunts his more respectable counterpart with the fact. " 'Ah, Mr. Heyst,' he said, 'you and I have much more in common than you think' ": a remark so galling to the usually undemonstrative Heyst that as he reports it to Lena he strikes the table with his fist. But galling or not, the fact of what they have in common remains. Just as through most of his adult life Heyst has lied to himself about his disinterest in worldly things, so now he finds Mr. Jones lying to him, far more flagrantly and with a baser motive, but telling substantially the same lie; and it makes him acutely uncomfortable. He wishes that Mr. Jones were the commonest sort of ruffian, to whom one could "talk straight" and from whom one could at least hope for some humanity; but his own brand of inhumanity, which has "managed to refine everything away," gives him the capacity, possessed by no one else, to sense the full inhumanity of the Pursuer and terrible threat of the "reckoning" with which Mr. Jones confronts him.

Of course it is not the menace of physical force that chiefly appalls Heyst; far worse is the sense of a hold over him that is moral in nature, and this arouses in him not only revulsion but an intense curiosity. "I am he who is —" Mr. Jones tells him; and it is this enigmatic fragment — this rather than the practical question of what Mr. Jones proposes to do — which in the tense interval that follows fixes itself in Heyst's mind and to which he returns at their last interview. But already Mr. Jones, without naming names, has made his meaning clear. He, like Claggart, is a gentleman who has come down in the world. "Having been ejected . . . from his proper social sphere because he had refused to conform to certain usual conventions, he was a rebel now, and was coming and going up and down the earth."[25] All this is said in a jesting tone, and on the event level it *is* a jest; but on the symbolic level Mr. Jones' suggestion is also the book's suggestion: that as Pursuer he is not merely an unusually gifted and vicious bandit but also the realization and magnification, as pure Satanic evil, of the seeds of evil present in the soul of his victim.

Yet Mr. Jones is no abstraction, and the mysterious affinity between him and Heyst is further established by the reciprocal reactions of the second self to the first. It should be noted that Mr. Jones comes to Samburan only in a mood of greed and boredom, quite impersonally, just as he has gone to Sourabaya to victimize the innkeeper Schomberg. But at his first meeting with Heyst all impersonalism disappears. There is never any of the pained yearning that we have seen in Claggart gazing secretly upon Billy Budd; in Mr. Jones' shriveled psyche there is no capacity for even a momentary softening. But he *is* moved. For the first time in Ricardo's experience of him a hint of passion is shown by "the governor," the peculiar feeling that his pursuit of Heyst "constitutes a sort of test." When the test comes, however, Mr. Jones finds it considerably less enjoyable than he has expected. In the final "showdown" scene it is he, for all his overwhelming advantages, who goes emotionally to pieces; his voice becomes wild and shrill, his face glistens with sweat, his lips are dry and black. It is not ordinary fear, for ordinary frays and risks are like the breath in Mr. Jones' slender nostrils; it is something in the personality of this quiet, courteous man facing him which affects him, just as it is something in his own personality, rather than the threat of his concealed revolver, that at the same time affects Heyst.

If we miss the point of this affinity between them we are bound to find the ending an egregious piece of coincidence. Mr. Jones just "happens" to shoot Lena, despite his expert marksmanship, instead of Ricardo at whom he has aimed, whereupon Heyst, setting fire to the bungalow, immolates himself upon her pyre. On the level of pure event it is pure chance, as it is that Mr. Jones should "happen" to enter Heyst's life at the precise moment he does. But to read the story on this level is to miss the core of it (and it is no less an "inside narrative" than *Billy Budd*), to miss in particular the whole careful process by which the parallel and continuity between the two men are established. It is not Mr. Jones alone, but Mr. Jones and Heyst together, moving in a "spectral fellowship" to which Heyst could put an end if he chose (only he does not choose), who find Lena with Ricardo; it is over Heyst's shoulder that Mr. Jones fires his shot. But this is merely their association in the act; when we consider the force behind the act the association becomes even closer. It is the sickness in Mr. Jones' soul, divorcing him from all natural sympathy with his fellow creatures and leaving him only the substitute of perverted desire, that flares up in hysterical jealousy and (spoiling his aim a trifle) presses his finger upon the trigger. And it is this same sickness which, mutatis mutandis, has poisoned the soul of Heyst, has already before the coming of the bandits chilled and half killed his relationship with Lena, and now paralyzes him with doubt in her at just the moment when a single motion of his hand could save her life: a doubt which, stemming from the same cause, is the exactly timed accompaniment on his part to the jealousy of Mr. Jones. Heyst at the end is well aware of this sickness and the part it has played in bringing about the tragedy of Lena's death. His mood, as he stands over her with the sea captain Davidson, is one of guilt quite as much as of grief; and it is in this mood of guilt that he burns himself to ashes with the body of the girl to whom, while living, he could never wholly give himself.

The malignancy of the second self toward the first, as I have said, can never be adequately explained by a rational motivation. It precedes all motivations, as the Black Cat's malignancy toward its master seems to precede the latter's ill-treatment of it. Often, however, the second self advances a motive, apparently in large part for his own benefit, in an effort at self-understanding or at least at self-justification. Thus Mr. Jones convinces himself that he is justifiably taking revenge on Heyst, since Heyst belongs to that class of society which has hounded him out of his proper sphere. This fastening upon a motive is sometimes made a very important part of the second self's hold over the first, and what gives it its power is the second self's ability to see into his counterpart's soul, and see the traces of guilt that lie hidden there. Claggart's accusation of Billy is utterly false, yet there is that within Billy which for all the latter's conscious innocence does indeed constitute, as Claggart charges, "a mantrap under his ruddy-tipped daisies." Mr. Jones could not be accusing a man less inclined to persecute others, yet Heyst *is* guilty of pride, of aloofness, of dispassionate contempt.

We see this tendency depicted with especial effectiveness in the last of the examples we shall consider in the present category, one which unlike the stories we have considered thus far belongs to our own time: an American novel set against the background of modern, mechanized Manhattan, and applying the relationship between the selves to one of the major problems of modern society, the relationship between Gentile and Jew. It is interesting that the Jew, who by literary tradition has been a rather mysterious person, appears here as the first self, the comparatively reasonable and sympathetic viewpoint character, while the second self is a Gentile; and that for all our present tendency to think of the Jew as an almost symbolically wronged figure, the sense of guilt is not awakened by the Jew in the Gentile, but awakened by the Gentile in the Jew.

The novel is Saul Bellow's *The Victim*,[26] a deliberately ambiguous title, since a part of the story's purpose is to raise the question of which is the real and original victimization: that which we see the second self inflict on the first, or that which the second self accuses the first of having inflicted on him. Even before the second self makes his appearance the nasty overtones of anti-Semitism, and of a reciprocal anti-Gentilism, are present. Asa Leventhal, editor of a small trade magazine, is forced to leave his office one afternoon to go to the help of his sister-in-law. As he leaves he happens to hear his employer Mr. Beard complaining to someone else that Leventhal has behaved "just like the rest of his brethren." The remark arouses counter-resentment in Leventhal, so strongly that he does not return to the office later in the day, since "it might seem that he was trying to establish himself as one of the 'brethren' who was different." And as we become better acquainted with Leventhal we find that despite his physical bulk he is a very thin-skinned young man. His family background is unhappy; his father has been a brutal and selfish man; his mother (whom Leventhal resembles to an extent that sometimes troubles him) has gone insane; and he himself, caught in the economic paralysis of the Depression, has spent years of deprivation and humiliation. He has survived; he has, as he tells his wife Mary, "got away with it"; but in a sense he has not got away with it, for these dark times have left a smudge of their darkness on his spirit; and he often thinks of that part of humanity that did not get away with it, the part he almost became one with: "the lost, the outcast, the effaced, the ruined."

It is out of this Legion of the Lost Ones, this underworld of dingy shadows, that Leventhal's reverse counterpart emerges. It happens (as always) at an unfortunate moment, when Leventhal is particularly unready, with nerves on edge, easily caught off guard. His wife, on whose stability and good sense he is strongly dependent, is visiting her family in the South, and New York is sweltering in almost unbearable heat; he is worried about his brother's family, both worried and irritated about his brush with Mr. Beard. When he goes back to his empty flat that night the doorbell rings, but no one is below. Unable to sleep, he strolls to a nearby park, and finds someone near him, watching him steadily. Immediately Leventhal's mind, without the slightest apparent cause, jumps to thoughts of hostility and violence, and of counter-violence in case the stranger should "start something."

The stranger does indeed "start something," though for the present only in words. He proves to be not a complete stranger but a former casual acquaintance named Kirby Allbee, who accuses Leventhal of having come in response to his letter (a letter Leventhal has never received), come out of curiosity, wanting to see and not be seen, in order to have a look at "the results." What he means by "the results" involves a still more ridiculous accusation: that Leventhal, angered by Allbee at a party years ago (it was during the years when he was jobless and Allbee employed; and Allbee, drunk, made certain offensively patronizing remarks about Jews), took revenge by deliberately insulting Allbee's employer in an interview Allbee had arranged for him, thus getting Allbee not only fired but blacklisted, so that he has never been able to find another job. The man is obviously a crank, a drunken derelict, and Leventhal angrily denies both accusations and returns home. Here, in his postbox, he finds a note signed "Sincerely, Kirby A.," containing the information that Allbee would be waiting in the park where they have just met.

This is only the beginning, but already the main features of the relationship between the selves are present. There is the sudden appearance of the second self out of the shadows, with his intense, inexplicable concentration upon and animosity toward the first self, and with an equally intense and inexplicable reaction on the first self's part. There is the absurdly inadequate motivation of Allbee; the hatred he shows is not felt to be the result of the motive he gives for it so much as the motive is felt to be the result of — the excuse for — the hatred. There is the strange knowledge each has of the other: Leventhal's ability to recall Allbee's name after all these years; Allbee's awareness of where Leventhal lives, where he works, even where his wife has gone. There is the oppositeness between them; in person: Leventhal bulky and stout, Allbee tall and thin (here for once the first self is dark and the second self blond); in character: Leventhal serious, naive, clumsy, conscientious, Allbee mocking, sophisticated, undependable, coming apart at the seams; in situation: Leventhal the impoverished Jew who has pushed his way up in the world, Allbee the cultured New England Gentile who has simultaneously slid down to the bottom. And within the oppositeness there is already the hint of basic continuity. The same sense of persecution that was once so dangerously strong in Leventhal, and from which he is still far from free, faces him now in Allbee like his own magnified and distorted image; indeed there is an even more intimate connection, for (at least according to Allbee) it is Leventhal's sense of persecution by Allbee that led to Allbee's persecution by Leventhal. There is the indubitable objective reality of the episode, and at the same time on Leventhal's part a sense of unreality about it, of something grotesque and namelessly dreadful, the feeling "that he had been singled out to be the object of some freakish, insane process . . ." Finally there is the revelation, as Leventhal returns home and finds the note, that by some force he does not understand he has been brought to do, without knowing it, exactly what Allbee has wanted him to do.

Increasingly, in the chapters that follow, this mystery deepens. Allbee becomes steadily more convincing to us, and yet always — as compared with all other characters in the book — having a certain aura of strangeness about him, at least for Leventhal, and it is only through Leventhal's eyes that we see him. These eyes, admittedly, are not seeing things with the calm dispassionateness that they might; nevertheless Leventhal is not deranged as Mr. Golyadkin is, and it is only Allbee whom he sees in this way, just as it is only *by* Leventhal that Allbee seems interested in being seen. Step by step the latter forces himself, like the Frog-Prince in the fairy tale, into Leventhal's life, into Leventhal's very being, until the edges between their separate identities begin in a nightmarish way to haze and blur together.

Thus after a second visit to his sister-in-law Leventhal returns to his flat. He is in the midst of writing a letter to his wife when the bell rings. He goes through the motions (wholly for his own benefit, for he is quite alone) of wondering who it can be, but he already knows. Instinctively, as at their first meeting he thought of resisting physical attack, he now thinks of physical flight. A moment later he knows, without seeing or hearing him, that Allbee has entered the room, but he pretends not to know. Only when he has finished the letter does he appear to take notice of Allbee, who stands and smiles at Leventhal as though quite aware of what strange thoughts have been running through the latter's mind. Allbee admires the comfort of Leventhal's flat, so sharply in contrast to the vile holes in which *he* has been living; and all at once the image of such holes rises into Leventhal's mind with a vividness as though he were this moment touching such beds with his own flesh, drinking such coffee with his own lips, feeling the smeared, bleary winter sun with his own back and thighs. Allbee admires the photograph of Leventhal's wife, and looking at it (seeing qualities in the face that Leventhal himself has never seen until now) his eyes fill with tears; and we learn for the first time that his own wife is dead, killed years before in a motor-car accident, while visiting her family in the South, just as Leventhal's wife is doing now. This parallel is returned to from time to time in succeeding scenes, with suggestions by Allbee that the same thing may very justifiably happen to Leventhal's wife — justifiably, because, according to Allbee, it is Leventhal who is responsible for the tragedy. *His* wife went back to her family because she and Allbee were separated; and they were separated because Allbee could find no job; and he could find no job because Leventhal had insulted Allbee's employer Rudiger for the specific purpose of getting Allbee blacklisted, of ruining him. In a spasm of resentment he clutches and twists Leventhal's shirt as he talks, and Leventhal slams him away against the wall. It is Allbee, this time, who retreats.

But he retreats only for the moment, and only in his physical person. His insane accusation has imbedded itself in the young Jew's mind, and as Leventhal recalls the Rudiger episode he realizes that he did lose his temper, that he did deliberately infuriate the offensive Rudiger, who may very well have taken out his fury on Allbee. Certainly this was not the result that Leventhal intended, but could he just possibly without intending have at least contributed to it? He discusses the matter with people who have known both him and Allbee, and their constrained manner both puzzles and further troubles him; they evidently think there is something in the charge. Leventhal is outraged by what he considers their treachery. And so Allbee's sense of persecution, attributed by him to Leventhal's sense of persecution, reawakens and feeds the latter.

The pursuit continues, both the external one and the internal. Allbee appears in a restaurant and intensely embarrasses Leventhal by accusing the latter's nephew of stealing a jar of mustard. Taking his nephew on to the zoo, Leventhal is sure he is being trailed by Allbee; so sure (though he catches no glimpse of his pursuer) that once more, as at the mention of the flophouses in which Allbee has lived, he has the sense of almost being converted into Allbee, as though their two bodies were growing into one.

Half out of fear of being mistaken, he made no effort to catch Allbee. He tried to put him out of his thoughts and give all his attention to Philip, forcing himself to behave naturally. But now and then, moving from cage to cage, gazing at the animals, Leventhal, in speaking to Philip, or smoking, or smiling, was so conscious of Allbee, so certain he was being scrutinized, that he was able to see himself as if through a strange pair of eyes: the side of his face, the palpitation in his throat, the seams of his skin, the shape of his body and of his feet in their white shoes. Changed in this way into his own observer, he was able to see Allbee, too, and imagined himself standing so near behind him that he could see the weave of his coat, his raggedly overgrown neck, the bulge of his cheek, the color of the blood in his ear; he could even evoke the odor of his hair and skin. The acuteness and intimacy of it astounded him, oppressed and intoxicated him.[27]

Allbee prevails on Leventhal to let him live in the flat, helps himself to an extra key so that he can come and go as he likes, reads Leventhal's private correspondence, gets Leventhal to lend him money, persuades Leventhal to do what Allbee once did for him: to try to arrange an interview to get Allbee a job. Under the strain Leventhal, who has rebuked Allbee for drinking, most uncharacteristically gets drunk himself. Only when Allbee brings a woman to the flat while Leventhal is out, actually has an affair with her in Leventhal's own bed, does Leventhal at last rebel, and eject his tormentor, but he cannot eject the episode from his mind. The woman's scent remains in his bed; her curiously shaped eyes seem to be like his own eyes (the curious shape of his wife's eyes has also been mentioned); in themselves and in their women he and Allbee once more merge into each other, both in his mind and in the reader's. He goes to bed, barricading the door, the chain of which he has smashed on his way in. In the middle of the night he awakens to find the door open and the flat full of gas. Allbee is sitting in the kitchen; the gas stove is on and unlighted. For the last time Leventhal drives his pursuer out, out of his kitchen, out of his flat, and this time out of his life.

Not permanently out. At the close of the story Allbee makes an unexpected return, an Allbee as changed as Leventhal is changed. Their brief last meeting serves the purpose of clarifying for us the nature of the effect that their relationship has had upon them both: an effect very different from that of any of the other relationships we have considered in this chapter and one which, since it takes us into a different category of the second self, we must return to at a later point.[28] Through the greater part of the novel, however, Kirby Allbee is unmistakably the second self as Pursuer; less violent than Count Victor, less vicious than John Claggart or Mr. Jones; yet despite his personal insignificance, his weakness and irresoluteness and general depravity, to a certain extent just because of these things, perhaps the most implacable Pursuer of all.

In the figure of the Pursuer, then, we find the descendant of the most primitive type of Twin Brother, the evil second self who prosecutes his cause of ill will toward the first self in the most direct fashion possible, sometimes by betrayal, often by the threat or outright use of physical force: Count Victor perched on the shoulders of the fleeing Medardus, Mr. Jones prodding his revolver into Heyst's ribs, Allbee ripping open the front of Leventhal's shirt. Such a direct approach is frequently effective, but has the disadvantage (from the second self's viewpoint) that it can scarcely help, save in the case of such an innocent as Billy Budd, putting its victim on guard and arousing his resistance. There is also an approach, perhaps somewhat less ancient in origin but still very ancient, in which the evil second self assumes a less obviously menacing aspect and takes a more devious tack. It is this form to which we turn next.

4

The Second Self As Tempter

Among the pursuing second selves we have found two, John Claggart and "plain Mr. Jones," whose personalities are suggestive of an evil beyond their specific evil: evil on a supra-individual, universal scale. They are not in the least allegorical abstractions; nevertheless about both these fallen gentlemen there is something (Mr. Jones taunts Heyst with the fact) reminiscent of a more famous fallen gentleman, who, long before Mr. Jones, had been ejected from his proper social sphere for unconventional behavior, and was going to and fro in the earth.

In fact about the evil second self in any of his forms there is always implicit the same suggestion. The combination of things that gives him his special power to victimize the first self — his terrifying alienness together with his no less terrifying familiarity, his unaccountable malice together with his unaccountable insight — is the same combination which characterizes the spirit of Evil by whatever name it is known, that superhuman force of darkness in the universe from which, in the most primitive Twin legends, the uncanny Brother is thought to be descended, and from some taint of which even the most resplendent second selves of literature are never quite free. In the evil second self, who is at the furthest remove from anything resplendent, this suggestion of an archetypal darkness is very strong and at times, as in the two cases just cited, inescapable: not simply the diabolical in the loose sense of the word, but overtones of the source of all diabolism, and sometimes the Prince of Darkness in person.

For the Devil of modern and recent literature, however, the shortcomings in the role of Pursuer that I have mentioned have brought about a change in strategy from that of more primitive embodiments of evil. Generally speaking he prefers a more subtle and easygoing manner, seeks not so much to destroy directly as to coax or argue into an attitude that will result in self-destruction, and to this end he presents instead of the foul face of terror the fair one of desire. It is for this reason that he is so often known by the name that describes his chief instrument of destruction, the Father of Lies; or by the name which I am applying to this whole category of second selves, the Tempter.

This is not to say that all second selves as Tempters are literally the Devil. Nor, conversely, is the Devil always a second self. In fact, certain serious obstacles have had to be overcome to enable him to play such a role at all. The main trouble is that though as Evil Incarnate he does act out of a malignancy springing primarily from his nature rather than from any specific purpose, he also tends to apply this malignancy to all rather than one. For the concentration upon the single victim of the first self a personal relationship is necessary which earlier concepts of the Devil made impossible. The Lucifer of Dante, chewing tiny human sinners in the teeth of his three mouths; the Lucifer of Marlowe, before whom Faustus grovels in terror, or even this Lucifer's lieutenant Mephistophilis, beside whom Faustus is little more than a bumptious boy; the gloomy and awesome archfiend of Milton, looking down upon the human pair in the as yet unviolated Garden — to such figures as these the specific earthly victim is no sort of alternative self, but only a child, a pawn between the mighty opposites of Good and Evil.

One might suppose, then, that if the Devil were to play the role of second self, the first self could be no one but God. We have already seen some tendency, in unorthodox medieval Christian legend, to think of him as the second self of God the Son; we have seen him in Persian legend as the dark second self and oppressor of God the Brother; and in at least one early Hebraic legend (the Book of Job) we find him as something closely resembling the second self, the successfully tempting second self, of God the Father. But all this is either pre-Christian or deviant-Christian material. From the orthodox Christian viewpoint, making the Devil the second self of God would involve a difficulty even greater than that which militates against making him the second self of man. For God as Almighty and All-Good cannot be affected by Evil at all; there is simply no contest possible. The young Jesus who walks in the wilderness encounters Satan, but there is no indication that he is at any point influenced by Satan. In Milton's *Paradise Regained,* which enormously expands the apostolic account, Satan's schemes and threats are from the first hopelessly inadequate, and the invulnerability of Jesus comes dangerously close to smugness.

In the literature we are examining, therefore, all of which is influenced by Christian tradition, the concept of the Devil as full-fledged Emperor of Evil is not a very promising one for our purposes. He needs either to be pulled down to the human level or elevated to the divine. And as all readers of this literature know we have tended on the whole to do the former, allowing our revised version of the Infernal Potentate to retain minor vestiges of supernatural power, but giving him human qualities, human frailties, human limitations, and often a very excellent human wit. Such a Devil, as the result of such a descent, becomes available at last for the role of second self as Tempter of man.

But even when humanized the Devil does not automatically become a second self. He must first meet the requirements that have been described in the first chapter; and this means, above all, that he must combine in his person the logically irreconcilable opposites of subjective continuity with his first self and objective independence of him. It is failure to recognize the importance of this combination that has led writers on the subject (for example, Rank, Chizevsky, Vivas, Tymms)[1] to accept as a second self that most droll and sophisticated of Devils, the shabby-genteel visitor who appears in the room of Ivan Karamazov on the night before Dmitri Karamazov's trial for murder (the murder which Ivan, knowingly-unknowingly, has brought about).[2] In many respects he does seem to be Ivan's second self. He is not the Tempter-in-general, but the very particular Tempter of Ivan, tempting with Ivan's own enlightened rationalism carried to its logical conclusion. He is the reverse side of Ivan's indignant scepticism, which is really an outraged idealism that has turned in its disillusionment to intellectual mockery of the world. Ivan's Devil, on the other hand, is troubled with no outrage, because he has never been troubled with any idealism; he offers the temptation of that urbane peace of mind that seeks nothing, because there is nothing to seek. Amiably in control, showing an intimate knowledge of Ivan's words and secret thoughts, he uses Ivan's own mockery of the world to mock Ivan, demonstrating by implication the immaturity of the other's mockery in its incompleteness and painful intenseness.

All of this sounds like traditional second-self behavior. But Ivan's diabolical visitor is not Ivan's second self, and Dostoyevsky has been at considerable pains to make the fact clear. Ivan's visitor is believable, unforgettably and frighteningly believable; but he is never for an instant *believed*. This is not a splitting of hairs; the distinction is clear and the gap is wide. It is true that the experience of self-encounter is often accompanied by a certain sense of unreality on the first self's part; and we might at first glance appear to have the same thing in this scene, when Ivan keeps insisting that the Devil is not there, while at the same time being compelled to see him and listen to him. But actually it is not the same thing, for of the essence of compulsion is the fact that the person compelled knows better. At no time does Ivan fail to know better, and what is more important is that at no time does the reader fail to know better. The Devil of Ivan is a purely subjective phenomenon, and at the end of the scene this fact is deliberately underscored for us. When Ivan is awakened he finds that the candles, which in his nightmare had been as bright and fresh as ever, have almost burnt themselves out. The towel he has wet and pressed to his feverish forehead is perfectly dry and unused. The glass of tea he has thrown at his visitor is still before him on the table, unthrown. There has been no visitor.

By contrast, and to take us now into an unmistakable example of the Devil as second self, let us go back half a century earlier than the story of the Karamazovs, to that first great humanization of the Prince of Darkness, the figure who furnishes the original both of Ivan's Devil and of many subsequent Devils. This is, of course, the Mephistopheles of Goethe's *Faust:*[3] a figure of great importance in the literary evolution of the Devil; for he not only anticipates those that follow him, but in a most interesting way recalls and transforms those that precede him. Like Marlowe's Mephistophilis he derives his name from the early Faust account, yet though unlike Marlowe's subordinate demon he is *the* Devil ("Squire Satan," the Witch calls him), he is far less devilish in any traditional sense of the word. Like the Satan of Job he makes his first appearance not in Hell but in Heaven, in intimate colloquy with the Lord. But his relationship with the Lord is most unlike that which is presented in the Old Testament story. Here it is not the Lord but Mephistopheles who begins the exchange. The Lord is not tempted to test his servant by plunging him into misery; Faust is already in misery, the very *Streben nach dem Unendlichen* that will finally save him. There is no wager between Mephistopheles and the Lord save in the mind of Mephistopheles; the Lord explains why there is no possibility of Mephistopheles' getting Faust's soul, why the effort to ensnare Faust's soul will contribute to the latter's salvation; but Mephistopheles shows no comprehension. In other words, Goethe's Devil is at once placed on a level far below that of the Lord, below that of the Satan in Job or the Devils of Dante, Marlowe, and Milton; in fact, except for certain strategic advantages, he is placed very close to the level of his chosen victim, man.

Mephistopheles' first self, however, is not man in the abstract; the only possible counterpart of an abstraction is another abstraction, and there is nothing in the least abstract about Mephistopheles. His changes in appearance have no effect on the consistency and solidity of the being who assumes such changes. He is objectively real, not only for Faust but for all the other countless characters with whom he comes in contact. And yet his reality for Faust is not the same as his reality for other people. In this relationship we find, as we did not in the relationship between Ivan and his visitor, that all-important paradox of simultaneous objectivity and subjectivity. At the same time that Mephistopheles is "there," outside, he is also (for Faust) "here," inside; his voice rings both in Faust's physical ear and throughout Faust's mental and moral being like an emanation of that being; and it does so even at those moments, especially at those moments, when what he says is most violently opposed by Faust. For despite their working agreement their relationship is basically one of opposition, diametrical opposition in purpose, rising out of diametrical oppositeness of character. And of the essence of what opposes them to each other is the same colossal irony later to be exploited by Dostoyevsky: the fact that the chief distinction between the Devil and his human victim lies just in the spark of the *übermenschlich,* the more-than-human, that burns uneasily and clumsily within the latter, and of which the former is so completely devoid that he can think of it only as an amusing mistake. All Mephistopheles' supernatural activities are the merest mountebank's hocus-pocus, really as unnecessary to the story as the compact written in blood. Of the two it is he, the superhuman visitor, who is by far the more recognizably "human"; it is the human victim who has, in addition to his humanness, the superhuman cravings of which his Tempter knows nothing.

From any such cravings or problems Mephistopheles is completely free. In accordance with tradition he is given certain numinous qualities; thus in Faust's eyes a streaming trail of fire, the diabolical element, follows the black poodle which circles closer and closer about the aging scholar, and out of which Mephistopheles subsequently emerges. Nevertheless it is the shape assumed in this episode of their meeting, and not the magical trappings attached to it, that is significant. For a part of the central irony of which I have spoken is not only that the Devil is the most vividly human character in the play, but also that it is just his unqualified humanness that makes him diabolical. Mephistopheles is the dog in man, in the most literal sense of the word the cynic in man. His cynicism does not make him bitter. Exactly that which leaves Faust most dissatisfied is that with which he is most content: the life of here-and-now, the realm of the senses, the veil of Maya. He may have his kingdom in the lower regions, but he shows no interest in it; he is the Devil of this world; and exclusive preoccupation with and attachment to the things of this world constitute the temptation he offers and the damnation he threatens. There is an interesting contradiction here, since materialism so absolute becomes in the end destructive even of the material itself. Mephistopheles is not at all an enemy of the body of this world, but only of the spirit within; yet it is this spirit which gives the body life, and thus the contentment with body that would be the death of spirit would ultimately be the death of body as well. Mephistopheles recognizes the fact when he introduces himself as

> ... The Spirit that Denies!
> And justly so: for all things, from the void
> Called forth, deserve to be destroyed.[4]

Thus Mephistopheles, in addition to being Faust's complementary opposite in character, exactly complements, in what he seeks to give Faust, that which Faust is seeking for himself. Faust seeks Life, which he can find only in Death; Life-in-Death; Mephistopheles seeks to reverse the process by giving him Death-in-Life. Faust seeks to transcend his physical limitations, even the boundaries of Space and Time, to "flow through Nature's veins in glad pulsation." Mephistopheles seeks to reconcile him to his physical world, make him at last cry out to some aspect of it the fateful words, *"Verweile doch, du bist so schön!"*[5] In his own terminology, Mephistopheles will help the human grasshopper to fly about over the grass in order to give him a richer sampling of its contents and make him the readier to settle into it again, to bury his mortal nose in the mortal dirt where it belongs.

But contrasting however profoundly with Faust in character and function is not in itself enough to make Mephistopheles Faust's second self. There must also be that peculiarly personal relationship between them which the Devil's role as corrupter of all mankind militates against, and there must be in this relationship that strange and special closeness which more than any other feature draws the two together into one. So far as the personal relationship is concerned, it, like the irony at the heart of it, is present from the outset. Whatever may be Mephistopheles' official role, he shows none of the general interest in the cause of evil that we would expect of him. He makes no real effort to tempt other people save to the extent that they will serve his purposes with Faust. Indeed for Faust's entire long lifetime the Prince of Darkness shamefully neglects all his other duties, and devotes himself exclusively to the effort to ensnare this single soul. And even for this purpose his motivation — in the sense of anything to be gained from the tempting, beyond the pleasure of the tempting itself — is wholly inadequate, as Mephistopheles himself realizes. "The loss of thee were really very slight," he tells Faust in a candid moment, and we must certainly grant his logic; can one soul among so many thousands and millions possibly be worth this monumental labor? Yet Mephistopheles, without seeming to know why (even ruefully suspecting in the back of his self-confident mind that he will in the end be cheated out of his prey in any case), never acts on this logic; he remains throughout the untiring servant, the inseparable companion; and what holds him to Faust seems to be something far more compelling than the bargain they have struck. The same thing is true of what holds Faust to him. Along with the ecstasy of discovering the godlike within him, Faust realizes that God has given him another and more humbling gift:

> ... the comrade, whom I now no more
> Can do without, though, cold and scornful, he
> Demeans me to myself, and with a breath,
> A word, transforms thy gifts to nothingness.[6]

Nor is he referring merely to Mephistopheles' usefulness to him in his pursuit of Margaret. When Mephistopheles demands of him,

> Poor Son of Earth, how couldst thou thus alone
> Have led thy life, bereft of me?[7]

Faust has no answer. It is Mephistopheles as part of his soul, not Mephistopheles as instrument to gratify his desires, who has become indispensable to him.

As always, then, what makes their relationship so intensely personal a one is that mysterious affinity that is like the reverse side of the mysterious opposition. And one sign of this affinity, as always, is their mutual insight into each other's secrets: the insight that enables Faust (unlike Wagner who is watching with him) to see the strange light streaming from the poodle's tail, to sense the presence of the Evil One and make the latter roundly sweat before emerging from canine into human form; the still keener insight that enables Mephistopheles to know about Faust's hidden thoughts of suicide, to know all the innermost workings of Faust's mind, and to use this knowledge in the best second-self tradition to mock Faust and to puncture his bubbles of sentiment and fine feeling. It is an understanding of only one side of Faust, and an understanding that takes intellectual form, yet it is far too penetrating and intimate to be achieved by intellect alone; it is the special understanding — like that of Mr. Jones for Axel Heyst, Allbee for Leventhal, and so forth — that can come only from participation in the thing understood. Throughout the Margaret scenes in particular, the objective Mephistopheles and the subjective Mephistopheles are almost impossible to separate. It is with Mephistophelean bluntness and brutality that Faust first demands possession of Margaret; it is with Mephistophelean self-centeredness and disregard for others that he gives Margaret the potion, actually the poison, to put her mother to sleep; it is with Mephistophelean will ("Thrust home!") that he stabs Valentine to death.

Repeatedly Mephistopheles taunts Faust with this overlapping of their personalities;[8] Faust himself, he comments judiciously, wouldn't make a bad Devil except for his insipid tendency to despair. At other times he takes a more positive and more intimate pleasure than simply that of mockery. "Well, well, — tonight — ?" he asks just after Faust has made his assignation with Margaret. "What's that to thee?" Faust demands angrily, and Mephistopheles answers:

> Yet my delight 'twill also be![9]

To suppose that his delight will be that of the Devil entrapping his victim's soul is to do considerable damage to the context. Faust does not damn himself by the seduction of Margaret or the murder of Valentine, nor does Mephistopheles ever claim that he does. Mephistopheles' delight is not that of one who will profit from the transgression, but that of one who will share it.

But the main example I wish to consider of the Devil as second self occurs not in Goethe's work — where the relationship between the selves is merely one of many elements — but in a work which centers throughout in this relationship, and with some of the most remarkable effects in all the literature of the second self. This is James Hogg's long-neglected novel, *The Private Memoirs and Confessions of a Justified Sinner,*[10] which appeared shortly after *Faust, Part I,* and bears certain marked resemblances to it. Here, however, there are really two relationships, interlinked by the fact that the second self of the one relationship (presented to us at the outset by the Editor's Narrative) becomes, in this second self's own confessions, the first self of the other relationship; and that this person's victimization by *his* second self, the Devil-Tempter, is achieved in large part by the Devil's taking on the appearance of his victim's victim, the first self of the first relationship; so that in a beautifully symmetrical way the two victimizations are made continuous with each other. Thus, though for once we are dealing with three characters instead of the usual two, we are dealing with the same basic selfdom that is present in all second-self literature. Between the opposite poles of this self, innocence and viciousness, the central "point of identity" is poised, though drawn strongly and at last hopelessly into the camp of the latter.

The central character is Robert Wringhim, legally the younger son of the Laird of Dalcastle, but actually the natural son of Lady Dalcastle by her "spiritual adviser," the hypocritical and self-righteous Reverend Mr. Wringhim, who has baptized his bastard with his own name and brought him up in his own household to his own stern religious principles. Thus Robert "was taught to pray twice every day, and seven times on Sabbath days; but he was only to pray for the elect, and, like David of Old, doom all that were aliens from God to destruction," especially the Laird of Dalcastle and his elder son. The relationship between the latter, George Colwan, and the protagonist, who is brought up to hate and curse him, is the same that we have already found between Medardus and Count Victor and that we shall find again in many other examples: that between legitimate and illegitimate half-brothers. This, in turn, is the same relationship that exists between the Twin Brothers of the most primitive legends; the uncanny or second-self Twin derives his uncanniness from a secret adulterous union of one parent (usually the mother) with a being of supernatural powers. In Hogg's story the Reverend Mr. Wringhim is not possessed of supernatural powers, but he fancies and advertises himself to be, and in so doing no less profoundly influences the character of his son. He not only has prayed to God that Robert may be admitted into the company of the elect, but has wrestled with God and at last prevailed over him, gaining the assurance "that I (Robert) was now a justified person, adopted among the number of God's children — my name written in the Lamb's book of life, and that no by-past transgression, nor any future act of my own, or of other men, could be instrumental in altering the decree."[11]

This assurance, nurturing the seed of pride already present in the young man's soul, plays a vital part in his motivation. In the Editor's Narrative, which constitutes the first part of the novel, however, we know little or nothing of Robert's motivation; so far as his relationship with his half-brother is concerned it is the latter's viewpoint we share and the latter with whom we tend to identify ourselves. George Colwan, then, is the first self here, the wholesome and understandable brother, while Robert

Wringhim plays the role of alien and uncanny intruder, possessed of insight and actuated by antagonism that go beyond anything explainable by the external situation.

Their paths first cross when one day George, who is playing tennis with friends, finds himself attended by a young man dressed in black, who stands so near him as seriously to impede his movements, watches him with a fiercely malignant eye, and refuses to step aside. Next day the same intrusive being makes his appearance, immediately at George's elbow on his right hand, distracts him by jeers and taunts, and after precipitating a physical altercation which brings the game to a close insists on marching along with the party, always by his brother's side, to the Black Bull Tavern, where he actually tries to force his company on the group at dinner. On the third day, when George and his friends once more go to play tennis, young Wringhim once more appears in his wonted station, and once more the game is spoiled.

And so it goes on. No matter how carefully George conceals his intention of going to this place or that, in some unaccountable way his half-brother seems to know about it, know "all his motions, and every intention of his heart, as it were intuitively . . . he had never sat or stood many minutes till there was the selfsame being, always in the same position in regard to himself, as regularly as the shadow is cast from the substance, or the ray of light from the opposing denser medium." [12]

The obsessive, subjective side of George's second self is strongly suggested by such episodes. But this is merely one side of Robert in his relationship with George; at no time does he become a mental content only, any more than he becomes an objective individual only. This two-sidedness of the minister's son becomes especially strong for the laird's son when the latter, having made a dawn excursion to the top of Arthur's Seat, sees to his right, in the clouds, a vast apparition of his brother, though twenty times the latter's size, cautiously approaching as though to spring on him. George flees in the opposite direction, and in doing so collides with the *real* person of Robert, who has been creeping up on him where he sat on the brink of the precipice, obviously planning to push him headlong from the cliff.

Thus far the role of Robert Wringhim as second self has been clearly that of Pursuer, like those of the figures we considered in the last chapter. But unlike them, Robert plays the part of Pursuer only incidentally to his part of Tempter; and that to which he constantly tempts his brother and other-self is the very pride of which he is such an unwholesome exemplar. [13] Pride is not natural to George as it is to Robert; and even when it is aroused in him it takes only a fleeting and unoriginal, pugilistic form; but this is enough to prove his undoing. His culminating mistake comes when, celebrating with his friends at the tavern, he quarrels with a member of the party named Drummond, who leaves. Within a few minutes someone appearing to be Drummond returns, and calling George to the door challenges him. George steps out alone into the night, is maneuvered by the psuedo-Drummond over to the mouth of a dark entry, where his half-brother, a meaner Faust, stabs him to death from behind.

This is the account given by the earlier part of the book, which concentrates on the relationship between George and Robert. The second part, comprising the memoirs and confessions of Robert, includes reference to this relationship, but only as a very secondary aspect of another relationship, which has already been alluded to but not explained. The crossing of paths of the two brothers, we now learn, has been both preceded and brought about by another crossing of paths, the latter taking place on that greatest day of Robert Wringhim's life, when it is announced to him by his reverend father that he has at last been accepted into the company of the elect, who can do no wrong. In his joy he bounds out into the fields and woods to pour forth his gratitude to the Almighty, but it is a singular sort of gratitude that emerges. "An exaltation of spirit lifted me, as it were, far above the earth and the sinful creatures crawling on its surface; and I deemed myself as an eagle among the children of men, soaring on high, and looking down with pity and contempt on the grovelling creatures below." [14]

It is at this moment that a young man of mysterious appearance approaches him, and from this young man emanates a mysterious power that draws Robert toward him as though toward a magnet. As they come nearer, Robert stands amazed: the other young man is in all respects the exact replica of himself. And not only does he resemble Robert in person, but as they enter into conversation he exactly subscribes to all Robert's beliefs, indeed carries them so far that Robert is slightly taken aback by the extremity of his own ideas. At their next meeting, the stranger, who gives his name as Gil-Martin, no longer looks the same, and explains that his countenance has a way of changing with his interests; that a concentration on anyone else's features causes his own features to mirror them, and in so doing to give him access to the other's most secret thoughts, as has happened at his first meeting with Robert.

But if he is no longer like Robert in looks he is no less like him in religious principles, in fact so like him that he is more Robert than Robert himself. The latter rejoices in his new companion, is proud of him, finds soon that he cannot live without him, but for some reason never mentions him to anyone else. Yet the two are seen together by certain other people, among them one Reverend Mr. Blanchard, who when alone with Robert warns him against Gil-Martin so eloquently as almost to persuade him to drop the latter. By now, however, there is no dropping Gil-Martin, partly because he will not be dropped, partly because in his secret heart Robert has no wish to drop him. When Gil-Martin hears of the warning, he convinces Robert that a man so dangerous to the human race as Mr. Blanchard should be removed from it. By using Robert's own arguments he forces his young disciple to see it as a bounden duty, and further works upon his mind until Robert, from ambush, shoots the old divine through the heart.

This is only the beginning of Robert's career in crime, crime which, Gil-Martin assures him, is not crime at all but only a carrying out of the vengeance of the Lord. The next step is the fratricide which has already been described, and is now related again, though this time from Robert's viewpoint, explaining that the Drummund who challenges George is, of course, Gil-Martin. Now we learn that it is under Gil-Martin's direction and encouragement that the Justified Sinner has commenced to make life miserable for his half-brother, that, in other words, the temptation of George is only an incident in the more intensive and deadly temptation of Robert, and that, as I have pointed out, the second self who intrudes upon George, seen now in this wider context, also the first self intruded upon by a far darker and more malignant second self. The simultaneous relationship between Robert and these two counterparts, one light and one dark, is underscored by the following remarkable passage. In the midst of his persecution of George, Robert is seized with a strange illness. He suspects that he is bewitched, because

I generally conceived myself to be two people. When I lay in bed, I deemed there were two of us in it; when I sat up I always beheld another person, and always in the same position from the place where I sat or stood, which was about three paces off me on my left side. It mattered not how many or how few were present: this my second self was sure to be present in his place, and this occasioned a confusion in all my words and ideas that utterly astonished my friends, who all declared that, instead of being deranged in my intellect, they had never heard my conversation manifest so much energy or sublimity of conception; but, for all that, over the singular delusion that I was two persons my reasoning had no power. The most perverse part of it was that I rarely conceived *myself* to be any of the two persons. I thought for the most part that my companion Gil-Martin was one of them, and my brother the other; and I found that, to be obliged to speak and answer in the character of another man, was a most awkward business at the long run.[15]

Here we have precisely that sense, of being both one with and at the same time distinct from someone else, which is characteristic of all true second-self relationships, in this case complicated by there being in fact two such relationships at once, one so to speak enclosed within the other. It is interesting to notice how skillfully Hogg uses the device of relative position to suggest the difference between these two relationships. In both cases Robert's other self is always a little to his left, on the traditionally sinister or evil side. But in the case of George this is the position in which Robert as conscious instrument of the Lord's vengeance intentionally places him. In the case of Gil-Martin, the appearance from the left is always assumed on Gil-Martin's initiative, not on Robert's, nor does Robert ever seem aware of its significance.

But though Robert's other-selves are at opposite extremes, the one of decency and the other of depravity, the fratricide in which both temptations culminate soon sets in motion a process which begins to bring these extremes together. Thus far Gil-Martin has assumed various personalities: Robert's at their initial meeting, Mr. Blanchard's, Drummond's, and, after Robert has taken possession of the Dalcastle estate, Robert's again. As Robert, so Robert learns to his astonishment and horror, he has committed numerous crimes, seducing a young lady, ruining her family, even at last murdering both the seduced girl and Robert's mother and secretly burying their bodies. Appalled by these discoveries, Robert struggles to be free. "And yet to shake him off was impossible — we were incorporated together — identified with one another, as it were, and the power was not in me to separate myself from him." Robert's supreme horror, however, is not at the revelation that Gil-Martin has been assuming his own appearance in order to ruin him, but at seeing for himself Gil-Martin assume, more and more strikingly and persistently, another appearance: that of the brother whom Robert has murdered. This happens first in Robert's Dalcastle dwelling, again at the edge of the Colwan Wood, and again, climactically, in the course of Robert's wild and hopeless flight across the countryside, pursued by the forces of official justice but still more by other forces, above all the image of his dead victim worn by his living victimizer.[16]

Thus though in this story we have the very complicated situation of a protagonist who plays the role of second self to one character and first self to another, actually the central dichotomy is between Robert Wringhim as first self and his diabolical visitant as second, the latter using Robert's temptation of George to subserve his own temptation of Robert, a temptation which proves as successful as Mephistopheles' temptation of Faust is unsuccessful, and ends in Robert's suicide at the end of a hay-rope. In all other aspects as well there can be no question that Hogg's novel is validly an example of the literature of the second self, and one of the outstanding examples in our language. Even more than Mephistopheles, Gil-Martin, though obviously *the* Devil, sacrifices his function as Tempter-in-general and serves as Robert's particular Tempter, focusing his attention exclusively on this single victim. This personal, one-to-one quality of their relationship is stressed throughout; indeed Robert is often puzzled by the unremitting attention paid him by so mighty a potentate, but the latter assures him that the adherence to his cause of such a person as Robert is worthy of all the efforts he can expend. Even when Robert begs to be spared such efforts, Gil-Martin explains that he could no longer discontinue them if he wished. He is bound to Robert as the mother to her child, as the shadow to the substance. "I am wedded to you so closely," he tells Robert at the end, "that I feel as if I were the same person. Our essences are one, our bodies and spirits being united, so that I am drawn towards you as by magnetism, and wherever you are, there must my presence be with you." [17]

Thus though the Devil's objective reality is as unquestionable in this story as it is in *Faust* (Gil-Martin is frequently seen by people other than Robert, including some who give legal testimony to the fact), his subjective reality is no less unquestionable or important. He is the Lord of Evil; but he is also the embodiment of that particular evil which lies in Robert's own being, and which on that day of Robert's acceptance among the justified elect rises up before him at the same moment that it rises up within him. So intergrown in sympathy with the Tempter is Robert that it is no longer possible, once the fratricide is committed, to be sure whether the further crimes are carried out by Gil-Martin impersonating Robert or by Robert unconsciously behaving like Gil-Martin. Even when the crimes are done, Robert is not always horrified at them; in fact the worst of them have the opposite effect. At the moment when, disguised as Gil-Martin, and temporarily safe, he sees the body of his murdered mother and that of the girl he is said to have seduced and killed, he does not recoil at the sight.

I cannot tell how it was, but I felt a strange and unwonted delight in viewing this scene, and a certain pride of heart in being supposed the perpetrator of the unnatural crimes laid to my charge. This was a feeling quite new to me; and if there were virtues in the robes of the illustrious foreigner, who had without all dispute preserved my life at this time: I say, if there was any inherent virtue in these robes of his, as he had suggested, this was one of their effects, that they turned my heart towards that which was evil, horrible, and disgusting. [18]

But the turning of Robert's heart has begun much earlier than this, and the magic involved in the turning is one that we can recognize by now as far stranger than that of charmed robes or any other traditional brand of sorcery. It is the magic of the paradox which is the subject of our study: of the one who is also two, and the two who are no less indissolubly one.

The second self as Tempter, however, is not always officially the Devil. In fact it is probably desirable, on the whole, that he should not be, since even when he is so superbly humanized as Mephistopheles there can never be complete equality between a supernatural Tempter and a human victim. It may be partly for this reason that perhaps an even more memorable example of the second self as Tempter than Hogg's Gil-Martin results not from the humanizing of the Devil, but from the diabolizing of a human being.

Actually both things are done in the work to which we now turn, but it is the latter — the devilish human rather than the Devil as human — who constitutes the genuine second self. This is the character known as Smerdyakov, in Dostoyevsky's *The Brothers Karamazov*. The appearance of the official Devil in this novel has already been touched on, and I have explained that he fulfills merely half the basic requirement of the second self, possessing subjective but not objective reality. It is only in the light of Smerdyakov that the significance of this hallucinatory diabolical visitant can be understood. The latter is a sort of quintessence of that within Ivan's nature which has evoked out of some strange abyss in the external world the Caliban-like Smerdyakov, and which, once Ivan has succumbed to the Smerdyakov-temptation, comes to remind him mockingly of the fact, in amiable deferential chatter woven together (as it must be, since the weaver is simply a projected mental content) out of Ivan's own thoughts. The visit of the Devil in this novel, therefore, is a modern version of the damned soul writhing in the torments of Hell, save that Hell is merely Ivan's sitting room, and the torments are his own recalled ideas and phrases.

In this sense, and in this sense only, Ivan's Devil does play a part in the relationship between the selves, but is neither of them. The second self of Ivan is Smerdyakov, about whose simultaneous external and internal reality there is not the slightest doubt, and who is shown in important relationship with Ivan throughout the greater part of the story. Like all Dostoyevsky's major novels this is a story of guilt, and of the almost infinitely complicated roots and flowerings of guilt. The head of the Karamazov family is a well-to-do landowner and drunken sensualist named Fyodor Pavlovitch Karamazov, whose three acknowledged sons are the impulsive Dmitri, the intellectual Ivan, and the saintly Alyosha. In addition to these there is a fourth young man, bastard son of an idiot girl known as Stinking Lizaveta and, reputedly, Fyodor Pavlovitch; a young man called Smerdyakov after his mother's nickname and brought up in the Karamazov household. Thus, at least according to rumor, Smerdyakov bears the same relationship to the acknowledged sons which Robert Wringhim bears to George Colwan, that of illegitimate half-brother. In only one of the three, however, does he show any special interest, and this is the one whom the affected, epileptic Smerdyakov would seem least to resemble: the brilliant writer of articles advancing religious positions which at the same time they secretly ridicule; the stern, reserved, ultrasophisticated intellectual, Ivan.

And yet in a way, the way of opposites, they are not so different. Though in no sense a scholar, Smerdyakov since boyhood has shown signs of the same rational skepticism that characterizes the thinking of Ivan. To be sure Smerdyakov's skepticism is elementary by comparison; nevertheless, this very fact forms a bond between them; it makes the lackey look up to Ivan as an oracle and put complete trust in him, as in God Almighty; it makes him show off before Ivan by imitating his ideas in the hope of earning his praise; it makes Ivan take an amused interest in Smerdyakov, talk with him, instruct and encourage him in his skeptical temper. Above all Smerdyakov is impressed with Ivan's argument that human virtue is not dependent upon spontaneous love but only upon belief in immortality and God. Skillfully Ivan has made this assertion sound, to many churchmen, like an argument for the supremacy of the Church, but the uneducated Smerdyakov sees at once the other side of it, the important side: that if one does not believe in the religious hypothesis — and what enlightened skeptic could? — "the moral law of nature must immediately be changed into the exact contrary of the former religious law, and that egoism, even to crime, must become, not only lawful but even recognized as the inevitable, the most rational, even honourable outcome of his position." [19]

Unlike another Dostoyevsky hero, Raskolnikov, Ivan maintains his doctrine purely as a theory. Yet if he keeps the realm of theory separate from that of action, he does not keep it separate from that of will, will regarding one matter particularly. Fyodor Pavlovitch has fallen in love with a young woman of loose reputation, Grushenka; if he marries her she will inherit all his money and his sons will get nothing, whereas if he dies before remarrying his fortune will be divided among his sons. Furthermore if Fyodor were to die, his son Dmitri would probably marry Grushenka, leaving the way open for Ivan to marry his own beloved, Katerina Ivanovna, now betrothed to Dmitri. Not that Ivan, as the result of such motivations, ever threatens his father's life; indeed he saves it, when Fyodor is attacked by the infuriated Dmitri — and then almost immediately regrets his intervention. How easy it would have been, the thought flashes across his mind, to let one reptile devour the other, let someone else do the deed for him! This is the temptation of Ivan. So long as it remains only a thought it has no power over him. Only when it is presented to him with the additional pressure of an external agent who is at the same time an internal force, the evil impulse objectified as Ivan's second self, does it become enough to influence his behavior. This is the function of Smerdyakov.

That Smerdyakov should influence Ivan might at first glance seem strange. The young servant has a certain native shrewdness but no mental depth; to the contrary, there is at all times about this fastidious invalid a certain quality reminiscent of his idiot mother. Ivan's intellectual powers, on the other hand, exceed those of anyone else in the novel, and they are all the more acute for the fact that they are not merely intellectual, but rooted in and fed by profound tensions within his own character. A curious and uneasy mixture of his hysterical, religious mother and his hard-headed, materialistic father, Ivan, who seems the most self-possessed of the three brothers, is actually the least. His rejection of God and immortality is only an inability to believe, but for all his professions of atheism he is equally unable to disbelieve; the question, as Father Zossima perceives, clamors for an answer, and he can find none that will bring him certainty or peace. His moral nihilism, far from being a product of coldness, rises from despair of soul at the spectacle of cruelty and suffering and horror that he sees about him. He does not deny God, he explains to Alyosha; he would be most willing to accept God; but the world created by this God he cannot and will not accept. Even if all the horror is ultimately resolved, still the wrongs *will have been,* and he can never forget or forgive them.

And thus it is not despite his mental and moral superiority to Smerdyakov, it is because of this superiority, that Ivan is also in a sense inferior to Smerdyakov, as the complex man is always inferior to the simple one. For Smerdyakov there are no agonizing questions or self-lacerations. He takes the theory of the young master and carries it straight to the point from which Ivan recoils. If there is no God, everything is lawful, and the obvious path to follow is that of one's own advantage. But Smerdyakov's superior self-sureness and clarity of purpose are only the logical explanation of his ability to dominate Ivan, the explanation that applies to their relationship insofar as they are separate individuals. For the subjective side of such a relationship the logical explanation is never enough. On this side we are dealing not with twoness but with oneness, and so on this side — we see the process more clearly here, I believe, than in any other example of second-self literature — the influence of the second self upon the first is never separable from the influence of the first upon the second. Through each of their four interviews, and increasingly as the climax is approached, there is the inescapable suggestion that Smerdyakov the victimizer is also the victim, that the influence he exerts on Ivan is indistinguishable from a secret and quite unconscious influence which Ivan is exerting on Smerdyakov, and through Smerdyakov on himself. Ivan cannot connive in the killing of his father, but on the wordless level of communication that in these relationships always underlies the spoken one he can persuade Smerdyakov to persuade him so to connive, to connive without conniving; later on Ivan cannot face the fact of his own guilt, but he can in the same way persuade Smerdyakov to make him face it.

It is only on the eve of the murder that we get our first hint of the mysterious bond between these two young men, and of this intricate Chinese puzzle of influence within influence. Ivan, who has just unburdened himself to Alyosha in the famous tavern scene, returns to his father's house. He has been paying the latter an extended visit, and plans to leave the next day for Moscow. His father has asked him to make a detour to Tchermashnya in order to settle a timber deal, but Ivan has refused. Returning home that night he feels strangely depressed, is vexed at the fact that he cannot understand why, and is further vexed at the fact that his depression seems to have "a kind of casual, external character," like some insignificant object which the eye sees but the mind fails to recognize even though offended by it, though there is no such object in view. Suddenly as he approaches the house he sees Smerdyakov sitting on a bench in the garden gate, "and at the first glance at him Ivan knew that the valet Smerdyakov was on his mind, and that it was this man that his soul loathed." [20]

This inexplicability of reaction, and especially this antagonism out of all proportion to any visible reason for it, is as we have repeatedly seen one of the most familiar features of the "moment of encounter," when the paths of first and second selves cross and the duel between them begins. The moment of encounter is not necessarily that of initial meeting; Ivan and Smerdyakov have been acquainted now for a long time. Only by degrees has Ivan come to dislike the vanity and deviousness of the valet, not realizing that these things are, though in more naive form, counterparts of his own. Above all he has come to dislike a "peculiar revolting familiarity" which the other has begun to show toward him; "he [Smerdyakov] had obviously begun to consider — goodness knows why! — that there was some sort of understanding between him and Ivan Fyodorovitch."[21] But these have been preliminaries only. Now all at once the preliminaries are over, and as though at the stroke of a bell the two men are made known to each other, at least in their hearts. Now all at once Ivan feels more than a mere dislike, feels an intense, unaccountable loathing and a growing fear; Smerdyakov shows more than a mere familiarity, shows a sinister sense of his own power over his social and intellectual superior.

He displays this power in the almost hypnotic control he exercises over Ivan's actions. Despite himself the latter stops in the gate; despite his wish to tell the "miserable idiot" to get away from him he hears himself ask, softly and meekly, whether his father is still asleep; and thus, against his own will, he initiates the conversation that follows. In this conversation, as though carelessly wandering from one matter to another, Smerdyakov tells Ivan three things. First, that Fyodor Pavlovitch has placed three thousand rubles in an envelope and is keeping it in his room as an enticement to Grushenka to come to him, this being precisely the amount Dmitri needs to pay a debt, so that Dmitri now has a double motive for attacking his father: revenge if Grushenka does go to the old man and greed if she does not. Second, that the secret signals which Fyodor has arranged for his own protection have been revealed by Smerdyakov to Dmitri, so that the latter can have access to his father whenever he chooses. Third, that Smerdyakov, though he admits no one can forecast such things in advance, "feels certain" that he will have a long epileptic fit the next day, in which case there will be no one to protect the old man — no one, at least, provided Ivan himself is gone from the vicinity, and Smerdyakov has already covered this point by advising that Ivan comply with his father's wish to go to Tchermashnya.

Now, of course, there is nothing to be gained by going to Tchermashnya that cannot be equally well gained by going to Moscow; all that matters for Smerdyakov's purpose is that Ivan go somewhere. And since Ivan has already decided to leave, this first interview accomplishes nothing so far as the event level of the story is concerned. What it does accomplish — and in this it is very nearly the central scene of the whole novel — is to force Ivan to confront the real reason *why* he is leaving, to force him to hear, from someone else who has ceased being altogether someone else, his own innermost thoughts in terms all the more shocking for the slight veil of innocence impudently draped across them. Smerdyakov's ability to know these thoughts is as extraordinary as his ability virtually to enslave Ivan by doing so, even to make Ivan choose Tchermashnya over Moscow, meaningless as such a choice may be. But there is also the suggestion, as I have said, that this ability is not wholly his own, that his insight into Ivan is at least in part made possible by Ivan's unconscious insight into them both, and that he derives such power over Ivan in part from Ivan's unconscious power over him: that is, the power to give him such power. Thus at the end of their conversation Ivan starts toward the house, then turns quickly back. But the man he turns upon has become again the old Smerdyakov, bastard son of the idiot girl and himself not wholly free from idiocy. "All his familiarity and carelessness had completely disappeared. His face expressed attention and expectation, intent but timid and cringing."[22]

Yet he has had his will of Ivan, as Ivan on a more submerged level has had his will of Smerdyakov. In angry impatience Ivan goes on to his room. Once there, however, he very stealthily goes out upon the staircase and for perhaps five minutes simply stands there, listening to his father move about below, listening "with a sort of strange curiosity, holding his breath while his heart throbbed." All the rest of his life he thinks of this with repulsion, as the basest thing he has ever done. Next day he leaves.

The train flew on, and only at daybreak, when he was approaching Moscow, he suddenly roused himself from his meditation.

"I am a scoundrel," he whispered to himself.[23]

And so all happens as Smerdyakov has predicted: he suffers an epileptic fit; Dmitri comes to his father's house and taps out the signal on the window frame; the old man is murdered. When Ivan returns home and finds Dmitri charged with the crime he is assailed by unbearable nervous tension; he is on the brink of madness, and is already being visited by his hallucination of the Devil. And yet it is not the Devil, whom Ivan knows to be unreal, that particularly preoccupies him. It is the one man who has the knowledge to answer the questions that are raging within him; and irresistibly he is drawn, again and again, to this creature whom he despises and fears as he does no one else on earth.

At his first call Smerdyakov admits nothing, appears to explain everything in a perfectly logical fashion. No, he did not say that he was going to sham a fit, but merely that he was afraid of a fit, and this fear had been enough to bring one on. No, he did not urge Ivan to go away, but merely mentioned Tchermashnya because it was nearer than Moscow, and hoped Ivan would not go even that far. Thus the temptation appears not to have been a temptation after all, and Ivan's mind is set at rest.

But it will not stay at rest. Within a fortnight he begins to be troubled by the same doubts, half-defined doubts which only the hateful Smerdyakov can resolve. But his next call proves less satisfactory than the first.

Smerdyakov seems to resent his coming again, is insolent and sarcastic, openly accuses Ivan of having left in full knowledge that the murder would occur. Shaken to the depths of his being, Ivan is temporarily calmed again when he is shown a letter written by Dmitri which seems to establish beyond question the latter's guilt. For a month he scarcely thinks of Smerdyakov. He does, however, receive news that the former valet is very ill, and by a strange coincidence, as though the other's illness were reaching out across space to infect him, he becomes very ill himself. It is an illness that sharpens rather than dulls his thoughts, that reawakens all his doubts, that undermines and at last destroys his brief sense of security.

In this state of mind, torn between fear of what he will find out and desperate need to find it out, he pays his last visit to Smerdyakov. This time another singular change has taken place in Smerdyakov's manner; this time he is neither reasonable nor sarcastic, but eyes Ivan with a look of insane hatred and accuses him of deliberately playing a farce by coming here, having known all along what the true case is. And now at last the true case comes out, and it is no more a catastrophic revelation to Ivan than it is to Smerdyakov, though the reason for the former's shock is quite different from the reason for the latter's. In his anger at what he supposes to be Ivan's hypocrisy Smerdyakov admits in so many words what he has assumed has been tacitly understood between them from the start: that he, not on his own initiative but acting as Ivan's instrument and faithful servant, has murdered Fyodor Pavlovitch. He not only admits this but gives all the details, and even produces the three thousand rubles which he, not Dmitri, has stolen for his own "share." Ivan listens in frozen horror; for a moment it seems to him that his counterpart is a dream or phantom sitting before him, though only for a moment. But from this horrifying discovery by Ivan, and the fact that his horrified expression can no longer be interpreted as make-believe, comes an equally horrifying discovery for Smerdyakov: that Ivan has not until this moment consciously understood, that there has been no explicit league between them, that Smerdyakov can no longer justify himself as merely having followed the orders of one whose judgment he has always looked up to.

The difference between the reactions of the two men is interestingly in accordance with the difference between their natures. Ivan tries at first to defend himself, but it is a feeble defense, for his very complexity and depth force him to understand that there is a knowledge which the mind may not possess, but which the heart and soul may; and that in his heart and soul he has more than allowed himself to be tempted; he has sought the temptation, he has accepted it, he has embraced it; and he sits and listens while Smerdyakov, like a judge speaking simultaneously from without and from within, pronounces the verdict upon him. Dmitri, the scapegoat, is not guilty, though of course he will be convicted.

But I don't want to lie to you now, because . . . because if you really haven't understood till now, as I see for myself, and are not pretending, so as to throw your guilt on me to my very face, you are still responsible for it all, since you knew of the murder and charged me to do it, and went away knowing all about it. And so I want to prove to your face this evening that you are the only real murderer in the whole affair, and I am not the real murderer, though I did kill him. You are the rightful murderer.[24]

But though Smerdyakov pronounces this verdict, and supports it with evidence, chiefly in the form of an insight into Ivan's nature that brings the blood rushing to Ivan's face, the valet himself seems less convinced by his own case than does the man he has condemned. There has come over him a strange dullness, a half-heartedness. For in this matter Smerdyakov's comparative simplicity and directness do not work to his advantage, but quite the reverse. The strength that has been given him by the belief that he was the chosen instrument of his god among men, putting into practice the godlike doctrine that "all things are lawful," has entirely deserted him. His god did not know; his god did not dare ("You won't dare to do anything, you who used to be so bold!" he cries bitterly); his god was not a god. And all at once Smerdyakov is shrunken and alone, and into the place of the man-god he has listened to and worshipped has moved another and older god, the unseen third that as he tells Ivan is between them now in the room, the God of Vengeance.

But the bond between them is far from broken. After Ivan has left the room, Smerdyakov hangs himself from a nail in the wall. Ivan, on the other hand, destroys himself in a characteristically more complicated way. Back in his lodgings he is visited and tortured by his hallucination of the Devil, the Devil of intellectual pride and moral self-sufficiency. Next day, going to Dmitri's trial to give evidence in his brother's favor, he is afflicted by the same Devil, not as an hallucination but as a force working within him, making his testimony — potentially so vital to Dmitri's case — at first reluctant, then more and more incoherent, and at last breaking off in complete and violent madness. The diseased lackey has been more successful than Goethe's *Junker Satan*. For like Smerdyakov, Ivan in destroying himself protects himself, holds back from making the full amends that would free him; even from beyond death the second self as Tempter (who like the slain Twin Brother never dies so long as his counterpart lives) keeps his hold upon the Tempted, remains the stronger of the two.

5

The Second Self As Vision of Horror

The last two chapters have presented the evil second self in his active roles of Pursuer and Tempter. In a third role, to which we now turn, he is no less evil, but far less active in prosecuting evil. This fact should not be interpreted as a comparative kindliness of nature. Frequently the inactive second self is as terrifying to the first self as either of the active ones, and as destructive in his effects. Frequently too he is just as malicious as any John Claggart, Mr. Jones, or Gil-Martin. The essential difference is that, while never indifferent to the first self, he seldom takes positive steps to destroy the latter. Even when he does take such steps, these prove relatively unimportant; and what he uses as his real weapon, though perhaps quite unconsciously, is not any of the things that he does, but the thing that he is.

Now obviously there is bound to be a certain overlapping between this type of second self and both of the other evil second selves we have considered, as well as to a lesser extent between this and all other categories of second self, whether evil or not. The nature of the relationship between the selves demands that their effect on each other should always stem centrally from inward identity rather than from external event. There is nothing to be surprised at in such overlapping; what we are studying is the various aspects of a single being, in an effort to understand this singleness lying beneath the apparent contradictions of his many-sidedness. The differences will never be absolute. In ways Claggart tempts Billy Budd as well as pursues him; in ways Gil-Martin pursues Robert Wringhim in the course of tempting him; both Kirby Allbee and Smerdyakov belong in some respects to the present category. Neverthless there are distinctions and important ones; and in general it may be said that the second self of this chapter differs from all others in that, being evil, he affects his counterpart with this evil only incidentally (if at all) by blows or stratagems or enticements, and primarily by personality; by the revelation, willed or unwilled, of what he is and of what therefore the first self must also be. Such actions as he may take are important chiefly as they disclose his nature, and thus force upon the first self the sickened recognition that there, not but for the grace of God but now forever bereft of the grace of God, go I. The evil that in the first self lies at a reasonably comfortable distance beneath the skin of good deeds or good intentions or at least self-justification appears in the second self covered by no skin whatever. Placed thus before him in merciless magnification, the excluded component of the first self's soul confronts him with the last of the specifically evil aspects we shall consider: the second self as Vision of Horror.

Undoubtedly the vision that is supremely horrible for us all, perhaps in a broad sense the only vision that is horrible for any of us, is that of Death. To say this is not to contradict the suggestion made in the last chapter, that the evil second self is always implicitly the Devil. Basically the Devil *is* Death; not physical death but inward, spiritual deathfulness encased by physical life; Death-in-Life in however busy a stage of decay. In the examples we are about to take up, however, the deathfulness of the second self is not particularly busy, or at least not particularly effective because of its busyness; it is effective above all in simply being, and, of course, in being recognized.

A famous example of such deathfulness in the second self takes the form of an "animated inanimate duplicate" like the shadow of the scholar and the mirror image of the student Baldwin, in the stories by Andersen and Ewers respectively. Here the duplicate is a painted portrait, and the work in question is Oscar Wilde's *The Picture of Dorian Gray*.[1] Essentially what we have in this novel is the old story of Narcissus with which we began this study, the Narcissus legend reset in the framework of Victorian England. But Wilde's novel makes certain changes in the original plan that give it far better title to be included in the literature of the second self. In the first place the youthful hero sees his own image not in a mirrored reflection that his smallest touch will destroy but in the apparently fixed and permanent form of a picture. In the second place, this later Narcissus stares more deeply and sadly than did the legendary one, and he does not become the victim of what to the modern reader is a naive mistake. He does not fall in love with "himself" (at this point the picture is nothing but a picture) but with his own beauty, as it is revealed to him by Basil Hallward's masterpiece. And at once this love brings him grief rather than joy, for like Keats he knows that Beauty is accompanied by the handmaidens Decay and Death, the processes of becoming ugly that are inseparable from the process of becoming beautiful. He wishes that in his case alone this inseparability might be broken, and transferred to the picture. Magically his wish is granted. Dorian remains physically untouched by Time; it is the portrait that shows his age.

Thus far we have only a fairy tale; it is the psychological and moral consequences of this miracle that constitute the real story. The change that takes place in the portrait is far more than one of physical aging, for the story is far more than one of Dorian's growing old by proxy. Centrally it is the story of Dorian's gradual corruption, in part by the Wildean philosophy of sensationalism to which he is introduced through his friendship with Lord Henry Wotton, in part by his immunity from any visible signs of evil behavior. In fact the figure in the portrait does not really become that of an old man (Dorian never gets beyond the age of forty) so much as that of an infinitely decayed man, an embodiment of that deathfulness which is the horror of the Vision of Horror, all the more loathsome in this case for certain lingering traces of the original beauty it has lost.

It is true that the second self of Dorian Gray is less mobile than the shadow of the scholar or the mirror image of the student-swordsman. But it is Wilde's very restraint in confining the animation of the duplicate strictly to appearance (almost as though the portrait were being retouched from time to time by unseen brushwork) that makes this animation so convincing. Indeed, in respect to the capacity for physical growth and change the portrait is the animate one of the two, while Dorian is as inanimate as painted canvas, though only in this one respect. In other words, the portrait is no mere allegorical abstraction of Dorian's soul, the true foulness of which lies hidden behind the fair-seeming screen of Dorian's body. His being is bound to Dorian's by the unbreakable chain of shared identity; he is as subjectively real, for his original and for us, as Dorian himself, for the reason that he *is* Dorian. But at the same time he is no less objectively real, as a completely independent being whose nature and will and purpose are diametrically opposed to Dorian's own. For all the influence of Lord Henry Wotton, Dorian remains fundamentally a sympathetic person; he blunders into evil rather than courting it, and in the forbidden garden of his untouchable beauty he sins much as Milton's Eve devours the forbidden fruit, not cynically but hysterically, and with a good deal of incredulous remorse. This is the Dorian-self. The portrait-self is not in the least either sympathetic or hysterical. His visible degeneration in no way detracts from his strength in the duel between them; it constitutes his strength, or more accurately it constitutes the weapon of which his strength makes use, and with which he brings about the step-by-step destruction of his original.

All readers of the story will recall how he accomplishes this task. With systematic meticulousness he collects and registers in his own person each smallest depravity of the Dorian-self. But this is merely the initial and comparatively mechanical step. At the same time that he mirrors the depravity he carefully excludes all traces of the remorse, the genuine and deeply painful self-reproach that struggles for existence against Dorian's selfishness. Nor does he do this in an effort to arrest Dorian's downhill course; to the contrary, one gets the impression of a silent satisfaction that gleams through the decaying features, at each sight of which Dorian's inward panic and demoralization increase.

One evidence of this demoralization, and of the malignity of the second self who has brought it about, is Dorian's murder of Basil Hallward, the artist. This is no calculated crime designed to cover up the secret, but an impulsive one springing from an uncontrollable fit of hatred that sweeps over him as he glances at the picture, "as though it had been suggested to him by the image on the canvas, whispered into his ear by those grinning lips."[2] But a more interesting evidence is that the first self is not only terrified by the malice of the second self who mocks him with the fact of their basic sameness, but to some extent infected by it, and mocks his counterpart in turn with the visible difference between them. Often, immediately after one of his wild orgies that leave him so wonderfully unmarked. Dorian unveils the portrait, and holding a hand mirror beside his own lovely face compares it with the unlovely face beside it. He does this partly for the satisfaction he derives from his own appearance. But he derives an equal and even less wholesome satisfaction from the other's appearance.

He would examine with minute care, and sometimes with a monstrous and terrible delight, the hideous lines that seared the wrinkling forehead, or crawled around the heavy sensual mouth, wondering sometimes which were the more horrible, the signs of sin or the signs of old age. He would place his white hands beside the coarse and bloated ones of the picture, and smile. He mocked the misshapen body and the failing limbs.[3]

Mockery, however, as usual comes more naturally to the second self than to the first, and even when the latter achieves it briefly his real attitude continues underneath, one of the horrified revulsion which dogs him through the rest of his tormented life, to his last desperate effort at escape: the stabbing of the picture which, like Baldwin's shooting of the mirror image, destroys not the second self but the first, and in this case restores to the former the flawless youthful beauty that has been temporarily and fatefully entrusted to the latter.

But as we have already seen, the inanimate duplicate, however skillfully animated for artistic purposes, is bound to have certain short-comings when converted into a living personality. We tend to feel a certain trickery about it, and to hold back from full emotional partici-pation. As always, it is the human second self who is the most satisfactory counterpart of the human first self.

This is not to say that he will be human in the best sense. As evil second self he is bound to be rather the reverse, and may be of such nature that we apply to him our arrogantly misleading word "inhuman," by which we mean simply that aspect of humanity we would like to disown. But inhumanity is not the province of beasts; beasts, unless they are humanized for fictional purposes, know nothing of it. Inhumanity is exclusively human, the dark jungle-recess of the enlightened psyche that uses its light of reason as the instrument of its own darkness. Inhuman-ity is what the deathfulness I have mentioned consists in: the abdication or perversion by the human being of his capacity to be human.

Let us take first a relatively mild illustration of such deathfulness in the literature of the second self, F. Scott Fitzgerald's *One Trip Abroad*.[4] Here we have an unusual plan in that both first self and second self consist of two people each, so that altogether there are four characters involved in the relationship, though substantially each pair functions as a unit. The young American couple Nicole and Nelson Kelly, on the strength of Nelson's inheritance of half a million dollars, have gone abroad to live. In their travels they repeatedly encounter (but never meet) another young couple of their own age and apparently in much their own circumstances. The other couple attract their curiosity, impress them with a sense of familiarity, though they cannot explain why. The others seem at first such a charming pair, the kind of people it warms one's heart to see. But by degrees there comes a change; the others have become harder-looking, dissipated and demoralized, decide Nicole and Nelson, who themselves by the same gradations have begun going to seed. The difference between the two couples is that the unnamed strangers display all the unfortunate

qualities of Nicole and Nelson in heightened form: all their gross immaturity, their increasing vulgarity, their bewildered lack of discipline and
direction, their small, spoiled self-centeredness. Such things are painful
for the protagonists to watch, though at first they have no clear idea why.
Only at the end, when they are attempting to find their lost health and
peace of mind in a stay at Lake Geneva, does understanding come.
Walking together outside the hotel after dinner, they stand looking over
the Alps, at a sky alive with summer lightning. Suddenly in a flash of
it they again catch sight of the other couple, and this time they cling
together in terror. It is Nicole who puts into words the nature of their
vision.

> "Did you see?" she cried in a whisper. "Did you see them?"
> "Yes."
> "They're us! They're us! Don't you see?"
> Trembling, they clung together. The clouds merged into the dark mass of
> mountains; looking around them after a moment, Nelson and Nicole saw
> that they were alone together in the moonlight.[5]

The disappearance of the strangers does not necessarily imply anything hallucinatory about them; in fact there is a good deal of evidence
throughout the story that they possess objective as well as subjective
reality. They are seen by and in company with people other than the
Kellys; they cause an uproar in the crowd at the café where (unlike the
Kellys, who fight in comparative private) they engage in a public brawl.
Nevertheless their reality is at best rather pallid; they are never sufficiently
developed as characters to become any sort of counterbalancing force in
the story; and, above all, the deathfulness of which they give a vision is
not particularly horrifying. Cases of arrested development are pathetic,
but in themselves no more than that.

Certainly both horrifying and unforgettable is the embodiment of
deathfulness that appears in Thomas Mann's *Death in Venice:*[6] the series
of death's heads, each in a different version and worn by a different
physically living man, that runs through the story as the quasi-musical
background of Aschenbach's passion for the Polish boy Tadzio; Death
playing the role of the hero's counterpart, walking in various guises by
his side, both within and without, revolting yet fascinating him, and
beckoning him to their final meeting place. But the different manifestations of Death are not welded together into a single personality, nor is
their interest concentrated exclusively enough on the protagonist, to constitute a clearly individualized second self.

The figure of Babo, the diminutive negro slave of Melville's *Benito Cereno*,[7] comes closer. Beneath the surface of doglike loyalty and devotion to his master (Babo stands always beside him, attached to him like an extra limb, watching the smallest expression of his face), is a hatred so profound that it is almost joyous, at times almost amorous. And yet for this hatred no reason is ever given; actually it was Don Benito's leniency toward the slaves that made the mutiny possible. Indeed Babo, in order to feed this unmotivated hatred, goes far beyond any useful intimidation, that is, intimidation designed to keep his former captain from betraying the secret that captain and slave have reversed roles. He invents such refinements of mental torture — for example, in the shaving scene when he brandishes a naked razor over Don Benito's throat — as to terrify his victim into inconsistencies that very nearly reveal the true situation; and Babo is far too shrewd not to realize this. His viciousness, in other words, is not serving the cause of strategy; it is serving the cause of viciousness. And similarly in the case of his victim and opposite, Benito Cereno, the effect goes far beyond anything that the presumable cause can explain. For what really characterizes the white man's behavior is less fear than horror: horror not primarily at Babo's threats but at Babo himself, at the sight of the face ever opposite his own, the nature of whose darkness (and implicitly also of the white man's darkness) has forever left its stain on his mind.[8] What is lacking here, for our purposes, is sufficient knowledge of the reactions of the first self, since the story is told by a character who for the most part completely misunderstands the relationship between the Spaniard and his former slave, and does not suspect the dark under-force of human savagery that has seized control while the captain slept.

In the modern story by Katherine Anne Porter, *Noon Wine*,[9] there are shifts of viewpoint within the story as a whole, but that which is held to throughout the section in which the encounter between the selves occurs is the viewpoint of the protagonist and first self, Mr. Thompson. Mr. Thompson (never referred to as "Thompson," since he would never think of himself in so unceremonious a way) is the owner of a small, impoverished farm in South Texas. His wife is ill, and he himself without efficient help, so that the farm has been going steadily downhill. With the arrival of a new hired hand, a silent and hard-working Swede named Olaf Helton, things take a turn for the better. Nine years pass in this way. Then one day a stranger comes to the Thompson farm, announces that Helton is an escaped lunatic who has killed his own brother, and asks Mr. Thompson's help in taking Helton back into custody. In the midst of this conversation Helton himself appears, the stranger draws a knife and apparently stabs the hired man, and coming to the latter's defense Mr. Thompson strikes the stranger over the head with an ax, killing him. Mr. Thompson is legally innocent of murder, but he is a suspect person from then on in the minds of all other people in the community, including his wife and children, and in his loneliness he is driven to suicide. These are the events of the story: the story (like that of *Crime and Punishment*) of an ax-murder and its consequences; except that, unlike Raskolnikov, Mr. Thompson has acted without premeditation and indeed with a laudable motive, for he has unintentionally killed in the effort to prevent a killing, and the consequences seem monstrously unfair.

But in this summary of the plot I have purposely omitted, not the role of the second self (the stranger), but his role *as* second self, which alone gives significance to what would otherwise be an unfortunate blunder. In order to understand this role let us look in more detail at the character of the first self as shown to us before the stranger's arrival. Mr. Thompson is "a noisy proud man who held his neck so straight his whole face stood level with his Adam's Apple."[10] But he is not proud in the sense of being aggressive; what he wants is merely the good opinion of others, on which he is wholly dependent; like Sinclair Lewis' Babbitt he is a decent but immature person, fatuously accepting opinions he has not thought through, heartily using the phrases and stale, tired witticisms of the society to which he must feel he belongs. He is not immoral, but in small ways, the only ways in which it is tested at first, his moral sense is a lethargic one. He has a family to support, but he does not go very actively about doing so, and when possible will slip off to town for a little amiable visit to the "hotel," or local saloon. Instead of doing what needs to be done, he will sit for hours and worry about the fact that it is not getting done, while the farm goes to rack and ruin. He is not a bad man; he is rather a self-justified man, whose house of justification is built upon the sand of his shallowness.

The stranger, the alien intruder who comes into the Thompson world on that hot August afternoon, is a certain Mr. Hatch, a name suggestive of both the hatching of mischief and a trapdoor waiting for the unwary foot, a trap which in this case is baited with Mr. Hatch's personality. It is a personality that seems somehow familiar to Mr. Thompson, though he cannot say why; it is also one that Mr. Thompson finds himself instinctively disliking, though again he cannot say why. As a matter of fact it is a personality that has much in common with Mr. Thompson's own; like Mr. Thompson, Mr. Hatch is loud, jovial, hearty, and fatuous; they seem two of a kind, and so in a sense they are. But in another sense Mr. Hatch is the exact opposite of Mr. Thompson, not the other side of the total human personality but the other side of that limited fragment of it we have already met in Mr. Thompson. Where Mr. Thompson's joviality, if a little overdone, is in the main genuine, Mr. Hatch's is wildly uproarious and as empty as a drum. Where Mr. Thompson's egotism is generally innocuous, Mr. Hatch's is insistent and insufferable. Where Mr. Thompson is sometimes tactless, Mr. Hatch, under a thin veneer of geniality, is deliberately insulting, with a fine sixth sense for just those points where the other is most vulnerable: his penny-pinching, his petty pride, his tendency to justify himself on the score of his wife's illness. Where Mr. Thompson is not above shifting responsibility onto the shoulders of others, chiefly Helton, and profiting from their work, Mr. Hatch does no work at all, but devotes himself, under the guise of supporting law and order, to the sordid business of tracking down escaped inmates of mental institutions and prisons for the sake of the rewards. Where Mr. Thompson is a man of good intentions that don't get very far, Mr. Hatch is a man of thoroughly evil intentions that are thoroughly efficacious.

In every way, then, Mr. Thompson sees before him, though he never understands the fact, his own character traits turned inside out, turned sour and decadent and vicious, in this shrunken fat man with the piglike eyes and the brown rabbit-teeth, who seems to know his thoughts before he utters them. He hears his own words in the other's mouth, but his own words skillfully distorted until he seems to have been saying, though he knows he has not, the most terrible things,[11] as for instance that his wife in her illness is a burden to him and that he would like to be rid of her. He begins to hate this man with a hate that fills his whole being. And when he finds that Mr. Hatch, in addition to all the rest, constitutes a direct threat to the inoffensive Helton, the prop and mainstay of the Thompson household, the hatred floods into his brain and explodes, like that of Billy Budd, in an instant of violence catastrophic for them both.

In *Noon Wine* we have the advantage, as we have not in *Benito Cereno,* of knowing directly the thoughts of the first self and being able to trace in detail the effect exerted on him by the second self. But the mind, and consequently the thoughts, of such a first self as Mr. Thompson are rather limited in nature. In Conrad's novel *Lord Jim*[12] we go back to the method of inference, but inference drawn for us in this case by someone (Marlow) whose deep understanding of the first self, as well as his knowledge of the second self and (from the latter) of the encounter between them, tells us far more about the relationship than we ever learn about that of Benito Cereno and his dark counterpart, and really more than we ever know about that of Mr. Thompson and Mr. Hatch.

Though the second self of *Lord Jim* makes an even later appearance than does the one of *Noon Wine,* there is a certain atmosphere of second-selfdom that runs through much of this story.[13] Thus the disgrace of Jim, when first mate on the *Patna,* in having participated in the desertion of his ship under emergency conditions, and the compounding of this disgrace by his insistence on standing trial alone, presenting himself in his shame before the world throughout the whole useless inquiry, have a far more comprehensive effect than he ever knows. He is not just a ship's officer guilty of dereliction of duty; he is also the kind of young man each of the elder shipmen attending the trial has been; he is, as Marlow the narrator puts it, "one of us." And he has fallen, not as a common criminal from whom they can easily divorce themselves, but as one of them might have fallen, perhaps *has* fallen, but without being caught as Jim has been, yet at the same time with the sense, whether or not conscious, that "from weakness that may lie hidden, watched or unwatched, prayed against or manfully scorned, repressed or maybe ignored half a lifetime, not one of us is safe."

Thus the elderly French lieutenant refuses to consider the possibility that the "honor" to which he clings may perhaps consist in the covering up of a past dishonor, but the very resoluteness with which he rejects the idea is clear indication that he has had to reject it before. Marlow on the other hand accepts the idea, and his acceptance leads to a friendship with Jim that lasts throughout the latter's life. But one who can neither reject it nor accept it is one of the two assessors who preside at the hearing and pass judgment on Jim. This is Captain Brierly, "Big Brierly," the last person who might be expected to associate himself with Jim. "He had never in his life made a mistake, never had an accident, never a mishap, never a check in his steady rise, and he seemed to be one of those lucky fellows who know nothing of indecision, much less of self-mistrust." This, however, is all on the outside. Inside, as he sits listening to Jim with his self-satisfied contemptuous air, Brierly is listening to a different hearing, and the man in the witness box is apparently himself. And on himself he passes a judgment heavier than that which is passed on Jim. Shortly afterward he leaps over the rail of his own ship to his death.

None of these cases, however, constitutes a true first-self-second-self relationship. Such a relationship must always be reciprocal; there must be on both sides some sense, however unconscious, of the basic oneness. Furthermore, in none of these instances is even the one-sided closeness quite close enough.[14] Nevertheless they do serve to prepare us, emotionally, for the emergence of a true second self at the climax of the novel. Here Jim plays the part of the first self. Having managed both to flee from his disgrace and to redeem himself by meeting new tests with courage and success, having learned even at the end of the earth to keep himself afloat in the destructive element of his own romanticism, having in Stein's words followed the dream, and again followed the dream, *usque ad finem,* he has become Lord Jim, the unofficial leader of the small fishing village of Patusan, where (though nowhere else in the world) he is accepted, looked up to, needed, and loved. To Patusan, on a raiding mission with a boatload of sea-wolves scarcely less depraved than himself, comes one "Gentleman Brown," a ruffian and pirate intent on stealing provisions and anything else to be found, even if it means toasting a few toes in the process. Brown and his gang meet with an unexpectedly hot reception and barricade themselves on a hilltop where, though still dangerous, they are effectively trapped. Jim, as leader of the natives, negotiates with Brown, unwisely takes Brown's word that the invaders will go peacefully back to their schooner, and prevails on the natives to let them depart. On his way Brown treacherously massacres the party of Dain Waris, son of the native chief Doramin. Jim, presenting himself unarmed before Doramin to answer for his mistake, is shot and killed.

But as in *Noon Wine* the events of the encounter become meaningful only in the light of the characters involved and the relationship that is developed between them. Again, the two men are diametrical opposites, both separated and linked by their oppositeness. Jim is the romantic dreamer who in unreadiness of soul has failed his dream, and then unexpectedly has realized his dream, in a way and in a place that forever cut him off from the world for which he has longed to justify himself, so that in Patusan he has received simultaneously the punishment for his cowardice and the reward for his courage. But this solution in no way ends his striving. He remains at the end what he was at the beginning, the romantic dreamer, who by now has learned something of the immense involvement of dreams in life, an involvement which one must control or be controlled by; and he dies in the exercise of this control.

Like Jim, Brown is no ordinary man, for if he were he could be the opposite only of another ordinary man, as Mr. Hatch is the opposite of Mr. Thompson. Brown too has had his romantic and even poetic streak, but always tinged with cruelty, and by the time he makes his appearance in this story, sailing out of the unknown sea like another Mr. Jones (it is interesting to note the anonymity of the two names), all the poetry of Brown's nature has been channeled to serve his "natural" inclinations. It has not disappeared; it has simply made him capable of being evil with a flair, with imagination. Jim dreams of heroism, of loyalty and service, of proving trustworthy under test; Brown dreams of rapine, of murder and torture when they serve his ends, and, when his victims have the effrontery to resist being victimized, of revenge. Jim is honest and trusts others; Brown is dishonest and trusts no one; hence each misjudges the other. But this mutual misjudgment should not be overemphasized; beneath it, and far more important in the effect they have on each other and their subsequent decisions, is a mutual understanding. This comes, of course, only when they at last confront each other, across the creek that has been so fateful in Jim's career. Up to this point Brown has had nothing particularly against Jim, has never laid eyes on Jim, and has assumed from what he has heard that Jim is someone like himself, another pirate who can be persuaded to share the takings. Instantly now he knows better, and his immediate reaction is hatred. He hates Jim's youth, Jim's innocence, Jim's clarity of eye and cleanness of person, all the qualities that so mercilessly point up his own lack of them. And yet, as always in the relationship between the selves, neither envy nor any other rational motivation is enough to explain the hatred that fills Brown at his first sight of Jim. Above all it seems to be hatred as a first principle, born into the soul and waiting for this moment, the implacable hatred of the dark second self for his Twin Brother of light. And out of this hatred comes the shrewdness that enables him, not to pull Jim down to his own level, but at least physically to destroy him.

Not, as I say, that Brown has any knowledge of Jim's past; his performance would be far less impressive if he had. What he has instead is instinctive insight, an insight which enables him, as Mr. Hatch was able to do with Mr. Thompson, to probe the needle of his taunts into the most sensitive spots of Jim's being. It is an insight even more inexplicable on rational grounds (for example, as mere shrewdness or "knowledge of men") than Mr. Hatch's, for Brown not only does not know the details of Jim's case but completely misinterprets them; but this is an insight that has no need of factual accuracy. Over and over he returns to the essential point. Jim has asked what made him come here. Hunger, Brown answers — as indeed it has, though hunger less for food than for rapine. "And what made you?" he demands. He cannot know the particular kind of hunger that worked on Jim, but he knows, without knowing why he knows, that there has been a hunger there, and with satisfaction he watches the reddening of Jim's face as their two cases are thus linked with each other. He pursues his advantage. They are both as good as dead men; therefore "let us talk on that basis, as equals."

And when Jim wants to know what Brown has done "out there" that has made him a fugitive, Brown gives an answer that cannot but sound, within Jim's mind, like the echo of what would have to be Jim's own answer to the same question, the answer that in the past he must have given himself with so many different accents of self-reproach: "I am here because I was afraid once in my life." It is, Marlow says, as though Brown were possessed with some sort of diabolical inspiration.

When he asked Jim, with a sort of brusque despairing frankness, whether he himself — straight now — didn't understand that when "it came to saving one's life in the dark, one didn't care who else went — three, thirty, three hundred people" — it was as if a demon had been whispering advice in his ear.[15]

And so one is. But the demon, of course, is not outside Brown but inside him. It is that within Brown which understands Jim, understands that part of Jim which is vulnerable to him because it is also part of him, degraded and distorted but nonetheless there.

Of Jim's attitude toward Brown we know only what the dying Brown tells Marlow, and what Marlow infers from this account; in other words, we for once know the thoughts of the second self more directly than those of the first. But by now we are so well familiar with the workings of Jim's mind that we can have little doubt as to the validity of Marlow's interpretation of it. At first there is plainly the bitterness of the thought that it should be such a man as this, this posturing cutthroat across the creek from him, who has come to him at last from the self-righteous world by which he has been condemned. By degrees, however, though his disgust does not pass, it broadens, as deftly, touch by touch, Brown points up the parallel between them; it becomes a terrible sort of sympathy which forces him to see the Jim that is in Brown, while at the same time remaining disgust; a double disgust now, not only for the Brown across the creek, but for the Brown that is in Jim. Through Brown's talk there runs "a vein of subtle reference to their common blood, an assumption of common experience; a sickening suggestion of common guilt, of secret knowledge that was like a bond of their minds and of their hearts."[16] Jim's reaction to the experience of self-encounter is, of course, quite the reverse of Mr. Thompson's. A far deeper and more sensitive person, he is not moved to violence against his loathsome counterpart; in justice if not in wisdom (and he is aware of the unwisdom of his course) he is unable to punish the other in any way; he is compelled to spare this second self just as he was spared, and to give Brown the same "clear road" that he was once given.

But in using such words as "parallel" and "understanding" to describe the relationship between these men I do not mean simply that the two "identify" themselves with each other.[17] There *is* such mutual identification; there always is in these relationships, at some level of consciousness, and Conrad is rather explicit about pointing out its presence in this one. But identification by itself is a purely psychological and explicable phenomenon, and is it never enough to give us a first-self-second-self relationship. It is not this *identification* with each other that counts, but the gradually strengthening suggestion of their *identity* with each other, identity in separateness, as though each while remaining on his own side of the creek that runs between them were simultaneously reaching across it, not just with calculating shrewdness or awakened conscience but with a part of his being.

The second self is always mysterious in function as well as in character. But by now we can see that there is a particular mystery about the second self in the present category. The Pursuer has his job of pursuing, the Tempter of tempting, but what is the proper job of the Vision of Horror? It is merely to present himself as he is, often without conscious knowledge of either what this is or what effect it is having on his victim. The result is that generally there is a disparity between what he intends to do or appears to be doing on the plot level of the story and the far more important role he plays on the level of his relationship with the protagonist. In the last three examples we have taken up — Babo, Mr. Hatch, and Gentleman Brown — this disparity has led to complications that the second self could not possibly have foreseen. In other cases the disparity goes so far as to make us wonder a little at first glance what the second self is doing in the story at all.

Such a case is the main example that we shall consider in this chapter, another of Dostoyevsky's novels, this time *Crime and Punishment*.[18] The figure I refer to is Svidrigaïlov: the wealthy landowner who has made dishonorable proposals to Raskolnikov's sister Dounia while the latter was a governess in his household and who, having followed Dounia to Petersburg, visits Raskolnikov and asks him to act as intermediary between them. Like Mr. Hatch and Gentleman Brown he makes a singularly late entrance, when the story is already more than half over; unlike them, however, he does not take the course of events into his hands when he does enter. His only connection with Raskolnikov's problem, the problem of the murder in which the whole novel centers, is his overhearing of the latter's confession to Sonia, and this information he makes only a half-hearted gesture to use (in any case a gesture of which Raskolnikov himself knows nothing). He appears infrequently and irregularly, and the longest scene in which we see him, that of his suicide, might well seem to have no bearing on the story of Raskolnikov, but to interrupt the latter at the moment of its climax. Except for his suicide, and a generous doling out of five percent bonds to the Marmeladov family, he does little but sit and chat with Raskolnikov, chiefly about himself, his ideas, his little shabby sexual peccadillos. On the event level, if one were to set about cutting this novel, surely the Svidrigaïlov sections are what one would drop first.

And one would drop, if not the heart of this book, something very like it. For once again, but more than in any of the other cases we have examined, the importance of Svidrigaïlov is to be understood only in the light of his relationship with his first self. There are other close relationships in this story, electrically close ones; but the closeness of relationship between Raskolnikov and Svidrigaïlov is of a completely different order, and there is nothing else like it in the novel.

Nor is there anything quite like it in any other Dostoyevsky novel, either. Here alone, to the best of my knowledge, Dostoyevsky makes use of certain almost musical devices to "sound the theme" of Svidrigaïlov in a preparatory way before we even meet him, and later on to link up the Svidrigaïlov theme with the Raskolnikov theme.[19] I have said that Svidrigaïlov does not enter until late in the story, nor does he, as a person; but as a name and as a value associated with the name he enters Raskolnikov's mind far earlier, well before the murder. Smarting from the sense of his poverty and uselessness, Raskolnikov is still more embittered by a letter from his mother, telling of the way Svidrigaïlov has insulted Dounia, and of the fact that Dounia is about to marry a well-to-do businessman named Luzhin, a man of about twice her age. It is the news of this engagement that seems mainly to disturb Raskolnikov; he paces the streets and mutters to himself, almost wholly taken up with this idea, the prospect of Dounia's selling herself to a complacent middle-aged sensualist for her brother's sake. Suddenly he sees a young girl, who has been made drunk and seduced and turned loose to wander by herself, being followed by a well-dressed, middle-aged gentleman who evidently intends to take advantage of the situation. One would expect Raskolnikov, seething with resentment against Luzhin, to make the obvious connection, but he does not. "Hey!" he bursts out. "You Svidrigaïlov! What do you want here?" — Not that the gentleman *is* Svidrigaïlov, or that Raskolnikov thinks so. But in a less specific sense, the thematic sense, the gentleman is not entirely *not* Svidrigaïlov, either. For while the Svidrigaïlov who, much later on, makes his first appearance in Raskolnikov's garret room is carefully distinguished from the earlier pursuer of young girls, he is carefully linked with him as well. He is older, yet he looks much younger than his years; and, though he wears a beard instead of moustaches, like his predecessor he is thickly set and fashionably dressed, has pink cheeks and crimson lips.

This is Svidrigaïlov's double introduction, first as a symbol and then as a man, the line between the two being deliberately blurred for us, as it is for Raskolnikov, whose viewpoint we share in the scenes between them. A similar artful blurring, this one to suggest a different and vastly more important continuity, occurs at almost the end of the book, in the account of Svidrigaïlov's suicide. The room in which he spends the last night of his life is an unmistakable echo of another room: Raskolnikov's room, where he has first made the latter's acquaintance, a close and dirty and tiny room, so low pitched one cannot stand erect in it, and with soiled wallpaper (even the color of this paper, yellow, is the same) peeling from the walls.[20]

But such anticipations and echoes merely form the framework for the relationship between the two men; let us now look briefly at the relationship itself. We first see Svidrigaïlov when, in much the same way in which Mr. Hatch "happens" to come to the Thompson farm and Gentleman Brown "happens" to come to Patusan, he "happens" to pass within a few feet of Raskolnikov, whom he has been seeking but does not know, and hears Sonia use the latter's name. For a time he drops out of sight. Meanwhile Raskolnikov undergoes his nerve-racking interview with the police inspector Porphiry, and returning to his room has a nightmare of again going to the flat of the old pawnbroker, of striking her repeatedly with the same ax with which he has killed her but finding that this time she will not die, but only shakes with secret laughter at him. He awakes, but his nightmare seems to continue, for a stranger is standing in his doorway watching him. He pretends to be still asleep, but the stranger neither disappears like a dream image nor goes away as anyone else would; instead he noiselessly enters the room and sits at the table, perfectly at home, to wait. He is real, and yet for Raskolnikov he is not real as other real people are; throughout the interview that follows a certain nightmarish aura still surrounds him, to such an extent that Raskolnikov wonders, after he has gone, whether or not he could have been an hallucination.[21]

Considering the nature of this interview it is little wonder. Svidrigaïlov announces at once that he wants help in approaching Dounia, and Raskolnikov is properly indignant. But neither the practical motivation of the one nor the proper indignation of the other plays any significant part in their conversation. Held by a strange and growing fascination not unmixed with fear (he is afraid of Svidrigaïlov long before he is given any reason to be) Raskolnikov listens to his visitor chatter gaily away, about himself in large part, but by degrees we begin to realize that it is not wholly about himself, or rather that just in being about himself it is also about Raskolnikov; that this sophisticated dandy, though a complete stranger and making not the smallest effort, is showing a knowledge of Raskolnikov that Razumihin with all his friendship, Dounia or Sonia with all their love, Zossimov with all his medical skill, and Porphiry with all his keenness as criminal investigator, come nowhere near showing. To some extent the two men recognize this themselves, as when Svidrigaïlov, apropos of nothing. reveals that he has been seeing the ghost of his dead wife, to whose death he may have made a certain contribution. Raskolnikov, despite himself more and more engrossed, questions the other closely. When exactly has Svidrigaïlov seen the spectre? Was he awake when he saw it? Oh yes, quite awake, in fact *almost* able to hear her go out the door (just as Raskolnikov, in the nightmare that still half-seems to be going on, was *almost* able to hear the laughter of his own victim).

"What made me think that something of this sort must be happening to you?" Raskolnikov said suddenly.
At the same time he was surprised at having said it. He was much excited.
"What! Did you think so?" Svidrigaïlov asked in astonishment. "Did you really? Didn't I say that there was something in common between us, eh?"
"You never said so!" Raskolnikov cried sharply and with heat.
"Didn't I?"
"No!"
"I thought I did. When I came in and saw you lying with your eyes shut, pretending, I said to myself at once, 'Here's the man'."
"What do you mean 'the man'? What are you talking about?" cried Raskolnikov.
"What do I mean? I really don't know . . ." Svidrigaïlov muttered ingenuously, as though he, too, were puzzled.
For a minute they were silent. They stared in each other's faces.[22]

What they are staring at, these two men who have just met for the first time in their lives, is what each of them in his own way has just struggled to put into words: their simultaneous discovery of a kinship between them which neither of them can understand. If we are in any doubt that this is what is meant here, the point is made for us again and again as the story goes on. Raskolnikov, of course, fights against any admission of such a kinship, but Svidrigaïlov in the traditional manner of the second self readily acknowledges it; even takes pains, like Mr. Jones with Heyst or Gentleman Brown with Lord Jim, mockingly to point it out. In this initial conversation, for example, it is revealed that not only do both men pretend not to have seen people they do see (Svidrigaïlov understands Raskolinkov's pretending because he himself indulges in the same pretending) and see people they should not see (the ghosts of their victims), but both, while skeptical about life after death, are unable to keep from thinking about the subject. Surely there is no more extraordinary moment in the literature of the second self than that in which Svidrigaïlov, who has come to enlist Raskolnikov's aid in his pursuit of Dounia, and Raskolnikov, who has been on the verge of turning Svidrigaïlov out of the room, find themselves all at once embarked upon the subject of eternity. What if it is only like a dirty little bathhouse in the country, Svidrigaïlov muses, while Raskolnikov watches him in terror and anguish. Suddenly Svidrigaïlov laughs.

"Only think," he cried, "Half an hour ago we had never seen each other, we regarded each other as enemies; there is a matter unsettled between us; we've thrown it aside, and away we've gone into the abstract! Wasn't I right in saying that we were birds of a feather?"[23]

An equally remarkable instance of their mutual interest and insight, the deeper level of communication between them that runs along like a wordless counterpart of the audible one, is the scene of their final meeting. When Porphiry finally accuses him of the murder, Raskolnikov's first move is to hurry forth in search of Svidrigaïlov. He has not the slightest idea why. "What he had to hope from that man he did not know. But that man had some hidden power over him." Obviously the hidden power is not Svidrigaïlov's knowledge of the murder; the latter is not hidden, nor would it require any such pondering on Raskolnikov's part, nor does Raskolnikov even allude to it when he finds Svidrigaïlov. It is something else, something that draws him like an unseen hand on his arm, draws him to the right place without his knowing where the right place is. He starts out, logically enough, toward Svidrigaïlov's lodgings. Being preoccupied, however, he wanders off in an entirely unaccustomed direction, and at last finds himself outside a tavern, in the window of which sits waiting the very man he is after. Svidrigaïlov offers the explanation that he has told Raskolnikov where he would be and that the words must have registered on the latter's unconscious memory. But as it happens the words are nowhere in the text. Furthermore, Svidrigaïlov has a practical reason — his rendezvous with Dounia — for wanting to avoid Raskolnikov, a reason which might be thought to account for the fact that at Raskolnikov's appearance he plays briefly the same cat-and-mouse game of seeing yet pretending not to see that Raskolnikov has played with him at their first meeting. Yet this explanation, too, fails to stand up. For once discovered Svidrigaïlov makes no further effort to escape; he looks at his watch and speaks of an appointment, but in fact it is he who holds Raskolnikov, or in stricter fact it is both of them who both hold and are held, all practical considerations, as before, virtually forgotten. What follows is another long talk, chiefly by Svidrigaïlov and again chiefly about Svidrigaïlov, about the sort of man he is and, by implication, the sort of man Raskolnikov is. As Svidrigaïlov puts it (using exactly the phrase that Raskolnikov has just been thinking), they have come to each other "for the sake of hearing something new":[24] the same something they have stared at on the earlier occasion, the discovery of themselves in each other.

Not that either of them is necessarily aware in his conscious mind of the full meaning of this discovery, for all Svidrigaïlov's twitting Raskolnikov with the likeness between them. In any visible way they are not in the least alike. Their physical persons are contrasted at almost every point. Interestingly in this relationship, as in the one between Leventhal and Allbee, the traditional color contrast between the first self as light and the second self as dark (e.g., Heyst and Mr. Jones, Billy Budd and Claggart) is reversed. But it is reversed only in externals, for the external fairness of Svidrigaïlov is made to emphasize his internal darkness. Raskolnikov with his dark hair and beautiful burning dark eyes is a far more wholesome figure than Svidrigaïlov, with hair such a light flaxen it seems almost white, and eyes of cold blue with a heavy fixed expression. Raskolnikov is young, slim, and well-built; gaunt with hunger and dressed in rags. He has a pale, refined, mournful face that like his eyes reflects the intensity of his feelings. Svidrigaïlov is advanced in middle age, thickset, with high shoulders that make him seem to stoop a little; he dresses in fashionable clothes and dainty linen, is something of a fop; his cheeks are pink and lips bright red, but his face as a whole is strangely, unpleasantly masklike. While Raskolnikov is taciturn and speaks, when he does, with earnestness that often rises to passion, Svidrigaïlov rattles on with the gay savoir-faire of an idle country gentleman.

An even sharper contrast is the one between their characters. Raskolnikov has committed a monstrous crime, acting from a motive that he himself cannot altogether understand; a motive compounded of need, wounded pride, bitterness at "the world" for its treatment of him and his mother and sister, and (explosively mixed in with the rest) philosophy: the doctrine that the strength of the strong entitles them to take what it enables them to take; the Napoleonic doctrine which, as he learns, is applicable only to a Napoleon. He has sinned, but not as the result of a temptation; instead, like Macbeth, he has forced himself to sin out of a perverted sense of duty, and despite the utmost reluctance and loathing. But he is no more a Macbeth than he is a Napoleon; instead of being led on to further crimes he is led into the agonies of isolation, into self-destruction and ultimate self-renunciation. In all this there is an intensity about Raskolnikov, a genuine and desperate struggle to find the right way and the true value, and — for all his confusion, his irritable egoism — a blundering nobility as well.

Who could be more different from such a picture than Svidrigaïlov? Far from forcing himself into a crime he abhors for the sake of proving to himself that he dares to do it, he has drifted from one ill-defined, sordid little transgression to another, from cheating at cards to abusing little girls, each transgression getting a bit more degenerate than the last; not for the sake of proving himself to himself but for the sake of bodily comfort, of sexual thrills (preferably illicit), of sadism (he looks forward to the humiliation he will inflict on the "unopened bud" to whom he is betrothed). He has suffered from no need, no self-reproach; yet there would be on his conscience, if he had any, considerably more than the possible responsibility for his wife's death: among other things, it would appear, the death of his servant Filka and the death of a child whom (like Stavrogin of *The Possessed*) he has violated and driven to suicide. Whereas Raskolnikov has confusedly reached for power, Svidrigaïlov has consciously dabbled, as a dilettante, in vice. Whereas Raskolnikov struggles to redeem himself, Svidrigaïlov seeks only to indulge himself, partly in the pleasure of shocking this over-earnest young man who is so clearly and diametrically his opposite.

And yet, as we have found in all the other diametrical opposites we have studied, the very oppositeness is a linkage, for it is the complementary oppositeness of the two halves of a single whole. All the striking ways in which these two men differ from each other are made possible by the ways in which to begin with they are like each other, the way in which at bottom they are identical with each other. These are the men who have attempted to place themselves beyond good and evil, and have acted accordingly. They have not said, "Evil, be thou my good"; they have simply taken the position that such a distinction is irrelevant to the man of emancipated mind. In accordance with this "master morality" they have committed their crimes not impulsively but deliberately; they have played the Napoleon, for whom all the rest of mankind is *chair à canon.* And too late, like Ivan and Smerdyakov who in their own way make the same mistake, they find that they are not Napoleons, that there is in their make-up a capacity for outrage of which they have not taken account, a thinness of skin and sensitiveness of soul that will not let them rest. Raskolnikov's hell is one of fire that burns him from within; Svidrigaïlov's, like Lucifer's in the *Inferno,* is one of ice, the frozen emptiness of boredom and jaded self-contempt; but it is no less hell, and no less terrible.

Thus Svidrigaïlov, in his very difference from Raskolnikov, is related to him with a particular kind of closeness that is not even approached by anyone else in the novel; and the crime and punishment of the one are, mutantis mutandis, the crime and punishment of the other. Svidrigaïlov is the reverse side of the Raskolnikov coin, the side that has long since been rubbed smooth and dim and more than a little dingy. Not that he is vicious in the way Mr. Hatch and Gentleman Brown are; his degeneration, and the effect of it on his counterpart's mind, are of a more subtle and appalling sort. He is Raskolnikov the earnest young student become a world-weary, middle-aged roué. He is Raskolnikov, the seeker of the meaning of life, become the seeker of thrills that he cannot find. He is Rakolnikov, the tense tormented man, gone slack at the seams, gone unbuttoned in soul.

Exactly what tangible effect he exerts on Raskolnikov's fate it is impossible to know with the clarity with which we can know the effect exerted by Dorian's picture or Mr. Hatch or Gentleman Brown; this is a far more complex story than any of those, and many influences are at work at the same time. We do know that, when despite himself Raskolnikov seeks out Svidrigaïlov in the tavern, he is still refusing either to confess his crime or to admit that it could have anything in common with the crimes of Svidrigaïlov; and we know that when we next see him, after the interview just described, he has reached the decision to give himself up. This, however, has been no part of Svidrigaïlov's intention, nor has it been brought about by any action he has taken. He has made no threat to expose Raskolnikov, has only once mentioned Raskolnikov's guilt and then not as a threat, and has dropped the subject at once. What he has done is simply to taunt Raskolnikov with the parallels between them, to lead him into outcries of revulsion at the things Svidrigaïlov is revealing about himself, and then to make him see the absurdity of such moral disapproval on the part of someone who has hacked two helpless old women to death with an ax. Raskolnikov has parted with the other in profound disgust. Consciously it is disgust with Svidrigaïlov, "that coarse brute, that depraved sensualist and blackguard"; but at the same time, relentlessly if not consciously, it is also disgust with himself. For the function of Svidrigaïlov, like that of all the other second selves we have considered in this chapter, is to force the protagonist to look full into the face of the Vision of Horror, and to see in it his own.[25]

6

The Second Self As Saviour

Often we welcome novelty, but we are still too near the forest primeval to be much at ease with genuine strangeness. The unknown, for most of us, tends to be automatically the sinister, and we use the word "dark" for both. This is doubtless why the second self, being the uncanny self, is in the majority of cases the evil self; actively evil as Pursuer and Tempter, more or less passively evil as Vision of Horror.

But the second self is not always evil. That he does not always bring evil about, at least in the final issue, we have already seen. The persecutions by Kamatha-Samvara have much to do with the evolution of his brother Marubhuti into the Lord Parsva. An argument can at least be made for considering the Billy Budd who with his last breath invokes God's blessing on the man who condemned him, and the Lord Jim who presents himself for execution at the hands of Doramin, deeper and better people as the result of their vicitimization by Claggart and Gentleman Brown. A much stronger argument can be made for considering that both Raskolnikov and Faust achieve major moral development through the friction of their relationships with their second selves. And in the case of Asa Leventhal no argument is needed, for the effect which Allbee has on his life proves in the end an entirely wholesome one; indeed long after this nightmarish experience the two men meet again and agree, partly in words and partly by implication, that the score is settled between them and consequently between each of them and the world, that whatever hidden debts and claims have rankled in their souls have been paid.[1]

In all these cases, however, the good effect which the second self exerts on the first is a by-product, indirect and accidental; he remains evil, he is actuated by malice, and his at least immediate effect is disruptive and destructive. In the present chapter we turn to that rarer but very important type of second self who is genuinely good, *un homme de bonne volonté*. There is nothing contradictory in such an idea. Often, if we have patience and courage, we may find that the strange does not menace us after all, and that the hand which approaches us out of the shadows holds a boon that we need, and offers it to us for our well-being. It is possible, as Thoreau realized in the solitude of Walden, to "be beside ourselves in a sane sense,"[2] and in a beneficial and healing sense as well.

This aspect of our subject is the second self as Saviour. Naturally I do not mean the most famous of Saviours, for, though Christ has sometimes been thought of as the counterpart of Satan or Judas-Satan, his stature would make it scarcely possible for him to serve as the second self of a human hero. Nevertheless I use the word "saviour" purposely, in order to suggest the Christ-like in man, which is always the essential characteristic of the good second self,[3] just as the Antichrist-like is always that of the evil second-self. The former is sometimes referred to as the *Schützgeist,* or protective spirit, but such a name does justice neither to his role as sharer of identity with the first self nor to the quality of his goodness, which may be anything but protective in the usual sense of the word.

Early and primitive versions of the good second self (and there are very few) do tend to concentrate on physical protection: the Twin Brother of Amerindian legend, for example, who must come to the aid of his counterpart in the latter's hour of need, who must save his life or, finding him dead, bring him back to life.[4] The function of Enkidu, on the other hand, is much more sophisticated. He does not save Gilgamesh physically, but awakens dormant possibilities within Gilgamesh; by the friendship and later the grief that he brings he opens the eyes of Gilgamesh to the fact of death, and sends the first self on his lonely quest through the underworld, the endless quest of man's soul. This comes far closer than any physical saving to the function of the good second self in recent and modern literature. As the evil second self carries the force of Death for the first self, especially internal Death, deathful contraction of the spirit, so the good second self carries the force of Life, especially in the sense of spiritual growth, even though to be internally effective the latter force may be externally fatal.

With this reversal in nature and function of the second self, there must be a corresponding reversal in the first self. As in rotating a sphere on its axis, we cannot alter the position of one side without equally altering that of the other. Therefore when the second self becomes good the first self necessarily becomes evil. But this does not mean that he becomes simply interchangeable with the evil second self. In all cases the first self is the one nearer to us, whose viewpoint we tend to share and to find the comparatively reasonable one, the "daylight" one. When he proves or becomes evil, even when he is as despicable a creature as Robert Wringhim, we feel him to be less absolutely vicious than benighted, someone like ourselves who has been corrupted, temporarily or permanently. We never feel this about Gil-Martin or Mr. Jones or Mr. Hatch; not because they are more evil but because they are more removed, separated from us by an impassable gulf of mystery. And one manifestation of this mystery further distinguishes the second self, good or evil, from the first: the fact that in all relationships between them it is he who, from a never quite understandable motive, possibly one that not even he can understand, works upon the character and life of the first self, rather than the other way around. The first self may strongly affect the second in an emotional way because of the bond between them (though this is often hard to be sure of since we know so little about the internal workings of the latter), but the result of this effect is to make the second self act on the first, who always remains essentially the recipient rather than the initiator in any important exchange of influence.

It is the mystery of the second self, then, that differentiates him from the first. But the mystery of the evil second self, which we have already examined, pales a little beside the mystery of the good one. For what we are dealing with in this category is a paradox within a paradox. The evil second self is at least all of one piece in that he is a dark figure in both senses of the word, both mysterious and malicious. The good second self is dark in the former sense, but the contrary of dark in the latter. What we must look for, therefore, is the backward-foremost situation in which it is the Power of Evil that is presented to us as the more familiar and at least more immediately plausible half of the twofold being, while the Power of Good appears as the uncanny and suspect counterpart, the alien intruder from the shadows.

This fact makes it difficult for us to recognize the second self as good, but of course the writer of a work in which such a second self appears would fail in his intention if we did not ultimately do so. The one for whom such recognition becomes almost insuperably difficult is the first self. Since the moral attributes of the selves are reversed, moral valuations are also reversed. From the viewpoint of the first self his own evil is the reasonable and justified, whether or not conventional, way of life, with which the influence for good exerted on him by the second self is bound to seem unwarranted, injurious, and sometimes immoral interference. As a result, the goodness of the second self means no less oppositeness between the selves than we have seen thus far, and certainly no less opposition.

The ways in which the second self as Saviour prosecutes the cause of goodness on behalf of the first self are interestingly akin to the ways in which the three aspects of the second self that we have considered in the last three chapters prosecute the cause of evil. The first way, again, is comparatively obvious and direct, and the second self who uses it corresponds, though for purposes of salvation rather than of destruction, to the second self as Pursuer. An example of such a benignant pursuit is given us in deceptively comic tone by Bernard Malamud's short story, *The Last Mohican.*[5] The American Jew, Fidelman, a self-appointed critic of the fine arts, is the viewpoint character and first self. He is a reasonable and well-meaning man who by hard work has saved up enough money to spend a year in Italy for the completion of his magnum opus on Giotto. Arriving in Rome, he is accosted by another Jew, Susskind, an impoverished refugee from Central Europe, now a citizen of Israel but averse to the effort demanded of him there and living as peddler and beggar on such scraps as he can pick up from tourists to the Holy City. In all respects he is the opposite of Fidelman — skeletally thin instead of comfortably plump, ridiculously instead of fashionably dressed, belligerently forward instead of politely reserved — the complementary opposite, with once more the basic sameness that makes such oppositeness possible, a basic sameness which Fidelman is most reluctant to acknowledge. It is not simply that both men are Jews, but that both are Wandering Jews, runaways and guilty runaways: Susskind from the responsibilities which he has undertaken as a citizen of the new Jewish state, Fidelman from the responsibility of facing and coming to terms with his own limitations. Fidelman has been obliged to confess himself a failure as an artist and has substituted the image of himself as art critic, an image which rests on one tangible foundation, the opening chapter of his projected book on Giotto, a document so important to him that he will not even let porters carry the new pigskin case in which it lies.

At once Susskind attaches himself to Fidelman. He has the effrontery to suggest that Fidelman give him a suit of clothes, the only extra suit Fidelman owns. When Fidelman does give him money Susskind is dissatisfied, gets Fidelman to increase the amount. Nor does he do this ingratiatingly. To the contrary, with relentlessly keen insight he forces Fidelman to admit that the mission which has brought the would-be art critic here is not quite what the latter would like to think it. Fidelman, it develops, is not a professor ("not exactly," he weakly qualifies), nor even a student, nor has he any better claim to being an authority on Giotto than has Susskind. Fidelman goes off in a taxi with the feeling that Susskind may be clinging to the spare tire on the back; and he is not far wrong, for soon Susskind appears in his hotel room, and when Fidelman flees from the hotel Susskind accosts him in a restaurant, always somehow knowing where he is, always returning to the insane demand that Fidelman give to Susskind his only other suit. Finally, while Fidelman is out for a walk, Susskind enters his hotel room, exactly as though he has some special knowledge of the fact that on this one occasion the American has left his door unlocked, and steals, not the coveted suit or anything else of tangible value, but the pigskin case containing the priceless first chapter.

Thus far we have what appears to be a case of the evil second self as Pursuer. At this point, however, the first self commences to pursue the second. Fidelman discovers where Susskind lives, and during Susskind's absence searches the miserable little hovel in the ghetto. But he finds no sign of the pigskin case with the fine critical chapter, the indispensable chapter, without which he is totally incapable of going on to produce the masterpiece which will justify his life. He needs a hot-water bottle to thaw out of him the dead cold of Susskind's room, but the cold remains in his mind, and that night in a dream he has a vision of Giotto's painting, *San Francesco dona la vesti al cavaliere povero*. Awaking, he hurries with the extra suit to Susskind, who in return gives him the empty brief case; the chapter has been burned. Susskind explains that he has done the other a favor. "The words were there," he tells the outraged Fidelman, "but the spirit was missing." And in the midst of angrily chasing the skinny derelict through the ghetto,

> ... Fidelman, stout and short of breath, moved by all he had lately learned, had a triumphant insight.
> "Susskind, come back," he shouted, half sobbing. "The suit is yours. All is forgiven."[6]

Susskind continues running; as he has said of himself, he is always running. But for the moment at least, by giving to his counterpart a new vision of himself and of the true nature of his responsibility, he has freed Fidelman from the need to run.

Another example of the second self as Saviour in pursuit of the first is the very different sort of beggar who drifts in and out of Strindberg's dramatic trilogy, *The Road to Damascus.*[7] Throughout this work virtually everyone whom the hero, the Stranger, meets is to some extent a reflection of him, even continuous with him.[8] But it is only the Beggar who plays the role of the Stranger's second self. The Stranger is aware of a certain inescapable resemblance between them, for all the fine clothes that he wears and the filthy rags of the Beggar; and this resemblance is confirmed for him by the lady who becomes his mistress. He resents the Beggar's referring to them as "we," just because he too knows they *are* a "we," a two-sided unit; he becomes acutely uncomfortable in the Beggar's presence and tries to get rid of him. But of course the Beggar is exactly the person who cannot be got rid of. Not only by his presence but in more explicit ways does this wretched collector of cigar ends, this wanderer in the footsteps of the wandering Stranger, point out the parallels between them. What is the Stranger, he asks, but himself a Beggar? For "if you can't laugh at adversity, not even that of others, you're begging of life itself." At last the Stranger can stand it no longer.

STRANGER (*as if to himself*). Who is it reads my secret thoughts, turns my soul inside out, and pursues me? Why do you persecute me?
BEGGAR. Saul! Saul! Why persecutest thou me?[9]

It is no accident, nor is it merely the mockery it seems at first, that these words — the words of Christ that blazed into the mind of Saul on the latter's Road to Damascus — should be spoken by the lowliest character in the play. The Beggar is not Christ; he is, rather, the Christlike other half of the lost Stranger, performing the same function of salvation through pursuit that Susskind performs for the unwilling Fidelman. By this time, however, the Stranger is no longer entirely unwilling. He tries, in accordance with the Beggar's advice, to believe for once in the Beggar's good intentions, and doing so gives him the strength to go on his way, though for the present it is only a way into darkness. What is needed by the Stranger, as was needed by the original Saul, is a vision of Light, and this is brought him (in Parts II and III of the trilogy) by the Beggar, no longer *as* the Beggar, but now as the Dominican who is also the Confessor, who leads the Stranger up the long climb to the monastery and attends him in his last hour. Thus the Saviour-Pursuer, recoiled from and reviled at the beginning, in the end has his will of the first self, bringing the latter back, in death, to the world from which he has been so long estranged.

In both these stories the evil of the first self consists chiefly of limitations rather than of anything positive, and hence is susceptible of cure. In a more famous example of the pursuing Saviour, Poe's *William Wilson*,[10] such a cure is conceivable in the early stages of the relationship, but gradually is made impossible by the hero's development. This development is one of increasing self-dedication to the cause of evil, which, like Milton's Satan, the first self embraces as his good. The result is a "transvaluation of values" in the first self's mind, causing the effort to save him to become for him a monstrous persecution, and arousing such resistance that in the end he murders both his Pursuer and himself.

The hero and first self of this story, William Wilson, meets at school only one rival to his dominance over all other boys in both studies and sports. The boy, as it happens, possesses the same name, not in itself a very remarkable coincidence since the name is such an everyday one, but becoming remarkable as the first William Wilson begins to discover other things they have in common: height, general stature and facial appearance, even date of birth. An intense rivalry springs up between the two boys, intense at least on the first self's part, though the second self so easily maintains equality with him in their various competitions that one might well suspect it to be really superiority. Not only does the second William Wilson cross the first in this way; he has an impertinent though very unobtrusive way of interfering with the other's purposes, and he makes this all the more galling by an unwelcome *affectionateness* of manner,[11] which the first self ascribes to conceit. At the same time, for all the first self's resentment and growing hostility toward his rival, he finds things in his own attitude that he cannot altogether understand. There is something at times strangely familiar about this second William Wilson, as though recalling memories so early that they antedate memory. There is furthermore an unexpected congeniality in their tempers which results in a confusingly heterogeneous mixture of emotions in the first self's feeling toward the second: with animosity a certain grudging esteem, with fear a real respect, and "a world of uneasy curiosity." They are inseparable companions, and under normal conditions they might have become fast friends.

But they do not, and for this fact the first William Wilson holds the second to blame. When the former makes fun of the latter's speech, which by some vocal weakness is restricted to a low whisper, the latter retaliates by mimicking the former in dress, words, actions, gait, manner, even voice; for though he cannot imitate the louder tones, his whisper becomes the very echo of the hero's own. And still more offensive is increased interference in the hero's affairs, often presumptuously becoming advice, advice later recognized by the hero to have been sound, but resented at the time as intolerable arrogance.

The climax of their rivalry comes when the first William Wilson goes at night to play a practical joke on the second, while the latter is asleep. Looking down at the other boy he is suddenly chilled to the heart at his sense of not only a resemblance but some much closer and stranger tie between them which he does not dare to name.[12] Stealing out of the other's chamber, he leaves the school at once. His flight has begun, but like Susskind and the Beggar the second self who would be his Saviour is not to be eluded or shaken off. As the first William Wilson, having largely freed himself from the influence of the second, sinks steadily deeper into dissipation, depravity, and crime, the second pursues, appearing in critical moments in his counterpart's career; at Eton checks him in the midst of a wild orgy by the mere stern whisper of his name; at Oxford exposes him publicly as a cheater at cards and forces him to leave in disguise. At last, at the Carnival in Rome, when the first William Wilson is planning the seduction of an elderly nobleman's young and pretty wife, a hand is laid on his arm and the familiar whisper sounds in his ear. Furiously dragging his tormenter into an adjoining chamber the hero stabs him through the bosom and, after his glance is distracted for an instant by someone's trying the door, turns back to see what appears to be a large mirror facing him, with his reflection in it, blood-stained and tottering. But then he realizes that it is no mirror. It is the second self, now unmistakable in his identity with the first; it is the pursuing Saviour who has failed, and whose failure, as he points out with his last breath, means equally destruction for them both.[13]

The allegorical element in this story is obvious, but should not be overemphasized.[14] To be sure the second William Wilson is the first one's "better self," but so, if not always this clearly, the second self as Saviour is bound to be, just as the second self in any of his evil aspects is bound to be the "worse self." But if he is a genuine second self, as I take the second William Wilson to be, he can never be simply translated into an abstraction, as "conscience" on the one hand or "innate depravity" on the other. What makes all the examples I am citing (unless I specify otherwise) works of creative literature rather than fictionalized moral tracts is the fact that they are first of all alive, living records of imaginative experience, of a relationship given a peculiar electrical excitement by the simultaneous separateness and sameness, attraction and repulsion, of the two beings involved in it.

In another group of examples the good second self resembles in technique the second self as Tempter; he is a more subtle Saviour than the ones we have thus far considered, realizing that the major task of salvation must be done by the person being saved, and enticing him by one means or another toward the inward state with which such self-salvation is synonymous. Naturally, as the second self who pursues in order to save is bound to seem objectionable and menacing to the first self who stands in need of salvation, so the second self who tempts for the same purpose is bound to seem devious, suspect, allied with the Devil or perhaps the Devil himself. It is for the latter that the unnamed intruder of Stevenson's *Markheim*[15] is mistaken by the first self, though he proves a very different Devil from the ones we met in Chapter 4. Similar in plan to Dostoyevsky's *Crime and Punishment,* this story begins with a murder, and again it is the murder of an old pawnbroker by an impoverished young man; again, also, the murder is merely the prelude to the real story, the story of its consequences in the mind of the murderer-protagonist. Markheim's need differs from Raskolnikov's in that he has brought it upon himself by a life of dissipation, but he justifies himself no less than the young Russian, not by the philosophy of Might Makes Right but by assuring himself that God, being just, will surely forgive him. Like Macbeth before the murder of Duncan, he is conscious only of the fear of earthly retribution, and he looks down with no stirring of conscience on the crumpled, blood-stained body that a moment ago was a living man.

But Markheim, in realms of his being of which he has not taken account, is no more immune to the monstrousness of his deed than is Raskolnikov. He has looked upon his victim, before plunging his dagger into the latter's heart, with infinite pity and a touch of horror; he has, for all the danger of doing so, delayed the stroke, trying to converse with the flint-hard old dealer, trying to penetrate the mask of everyday to some vestige of humanity within, trying as Raskolnikov tries to find some excuse for *not* doing the act to which his sense of duty to himself has brought him. And once the crime is committed, and he is alone and free to search for the pawnbroker's money, he discovers that he is neither alone nor free; on every side there are companions, there are watchers, there are reminders and compellers. As he moves about with a candle, the mirrors on all sides catch his reflection: once more the old device of the mirror, placing the self outside the self, as though independent of its original (Narcissus, Baldwin, William Wilson), in this case not only inimical but manifold, "as it were an army of spies." The silence is vexed by sounds other than clocks: his own stealthy footsteps — or is he positive they are his own? In the drawing room upstairs, going through the dealer's keys, he hears them again, and now in horror he knows they are *not* his own; they are mounting the stairs from below. Suddenly the knob turns, and, as

Markheim cries out hoarsely, a visitor, apparently taking this for an invitation, enters and shuts the door behind him. The outlines of the newcomer seem to waver slightly, to Markheim's terrified gaze, like those of idols in candlelight. Markheim has no doubt of the other's reality, but he has increasing doubt of the other's humanity; "and at times he thought he knew him; and at times he thought he bore a likeness to himself; and always, like a lump of living terror, there lay in his bosom the conviction that this thing was not of the earth and not of God." [16]

In other words Markheim, like Ivan Karamazov and Faust in their hours of extreme vulnerability, appears to be playing host to the Devil. And like those other diabolical visitants, Markheim's is no gloomy fallen Archangel but a poised, polite, cynical man of the world, precisely the sort of man Markheim ought to have been in order to carry out his plans with full success. At once he seems to take Markheim's side, gives him sound advice on how to proceed, urges him to hurry before the maidservant returns, offers to tell him where the money is hidden ("for a Christmas gift," as he sweetly puts it), and suggests that Markheim be content with the kind of scoundrel he is and act accordingly. All this is much the sort of thing we have seen other Devils doing, tempting to evil with plausible diabolical arguments that are articulations of thoughts already present in the first self's mind. But Markheim's visitor differs from the others in that he tempts in just the reverse direction from theirs, toward good instead of evil. By affecting to take the side of Markheim's viciousness he forces Markheim to face the fact of this viciousness, to stop deluding himself with notions of his justification or of good intentions to reform, and to see that the course he has taken can lead him only where it has always led him, steadily deeper into degradation and hopeless damnation. Nor is this done, as we have seen it done by Svidrigaïlov, out of malice; for as Markheim at last defies the diabolical counsel (the maidservant has returned, and the "Devil" suggests that Markheim murder her as well) and chooses the one door of freedom left open to him, that of self-renunciation, the features of the visitor "brightened and softened with a tender triumph." Markheim walks down the stairs and opens the house door.

> He confronted the maid upon the threshold with something like a smile. "You had better go for the police," he said. "I have killed your master." [17]

To be sure there is a certain allegorical flavor about the tempter of Markheim, just as there is about the pursuer of the first William Wilson. Nevertheless, the former is no more a mere personified idea than the latter, but from his first appearance, for all his mystery, he is a living, breathing, flesh-and-blood character in the story, perhaps even more vivid than his counterpart. It is true that he is perceived only by Markheim, as the Devil of *The Brothers Karamazov* is perceived only by Ivan. But it should be noted how careful Stevenson is to avoid stamping his visitant as "nothing but" a mental content; just as careful as Dostoyevsky is to do the opposite. The fact that the features of the visitor "faded and dislimned" as Markheim turns away to give himself up is not the same thing as his disappearance before Markheim's eyes. Indeed Markheim does not watch the transformation, even though we are told that the transformation takes place, and have it described for us. In other words, we are made aware of something (whether or not a supernatural something) happening to the visitor of which Markheim is not aware, something that must therefore take place outside the range of Markheim's experience, in the realm of objective reality.

In *Markheim,* then, we find the second self as Saviour assuming the guise of the Devil and apparently tempting *as* the Devil, but using the process of pseudo-temptation to accomplish his real temptation, which leads Markheim from the lostness of self-love to the triumph of self-conquest. A similar twofold tempting occurs in Hermann Hesse's novel *Demian.*[18] The ambiguity of the second self's name, Demian (*daemon, daimon,* with its suggestion of both guardian spirit and evil spirit), reflects the ambiguity of his character for the first self; while the first self's name, Sinclair (*sine claror,* without light), reflects the state of mind in the first self that causes this ambiguity and makes the process of his salvation so long and difficult. The light of Demian, to the clouded view of Sinclair, becomes itself clouded and suspect as Dark. For Light and Dark, and the intricate and confusing relationship between these realms, play a major part in the symbolism of this novel, as they so often do in the literature of the second self. From earliest childhood Sinclair has been conscious of two worlds: the world of light — the familiar safe, clean, orderly world of home and "family"; and all around this world the "other world" — the dark, passionate, monstrous, enigmatical world of "outside." It is the penetration of the former world by the latter that brings into Sinclair's life all that poisons and corrupts it, but that brings along with this a very different darkness, the darkness of wonder, which becomes his true if far less comfortable light.

Sinclair is first introduced to us as a naive little schoolboy of good family, being unmercifully victimized by an elder boy, Frank Kromer. At the Latin school with Sinclair is another elder boy, Max Demian. Demian, however, is more than simply another elder boy, for in ways he seems more of an adult than an adolescent, more of an adult than the adults, with strangely wise, bright eyes and features, at the same time both masculine and feminine, young and old, ageless as the rocks. Such things are impressive, but they do not endear Demian to Sinclair. Brilliant and magnetic as the former may be, he is no less than Claggart or Mr. Jones or Smerdyakov a creature out of the shadows, and these shadows continue to cling to him in both Sinclair's eyes and ours, despite his first clear intervention in Sinclair's life for the latter's benefit.

Enabling him so to intervene are two qualities that we have found to be outstanding characteristics of the second self in all the categories we have studied thus far. One is his special and inexplicable preoccupation with Sinclair, reciprocated by Sinclair's growing if uneasy preoccupation with Demian. The other is his insight, also going beyond anything explainable by logic or the facts of the case, into the working of Sinclair's mind and the state of his soul, this also coming to be reciprocated, though slowly and in lesser degree, by Sinclair's insight into Demian. Both these qualities appear in the intervention to which I have referred. At the depth of Sinclair's enslavement by Frank Kromer, when he is almost in despair with torment and humiliation, he encounters Demian. Sinclair is afraid to tell the nature of his trouble, but Demian reads it from his mind, speaks it aloud in words which seem to come from inside Sinclair's breast as well as from outside his ears.[19] Demian thereupon has a "little talk" with Frank Kromer, and the victimization immediately ceases.

Sinclair is restored to the comfortably safe home world that he still supposes to be that of light. His reaction to Demian, however, is not the overwhelming gratitude one might expect. The very act of saving has been so strange as to seem in itself a threat; he feels that Demian too, in a far more insidious way than Kromer, is a "seducer," tempting him somehow toward the same evil, dark world of which he fancies he has just washed his hands. But of course he has not. Rejected in the Demian-form, the dark world creeps upon him now in another form, that of his own secret guilty desires. And so, like Markheim's visitor, Demian must tempt on two levels and in two directions: on the apparent level, where Sinclair recoils from him in fear, toward the forbidding and the forbidden; and on the real level, of which Sinclair becomes only gradually conscious, toward maturity and wisdom. During this time, casually taking the seat beside his younger friend in confirmation class, Demian reappears on Sinclair's horizon, aware as before of the other's inward crisis. He tries to reconcile Sinclair to the process of growth, which is also necessarily a process of destruction; he tries to explain that the concept of Light untouched by Dark is an unreal fable and a childish self-deception, increasingly dangerous to one's self and others as one begins to assume the responsibilities of adulthood.

But again Sinclair will have none of such subtleties, nor is he ready for such depths. From the one-sided world of sheltered light he has gone over to the one-sided world of self-indulgent dark. Sent away to a different school he becomes a sort of lesser William Wilson, demoralized and dissipated, threatened with expulsion. It is at this point that the counter-temptation by Demian asserts itself across the distance between them. Struck with the sight of a girl who makes him think of a pre-Raphaelite Beatrice, Sinclair attempts repeatedly to paint her picture, and in the end realizes that the face he has painted is that of Demian, and in being that of Demian is something more.

And by degrees the feeling came to me that this was not Beatrice or Demian but — myself. The picture did not resemble me — it was not meant to, I felt — but there was that in it which seemed to be made up of my life, something of my inner self, of my fate or of my demon.[20]

More and more closely now the two selves are drawn together. Sinclair paints another picture, of the bird on the crest above the door of his home; it becomes, as he paints, a bird with a golden, hawklike head, working its way out of something that looks like a giant egg. He sends it to Demian, and one day finds a note inexplicably slipped between the pages of his book.

The bird fights its way out of the egg. The egg is the world. Whoever will be born again must destroy a world. The bird flies to God. The name of the god is Abraxas.[21]

Abraxas, Sinclair learns, is "a divinity on whom the symbolical task was imposed of uniting the divine and the diabolical." It is this union, this difficult integration with one another of the two worlds which for Sinclair have been so sharply antithetical, that constitutes Sinclair's salvation and that the influence of Demian enables him to achieve: the objective Demian (whose existence is never in doubt) working to awaken the subjective Demian in Sinclair's soul. It is at the moment of the physical Demian's death in the field hospital that the golden bird at last fights its way out of the egg, and the inward Demian is born.

The bandaging hurt me. All that has happened to me since hurt me. But my soul is like a mysterious, locked house. And when I find the key and step right down into myself, to where the pictures painted by my destiny seem reflected on the dark mirror of my soul, then I need only stoop towards the black mirror and see my own picture, which now completely resembles Him, my guide and friend.[22]

The examples of the second self as Saviour that we have covered thus far are analogous to the evil second self in his active aspects. A third group is reminiscent rather of the second self as Vision of Horror. Like the latter, these second selves have no conscious intention of influencing the first self as they do, and the kind of influence they exert could probably not be brought about by plan, for it is the result in each case simply of the impact of the second self's personality on the mind of the first self, as a vision of something in the latter's own personality as yet unknown or unacknowledged. Indeed the parallel goes further, for since the first self in these cases is the evil or at least limited self, the vision that he gets of his identity with the second self *is* for him a vision of horror, either mildly, as in the first example we shall consider, or catastrophically, as in the last.

The first example is another of Conrad's stories, *The Secret Sharer*,[23] the clearest instance of Conrad's treatment of the relationship between the selves, making frequent use of the terms "double," "other self," and "second self." At first glance it would appear to be the first self of this narrative, the young captain, who saves the second, but the counter-salvation that goes on at a deeper level is far more important. At the outset the young captain, unexpectedly, has just been given his command; he feels himself a stranger to his ship and something of a stranger to himself. While waiting for a wind that will let him sail he takes a night watch by himself, and while walking alone on deck notices a rope ladder that has been left hanging over the side. He is about to haul it in when he sees at the foot of it, floating in the water and flickering with phosphorescence, the naked body of a man. The man proves to be one Leggatt, formerly chief mate of a ship anchored in the same harbor. Without hesitation he explains that he has killed someone, an insolent sailor who goaded him to fury during the setting of a reefed foresail in a storm. He has no regrets; the man was a vicious troublemaker who deserved to die. He has therefore taken his chance to escape; has entrusted himself to the black, measureless ocean; and finally has made his way here (just as the captain has made his way), to the ladder that "happens" to have been left over the side.

The difference between the two men is immediately established. For all his desperate situation, this naked derelict from out of the sea is really far more determined, far less subject to self-doubt and hesitation, than the captain who receives him; in this sense, the inward sense, he is more "in command" than the captain is. It is such qualities that have brought him here, confronting his host with a test no less critical than that with which the pseudo-diabolical visitor confronts Markheim. Here, however, it is not the killer who is being tested but the one who has found the killer; here too, in view of the nature of the crime, the motive for turning the killer over would be less that of serving justice than that of serving convention.

The captain-narrator does not make the "proper" choice, and for the reason we must look to the peculiar effect which Leggatt exerts on him from the moment of their meeting at either end of the rope ladder. Something about this stranger, even before anything more is visible than the flickering phosphorescence of his body in the water, unaccountably appeals to the captain: the calm and resolute voice that comes up from below, the deliberateness with which Leggatt weighs the alternatives, whether to go on swimming until he sinks or to trust himself on board. The captain waits, and in the silence "a mysterious communication was established already between us two — in the face of that silent, darkened tropical sea." And this mysterious communication continues, even after Leggatt is on board, and they resume their low-voiced conspiratorial exchange; for the most important part of what is communicated goes far beyond the words that are spoken. Above all what is communicated, for the captain, is the increasingly weird but inescapable message that the man who has just risen to him out of the sea is not a stranger, but himself.

In part this is conveyed by physical appearance and juxtaposition. Leggatt is about the same age as the captain, the same height, the same build; the sleeping suit with which the captain clothes him, an exact duplicate of the captain's own, exactly fits him. So dressed, with their shadowy dark heads together as they whisper, they are like mirrored reflections of each other. And not only does the captain dress Leggatt in his own clothes; he also lets Leggatt sleep in his bed while he, supposedly in bed, sleeps on the couch; he lets Leggatt drink the early-morning coffee that he is supposedly drinking; and so forth, frequently with the confused sensation of being in two places at once.

But of course this is not a story about mistaken identity, but about the discovery of a shared identity. The physical parallels are simply the external manifestations of the really significant process that is going on in their relationship. The moment the captain makes his first move on the criminal's behalf, and after the fashion of Saint Francis and Fidelman clothes the naked man in his own garment, his sense of the true parallel between them is awakened and grows rapidly to a sense of continuity, even an uncertainty from time to time as to which is the captain and which is the criminal; and with this growth comes an increasing conviction of the rightness of Leggatt's cause, and increasing determination to do for the other what he can.

This is true sympathy: a "feeling with" to the extent of becoming one with, of being beside oneself in a sane sense. But for the average person, accustomed to our neat, orderly system of divisions, such sympathy puts a severe strain upon the kind of sanity to which he is used. The captain sits at his desk in the daytime, his double sitting exactly behind him out of sight, not in mockery as Golyadkin junior might have done, but because there is nowhere else to sit; and there Leggatt must remain, hour after hour, like a carbon copy. Often the captain has the feeling, so familiar among the symptoms of psychic disease, of looking at himself from outside. His strangeness to his ship increases, for just like a psychic disorder this experience isolates him even further from his men.

There is no way to put Leggatt ashore. The only chance is to let him slip off at night into the sea and make for the islands off the Cambodian coast. But first he must be taken near enough. Under the pretense of seeking the land breeze the captain changes course and sails toward the inhabited island of Koh-ring. Aware of the risk he is running, aware that his whole future as seaman is at stake, he presses on through the darkness, disregarding the fears of the helmsman, overruling the hysterical protests of his mate, on until "the black southern hill of Koh-ring seemed to hang right over the ship like a towering fragment of the everlasting night," on until he is sure that Leggatt has had his chance; and only then, with the fate of the ship balanced on a hair, does he swing away. For a moment he cannot tell whether the ship will respond or not. Then he catches a glimpse of white on the black water below him, his own floppy straw hat which he has put on Leggatt's head to protect the latter from the tropic sun, and which has apparently slid off when Leggatt struck the sea. "It had been meant to save his homeless head from the dangers of the sun. And now — behold — it was saving the ship, by serving me for a mark to help out the ignorance of my strangeness."[24]

Thus Leggatt, saved by the captain, has in turn saved the captain. But the episode of the hat, again, is only an external manifestation of the real saving. The story has begun with the statement of the captain's problem. Young, inexperienced in his new post, untrusted by his subordinates, unsure of himself, he knows that as yet he is captain in name only; he must win the respect of the men he commands before he can truly command them; he must "get the feel" of the ship before he can truly sail her. And it is the solution to this problem which Leggatt, rising out of the dark sea like a force from his own unconscious depths, has brought him; it is his supreme effort to meet the demands laid upon him by his relationship with Leggatt which solves not only Leggatt's problem but his own as well.

Already the ship was drawing ahead. And I was alone with her. Nothing! no one in the world should stand now between us, throwing a shadow on the way of silent knowledge and mute affection, the perfect communion of a seaman with his first command.[25]

The Secret Sharer is an exception to the general rule of second-self literature in that there is at no time any real opposition between the two main characters. The only thing that approaches it is the captain's appalled astonishment at the way in which, under Leggatt's influence, he is risking his ship, his men, and himself for the sake of a naked, derelict murderer he has never laid eyes on before. But we should not infer that there is necessarily less of such opposition in situations where the second self as Saviour works nonpurposively, through the impact of his character, than in those where he saves or tries to save as a matter of conscious intent. To the contrary, such influencing through personality often involves an opposition that may be literally carried to the death. Such is the case in the last two examples we shall consider in this chapter.

One of these is Melville's story, *Bartleby, the Scrivener*,[26] to which in the original version was added the subtitle (the significance of which will become apparent), *A Story of Wall Street*. The first self and narrator of this story is a far cry from the doubt-troubled young captain of *The Secret Sharer*. He is an elderly lawyer who never addresses a jury or pleads a case or does anything else that might invade his peace, but devotes himself to taking care of bonds and mortgages and title-deeds for the wealthy. He is not a brilliant man, or a dynamic man, but an eminently *safe* man, and his outstanding qualities are prudence and method. Even his chambers on Wall Street are adequate, prudently unexciting, and safely circumscribed, at one end looking out on the white wall of the interior of a skylight shaft, at the other looking out on a brick wall black with age and everlasting shade, so close that the interval between looks a little like a huge square cistern.

Our hero, then, is a dull old mole who has spent his life digging about in other people's titles and conveyances, and, far from objecting to the dullness of his existence, he is complacently contented with it, has grown sleekly fat on it. Even a shade duller than his own life is that of his two clerks, or scriveners, who spend their days copying out by hand the numerous documents with which the lawyer must deal. From sunrise to sunset, while the earth turns and the winds blow and men love and die, they sit at their high tables and copy. Unlike their employer, they show certain symptoms of rebellion against this reduction of man to a machine as the price of allowing him to live. Turkey, the elder of the two, is a model of industry until the lunch hour, at which time he not only dines, but wines, and through the afternoon works with a "strange, inflamed, flurried, flighty recklessness of activity," becoming guilty of numerous blots and errors. Nippers, the younger, is temperate, but suffers from indigestion and a general irritability, as well as a specific discontent with the table at which he works, which he can never adjust to suit him. Conveniently, Nippers is difficult only during the morning hours, so that his symptoms of rebellion alternate with Turkey's, like the changing of the guard. It is a sorry sort of rebellion in both cases, a mere impotent gesture of eccentricity, as empty and mechanical as the way of life it seeks to rebel against.

But another type of rebellion is soon to make its appearance. So many are the documents waiting to be copied that an additional scrivener is needed, and in answer to the lawyer's advertisement a young man named Bartleby comes one morning to the office and is engaged. A few words are exchanged concerning his qualifications, but none concerning himself. Indeed, Bartleby for all his colorlessness rises as much out of the sea of the unknown as Claggart and Mr. Jones. He surrounds himself with an air of pallid and austere reserve; in his wholly undramatic way he is perhaps the most mysterious of all the second selves we have met, and the lack of drama is of the essence of the mystery.

There are two parts of the process by which Bartleby comes to fill the narrator's horizon, and they go on simultaneously. One is the way in which he installs himself physically, as a permanent fixture, in the narrator's office. In this installation the narrator, like the traditional witch's victim, takes the initiative. Not only does he "invite" Bartleby by the advertisement, and then by hiring him, but he goes further. Though the other scriveners are kept in a room separated from the lawyer's by ground-glass folding doors, he places Bartleby's desk in his own room, next to a little window looking out on a wall, and enclosed in a high green folding screen. Bartleby's presence therefore, if not in his person, is always within the lawyer's vision. And by degrees it becomes apparent that this presence is not restricted to ordinary working hours. Bartleby never goes out to meals; he never goes anywhere. "He was a perpetual sentry in the corner," comments the narrator, though not realizing at this point quite how perpetual and faithful a sentry Bartleby is. One Sunday morning, however, when he stops in at his chambers, he discovers that Bartleby, who has somehow got hold of the extra key to the door, is living there. In much the same way in which Allbee takes possession of Leventhal's flat, Bartleby takes possession of the lawyer's office. At first the narrator ascribes the situation to Bartleby's poverty, but in Bartleby's desk he finds money, tied up in an old bandanna handkerchief.

The other part of the process by which Bartleby becomes a preoccupation crowding out all others from the narrator's mind is his opposition to the narrator's will. It is a rebellion which, though far quieter than that of Turkey and Nippers, is no mere gesture like theirs, but an absolute and inflexible defiance. A scrivener must not only copy, but also verify the accuracy of his copy, word by word; and it is this that even the narrator admits is dull, the quintessential dullness of the scrivener's dull existence. When called on for this part of his service Bartleby, to the thunderstruck surprise of his employer, simply refuses. He refuses in an interesting way, saying instead of "I will not," "I would prefer not to"; thus both emphasizing the bleak mildness of his manner and underscoring the monstrous fact of a scrivener's having such a thing as a preference at all.

The reaction of the narrator, for all his equable temperament, is strangely intense and ambivalent. On the other hand he is outraged, and as Bartleby persists he finds himself giving way to an impulse which he knows to be evil, renewing his first request and making new ones, attempting to goad Bartleby into even more outrageous rebellion. On the other hand, though he intimates that terrible retribution will follow, he finds ". . . something about Bartleby that not only strangely disarmed me, but, in a wonderful manner, touched and disconcerted me." What especially disconcerts him is the way Bartleby seems carefully to consider everything the narrator says to him, tacitly to grant the logic of it, but, because of "some paramount consideration" that takes precedence over logic, to persist in his refusal. The narrator's faith in the rightness of his cause is actually shaken a little, and for the time Bartleby wins, being exempted from any duties but copying. What is more, instead of being roused to fury at his discovery that Bartleby has taken over the office for living quarters, the narrator is struck with the thought of the other's friendlessness and loneliness. This is an emotion such as the elderly lawyer has never before known. "For the first time in my life a feeling of overpowering stinging melancholy seized me. Before, I had never experienced aught but a not unpleasing sadness. The bond of a common humanity now drew me irresistibly to gloom."[27]

But soon the habit of prudential common sense reasserts itself, and the sympathy with which Bartleby has "infected" the narrator gives way to fear and even repulsion. There is something morbid about Bartleby, and safety requires getting him much farther out of sight than behind his folding screen. This decision is strengthened by the narrator's discovery of a further infection; he has commenced using, involuntarily and not appropriately, Bartleby's word "prefer." "And I trembled to think that my contact with the scrivener had already and seriously affected me in a mental way." When Bartleby ceases even to do any copying, will do nothing but stand at his little window staring out with dead eyes at the dead wall facing him, the narrator summons up his resolution and gives the scrivener notice. But on the morning after what was supposed to be Bartleby's last day the recalcitrant scrivener is still there. Professional visitors begin to stare at this extraordinary creature who stands "like the last column of some ruined temple"; a whisper of wonder about him begins to go around; and the narrator, never a man of much moral courage, fears that his reputation is being damaged by this taint of strangeness. Seeing no way to persuade Bartleby to quit him, he quits Bartleby, removing to new offices. The last thing to go is the folding screen, and there still stands Bartleby, motionless in the stripped room, staring at the blank wall outside the little window.

Yet even left behind, Bartleby is not entirely got rid of. He makes no move to follow, but remains in the old office, and when ejected he remains in the building, sitting on the banisters by day and sleeping in the entry by night. Notified of the fact the narrator goes to him and for the last time tries to reason with him, even offers to take Bartleby to his home; but Bartleby would prefer not to make any change. The narrator washes his hands of all responsibility, and the police remove Bartleby to the Tombs. There he stands in the courtyard as he has done in the office, facing a high wall, refusing now to speak to the narrator, refusing to eat when the narrator pays the "grub-man" to feed him. A few days later the narrator visits the prison again, and finds the wasted Bartleby lying at the base of the wall, apparently asleep. He touches Bartleby, and realizes what sort of sleep it is, the sleep from which there will be no waking.

The effect that the narrator has on Bartleby is given us in far less detail, as we should expect, than the effect that Bartleby has on the narrator. But quietly and pallidly though it may be shown there *is* such an effect, and to notice the signs of what is going on in the second self is most important, in this story, to a full understanding of what is going on in the first. Toward everyone else who appears Bartleby is completely indifferent, but he is not indifferent to the narrator. For example, after the narrator has discovered that Bartleby is living in the office, and through this discovery has got some sense of the man's isolation from all the rest of humanity, he tries in a friendly manner to question Bartleby about himself. This friendliness, however, is chiefly in manner, for the narrator's initial sympathy has already begun to give way to fear, fear really of the sympathy itself, and the questioning is designed as a prelude to getting rid of Bartleby. Bartleby as usual prefers not to comply, but for the first time there is a sign of emotion on the cadaverous face, "the faintest conceivable tremor of the white attenuated mouth." When Bartleby announces that he will do no more copying and is asked for his reason, he does not give his formula-reply, that he would prefer not to, but for the only time in the story puts a question of his own to the narrator. "Do you not see the reason for yourself?" The narrator, noticing that Bartleby's eyes look dull and glazed, concludes that he must be suffering from eye-strain. But we have long since been told of the dimness of Bartleby's eyes, and even when the eyes have had full time to recover, Bartleby persists in his refusal; apparently, in other words, the narrator has failed to see the reason for himself, and when, taken to the Tombs from the deserted office, Bartleby is visited by the narrator, he declines even to look at him, and stands facing the wall at the foot of which he is to fall into his last sleep. " 'I know you,' he said, without looking around — 'and I want nothing to say to you'." [28]

Why should Bartleby feel such resentment against the man who has shown him such consideration, made every effort to help him? Resentment against a mechanized society for having crushed his spirit is no adequate explanation, for Bartleby's spirit is not crushed, and in any case his resentment is not against society but against the narrator. In fact it is the very pinpointing of this emotion, when seen against the background of the other writings we have considered in this chapter, that will enable us to find once more the same basic pattern of relationship. It is the pattern of a certain claim made by the second self upon the first, the demand that the latter not do something or that he do something or that he become something he is not but has within him the capacity to be; and of the struggle by the first self either to meet the demand or to resist it — sometimes both. The demand in this story is never put into words, but it is the thing of paramount importance for both selves from the beginning of their relationship to the end. Obviously Bartleby's demand is not for consideration or pity; he receives these. It seems to be rather for sympathy in the most complete sense of the word, sympathy which (like that of Conrad's young captain) follows through in active commitment, sympathy which *gives itself,* and which in this case by giving itself would complement and realize itself. He is not asking condonement of his rebellion; he is, doubtless quite unconsciously, demanding allegiance in it, and he is making this demand of the man, diametrically Bartleby's opposite, who has compromised with the soul-squashing monotony of the life of getting and spending to the point where he no longer knows it to be monotonous; who has faded almost indistinguishably into the dull gray landscape of profits and losses, desks and documents.

What is demanded of the narrator is, to put it into the simplest terms, that he save his soul; and this demand is made by Bartleby not as dispassionate observer but as co-owner of the soul to be saved. He rises out of the unknown to protest the grievous wrong that is being done to their shared being, rises both before the narrator and within the narrator to install himself at the heart of just those activities which have made the narrator what he is, and remains fixed there as a pale, silent ghost of reproach, the banner of passive insurrection planted at the center of the enemy's bastions. And under his influence the narrator's shell of comfortable complacency fits somewhat less comfortably; he is shaken a little in his confidence that his is the reasonable way; the long winter ice of conformity begins to thaw slightly; for the first time in his life he is touched with gloom at the thought of what such a life can do to a man, is moved to sympathy for a victim of it. But no sooner do the sympathy, and the insight that accompanies it, arise in him than, frightened and repelled by such painful things, he hurriedly enshells himself again, and resolves (a resolution embroidered with all sorts of altruistic sentiments) to put this Satan of salvation once and for all behind him. With even keener insight Bartleby seems to know exactly what has been going on; it is at this point that he shows his first sign of resentment; and it is shortly after this that, refusing even the limited concession he has made so far, he turns his face to the wall.[29]

In an epilogue the narrator mentions a rumor he has heard, that Bartleby was once a subordinate clerk in the Dead Letter Office; and he conjectures that the dreariness of this business has produced or heightened Bartleby's own natural dreariness, and that the continual handling of dead letters, striking their dead chill through skin and into blood, has produced a dead man. But this is the narrator's comment, not Melville's, and if read in the light of the story that precedes it it becomes, not an explanation of Bartleby, but an attempt at self-jusification by the man whom Bartleby has tried to save. For the essential irony of this novella is that Bartleby, who moves through the story like a walking corpse, is in fact the only living person in it, the only person capable of genuine "preferring." He is not a dead man, but a death's head, a memento mori to the dead of soul who surround him, only one of whom (the narrator) is capable of being stirred by the reminder; and even this stirring is only an intimation that flickers for an instant and then goes out. *Bartleby, the Scrivener* is light in tone, but is probably the bitterest story Melville ever wrote, all the more bitter for the fact that there is no anger in it; no blackness, only grayness, that in the end like gray dust settles back placidly over all.

The other example of a work in which the second self's influence for good is exerted on the first self chiefly through the impact of his personality, and in which the first self's resistance to this personality is carried to the point of death (though in this case his own rather than the second self's), occurs in Victor Hugo's gigantic novel, *Les Misérables*.[30] The relationship between the hero, Jean Valjean, and his nemesis, the police inspector Javert, might be thought to belong with those we have discussed as examples of the second self as Pursuer, with Javert as the pursuing and evil second self. But in this novel, so far as the relationship between the selves is concerned, a most peculiar thing happens. Through the book as a whole Jean Valjean is the protagonist and more than any other one person the viewpoint character. But in his relationship with Javert, though we are given neither viewpoint consistently, we know far more about and are far more involved in Javert's reaction to Jean Valjean than we are in the latter's reaction to Javert, and this becomes increasingly true as we approach the climax of their relationship. Our general sympathy is with Jean Valjean, but throughout his long persecution it is the man who persecutes him to whom we are always closer, whose attitude is presented to us as the human and understandable and to this extent reasonable one. Jean Valjean's attitude toward Javert, on the other hand, we must infer as something far less familiar to our experience, and in this respect he is almost as much of a mystery to us as he is to Javert.

Les Misérables is an immensely complicated work, of which the relationship with which we are dealing constitutes only one among many strands. But it is necessary that we study this relationship in the context of the novel as a whole, and to do so we must begin at a point considerably before the paths of the two men involved in it cross, indeed before either of them even appears. The whole first book, "A Just Man," is devoted to a character who, so far as participation in the plot is concerned, might seem a very minor personage indeed. Nevertheless the personality of this man, long after he is dead, reverberates through the entire work, becoming the main single influence in the life of Jean Valjean, and through him in the life of Javert as well.

The "just man" is the elderly Charles Myriel, the Bishop of D——. He is a genuine bishop, but his episcopal palace, his handsome income, and all his personal energies he has long since dedicated to the succor, both physical and spiritual, of the miserable.

The bishop is not literally the second self of the relationship we are studying. But in a very broad sense, which it is vitally important that we understand, he is. Long before the relationship between Jean Valjean and Javert begins, it is prepared for by a much briefer relationship between Jean Valjean and the bishop. What we have here, in other words, is something that structurally at least resembles the plan of Hogg's *Private Memoirs and Confessions of a Justified Sinner*. There, however, the central character shifts from the role of second self to that of first; here the reverse happens, with results far more remarkable and moving. In the earlier relationship of *Les Misérables,* Jean Valjean is the first self, showing qualities to be unmistakably paralleled by Javert, the first self of the later relationship; just as there are equally unmistakable parallels between the Bishop of D——, who in this earlier episode is Jean Valjean's second self, and the later Jean Valjean, who becomes the second self of Javert. It is a complicated plan, but not really an obscure one. We are still dealing with only two halves, the old division between the Light Twin and the Dark. This time the two extremes are represented by the diametrically contrasted figures of the saintly bishop and the "dog son of a wolf" Javert. But in their own persons the bishop and Javert never meet. Midway between them stands the figure of Jean Valjean, who possesses qualities of both, and who in the early part of the story shows his Javert-side in his encounter with the bishop, but who then, "infected" by the bishop, shows his bishop-side throughout his relationship with Javert. If this sounds mechanical, it is only because I am giving the skeleton without the flesh and blood that clothe it. Let us now briefly trace the way in which this change takes place.

To the home of the bishop, "Monseigneur Bienvenu" (My Lord Welcome), there comes one night a ragged wanderer, fierce-looking and harsh of voice, whose name is Jean Valjean. He is a recently discharged convict who has served nineteen years as a galley slave at Toulon; five years for stealing bread to feed his sister's starving children, fourteen years for trying to escape. Because of his yellow passport, which brands him as a dangerous exconvict, he has been refused admittance at all inns, refused by everyone, ejected even from a dog's house in which he has sought shelter. But by the bishop he is not refused. To Jean Valjean's astonishment the old man whom he accosts with hostile defiance treats him in return with every kindness and courtesy, has a place laid for him at his own poor table, has a bed made for him in the alcove next to his own room. For Jean Valjean the change is too abrupt, and the darkness of mind, the surly resentment that has been hardening within him for nineteen years, is too strong. In the middle of the night he steals into the bishop's room, takes the bishop's silver plate, and flees. He is captured by the police and brought before the bishop. But the bishop presses no charges. To the contrary, he insists that he gave the plate to his guest, and that he also gave him the two heavy silver candlesticks, which he now presents to Jean Valjean. As the officers leave he says in a low voice, "Jean Valjean, my brother, you no longer belong to evil, but to good. I have bought your soul of you. I withdraw it from black thoughts and the spirit of perdition, and give it to God." [31]

Like Judas, Jean Valjean has sold his soul for silver, but to the Power of Light rather than the Power of Darkness. The true transaction, however, has barely begun; and it is at this point that the Bishop of D——, dropping out of the story in his own person, makes his real entrance into the moral life of Jean Valjean. Utterly bewildered, torn by sensations he cannot comprehend, the exconvict wanders about the neighborhood, and at sunset he finds himself sitting in the midst of a large, deserted plain. A little ragged chimney sweep named Gervais comes past, tossing a coin in the air; it drops to the ground, and Jean Valjean, placing his foot on it, drives the child away. When he comes to himself, he is horrified; he searches the countryside for half the night, calling vainly "Little Gervais! Little Gervais!" At last he falls in exhaustion, and for the first time in nineteen years he begins to weep.

This weeping marks the climax and resolution of a struggle such as this man has never known: the struggle, on the part of the Jean Valjean who has been, to choke off the birth of the Jean Valjean who is to be. But it is already too late. The robbing of Little Gervais is not only an automatic gesture, but also an anachronistic one. "It was a curious phenomenon, and one only possible in his present situation, that, in robbing the boy of that money, he committed a deed of which he was no longer capable." It is an act which has damned him (it pursues him all the rest of his life), but which, in the sense of damnation that it forces upon him, also has saved him.

When he exclaimed, "I am a wretch!" he saw himself as he really was, and was already so separated from himself that he fancied himself merely a phantom, and that he had there before him, in flesh and blood, cudgel in hand, his blouse on his back, his knapsack full of stolen objects, the frightful galley-slave, Jean Valjean, with his resolute and gloomy face, and his mind full of hideous schemes. . . . He contemplated himself, so to speak, face to face; and at the same time he saw through this hallucination, in a mysterious depth, a light which at first he took for a torch. On looking more attentively at this light which appeared to his conscience, he perceived that it had a human shape, and that the torch was the bishop. His conscience examined in turn the two men standing before him, — the bishop and Jean Valjean. By one of those singular effects peculiar to an ecstasy of this nature, the more his revery was prolonged, the taller and more brilliant the bishop appeared, while Jean Valjean grew less, and faded out of sight. At length he disappeared and the bishop alone remained, filling the wretched man's soul with magnificent radiance.[32]

This bishop is, of course, a vision only, purely subjective, and so recognized by both Jean Valjean and the reader. But behind this vision is its objective original, the gently relentless Monseigneur Bienvenu, who not by any mere conversion but by an actual invasion of Jean Valjean's being with his own, and an awakening to predominance of the latent bishop-force present there, becomes the Saviour of Jean Valjean's soul.

Only after a considerable lapse of time do we again meet Jean Valjean. By now his situation, his personality, his appearance, his direction in life, are all completely changed. Even the name is different; it is now "Father" Madeleine, originator of a new process of bead manufacture, owner-operator of a large factory from which flows the lifeblood of the town of M. sur M., and, after several times declining the office, made mayor by the king. This success is of no importance except for what it enables him to do for others, for the bishop-self that has been brought to birth during the labor pains of self-division and self-confrontation has grown now to maturity. Like the bishop the new Jean Valjean lives simply and frugally and with but one aim — to give such help as he can to those who need help, especially that lowest substratum of the needy from which he has so recently risen, the miserable of the earth.

But Jean Valjean is not the only one who has risen from the depths. In the same town, as it "happens," is another man who has done so, though in a very different way. Not a galley slave himself but the son of one, born in prison of a fortune-teller, he has grown up with an inexpressible loathing for the class of people to which by birth he belongs, and motivated by this loathing he has found employment with the police, becoming in time an inspector and performing the useful duty of spy. His name is Javert. Years of pain and disgrace have made Jean Valjean at first resentful against his oppressors, later deeply sympathetic with the oppressed. But the same factors have had the reverse effect on Javert. As though to divorce himself as completely as possible from the dregs of society out of which he has come, he has developed into the fanatical supporter of established authority, the inflexible enemy of the slightest disrespect toward it. In persecuting transgressors he is absolutely without mercy, and just in this mercilessness he finds "his connecting link with humanity."

Such is Javert, not a sadistic man but a dedicated man, and in what he is dedicated to surely no one could be more the opposite of the sadly gentle, the tolerant and forgiving Father Madeleine. We must remember, however, that Father Madeleine is only the present version of Jean Valjean. And just as, earlier, the old Jean Valjean met his opposite, the bishop, who confronted him with the latent decency of his own nature, so now the new Jean Valjean meets *his* opposite, Javert, who confronts him with the former savagery of soul that Jean Valjean has put behind him. Each — the bishop and the police inspector — is the opposite of

Jean Valjean, but since in the interval between the two encounters Jean Valjean has reversed his character, they are opposites in opposite ways, that is, opposites of each other. Each, finally, in his oppositeness to the Jean Valjean whom he meets, is linked to him by a bond of identity with the part of Jean Valjean's own nature which at that point is buried deep inside him. The bishop anticipates the "Father Madeleine" of the future. Javert recalls the Jean Valjean of the past.

Hints of such a complicated linkage are given us, at this point in the story, by means of certain quasi-musical devices resembling those by which Dostoyevsky suggests the linkage between Raskolnikov and Svidrigaïlov. Thus the name of Javert, in its two dominant consonantal sounds, echoes in the same sequence the initials of the name which M. Madeleine has sought to leave behind him: Jean Valjean. Thus the three main changes in the appearance of Jean Valjean, now that he has become M. Madeleine, are the fact that he is clean-shaven instead of wearing the long beard in which we first saw him, the fact that he has discarded the leather cap that was pulled low over his eyes, and the fact that he no longer carries a cudgel. It is just these changes that are underscored for us by three main items in the appearance of Javert: the enormous whiskers that cover most of his face, the hat with a turned-down brim that hides his entire forehead, and the cudgel that he conceals beneath his coat. But of course the important parallels lie deeper. Though Javert is no exconvict but the pursuer of convicts, though he has become the watchdog of respectable society instead of its outcast enemy, his fundamental traits of character are in exaggerated form the same as those of the man who, on that fateful night, ate of the bishop's bread and stole the bishop's silver. There is the same resentment, except that it is directed downward rather than upward; there is the same hardness, except that encouraged by opportunities for exercise which Jean Valjean's never knew it has become even harder; there is the same gloomy habit of thought, the same animallike ferocity of temper, the same self-justification, which has become in Javert an almost maniacal self-righteousness.

Quite naturally, in view of these parallels, it is the Javert-side of Jean Valjean that Javert senses even before he knows the other man's true identity; and once he has learned this it is only the exconvict, the old Jean Valjean, that he can ever think of; all the rest is to him sheer hypocrisy. But ironically it is not the old Jean Valjean but only the new one, the one whose existence he refuses to acknowledge, that he can ever respond to. His initial response is not at all what we should expect of him, for it is explainable as a reaction neither to the mayor of M. sur M. that Jean Valjean nominally is, nor to the criminal he really is. Toward the former, Javert as worshipper of authority would normally feel the utmost respect; toward the latter he would feel the contemptuous severity he feels for all violators of the law. But in this case what he feels is an immediate and instinctive antipathy which he cannot understand, which is like that of certain animals to certain other animals, "'refractory to all the counsels of intelligence and all the solvents of reason, and which, whatever the way in which destinies are made, surely warns the man-dog of the man-cat, and the man-fox of the presence of the man-lion."[33] Mixed with (though not the cause of) this antipathy is a kind of fascinated suspicion, the feeling that he has seen this man before — as he has, since in his early years with the police he has served in the southern galleys.

Yet it is not this suspicion of a criminal past (criminal pasts are an old story to the police inspector), but M. Madeleine's humanity, his selflessness, his gentleness toward the helpless and especially the errant, that most outrage Javert; just as the humanity of the bishop so outraged the old Jean Valjean. And as we later learn, the reason for the former's outrage is the same as was the reason for the latter's: the fact that there is something in this narrow, implacable man susceptible of being touched by the bishop-spirit, and that the whole self to which he is used and with which he is so satisfied cries out in protest against the possibility. For all his rigid self-possession under all other circumstances, Javert is stirred to the depths by the mild, quiet M. Madeleine; he displays a personal hatred that gnaws him from within and rises to almost hysterical proportions. When the mayor refuses to let him send a prostitute to prison, Javert, most uncharacteristically losing his head, denounces the other with no evidence to support him, and puts himself in a most uncharacteristically humiliating position. When the mayor, in order to save someone who has been wrongly accused in his place, confesses that he *is* Jean Valjean, and Javert is appointed to make the arrest, the unholy joy of the police inspector, to whom the making of arrests is a routine matter, is so great that it amounts to an "internal earthquake." "Upright, haughty, and dazzling, he flaunted the superhuman bestiality of a ferocious archangel in the azure of heaven."[34]

Nor is Javert without his effect on Jean Valjean, to the extent that we are shown the second self's side of the relationship. Javert is the only person in the book capable of arousing, in the new Jean Valjean, some of the harshness reminiscent of the old (this in their dispute over the prostitute Fantine). Furthermore it is Javert who, bringing news of the false arrest of someone resembling the exconvict, precipitates an "internal earthquake" in his counterpart: a titanic struggle between self-justification and self-renunciation, the Javert-side of his nature and the bishop-side. For while Javert is a man of probity, he is above all a man of iron hardness, to whom the stability of the social order always takes precedence over the welfare of the individual. This is precisely the hardness which now, as the result of Javert's visit, rises within Jean Valjean, urging on him the view that it is not only his right but his duty to let the worthless old Champmathieu go to the galleys in order that he, M. Madeleine, may in his position of mayor continue to do good for the people of M. sur M. It is the Javert within that presents the argument to foil the Javert without.

I am saved, and all is settled. There was only one open door through which my past could invade my life; and that door is now walled up forever. That Javert, who has so long annoyed me, whose terrible instinct seemed to have scented me out, and, by heavens! had scented me out, the frightful dog ever making a point at me, is routed, engaged elsewhere, and absolutely thrown out! . . . After all, if some people are made unhappy, it is no fault of mine. Providence has done it all, and apparently decrees it. Have I the right to meddle with the arrangements of Providence?[35]

But this is only a brief spasm of self-assertion by the old Jean Valjean, and the argument of social expediency is soon rejected. Returned to the galleys for life, Jean Valjean falls into the sea beside his ship and is apparently drowned.

So for a time Javert too believes, but the thought of Jean Valjean remains in the back of his mind. Piecing together various scraps of evidence, he follows the trail to the parish of Saint Medard, borrows the rags of a begging exbeadle (for he is aware of and despises his enemy's charity to the poor), and kneels in an attitude of prayer in the beggar's usual place. As Jean Valjean approaches to put a gift in his hand Javert raises his head, and the two men, each with a violent shock of recognition, look into each other's eyes. Another long pursuit begins, but this time Jean Valjean, who has taken under his protection the daughter of the now-dead prostitute, a child named Cosette, does not give himself up, and for many years evades Javert. It is not until the Revolution of 1832, in the battle of the Rue de la Chanvrerie, that the two men again meet face to face. Javert has come in his capacity of spy for the established order and has been exposed and condemned to death. Jean Valjean has come in the hope of rescuing the young man, Marius, who is Cosette's betrothed. As Javert is being bound to a table, one thing takes his attention: the shadow of a man standing in the doorway. He turns his eyes, and again confronts Jean Valjean. When the time comes for Javert's execution, Jean Valjean asks permission to do the deed himself. He leads the other into a nearby deserted lane, where they are unseen by anyone else, draws out a knife (which Javert assumes to be for his own throat), cuts Javert's bonds, and sets him free. Javert, after a moment of gaping astonishment, rebuttons his frock coat, resumes his military stiffness, folds his arms and walks off. But before he has gone out of sight he wheels about. Jean Valjean is still looking after him. And suddenly Javert shouts: "You annoy me. I would sooner you killed me!" [36]

The famous episode that follows will be familiar to all readers. As the barricade falls, and Marius is wounded, Jean Valjean snatches up the unconscious young man and descends with him into the sewers of Paris. Through the whole system of loathsome subways he makes his way, carrying Cosette's bethrothed on his back, crossing the whole city of Paris, not by its streets but by its unseen under-streets, stifled by the fetid air, wading through the sea of excrement. On the other side of the river he reemerges, and, crouching on the bank, commences to bathe Marius' face. At this moment, in the same instinctive way in which Javert has felt the importance of the shadow cast from the doorway, Jean Valjean becomes aware of being watched from behind; he turns, and there is Javert. He makes no effort to escape. At his request, Javert helps him to convey the unconscious Marius to the home of the latter's grandfather and then, before taking Jean Valjean on to the police station, allows him to enter his own home for a moment, telling the exconvict that he will wait at the door. But when Jean Valjean, who has every intention of returning at once, glances out the window on the landing, he sees to his amazement — the same amazement with which Javert has found himself set free at the barricade — that the police inspector has disappeared.

The street is short, and physically the disappearance has been simple enough to manage, but psychically and morally it is the first act in Javert's life that has not been simple; and in its reverberations throughout his mind it is cataclysmically complex. The reader who wishes to see for himself the skill with which the character and fate of Jean Valjean are intertwined with those of Javert should compare the following section, the effects of his last meeting with Jean Valjean upon Javert, with the early section already discussed, the effects of his meeting with the bishop upon Jean Valjean. Not only are the two experiences of mental turmoil carefully paralleled with each other, but they are related to each other as result to cause, for it is the earlier agony of Jean Valjean that has led directly to the present agony of Javert. Like Jean Valjean, he has been "infected" by the bishop, but in his case it is the bishop in Jean Valjean, grown by now nearly as old as the bishop was then, and nearly as selfless. Like Jean Valjean, he is consumed by his infection as by an inward flame;

like Jean Valjean he wrestles with it and vainly tries to throw it off; but unlike Jean Valjean he cannot give in to it. For the first time in his life he sees before him not one road but two, and they run in directions contrary to each other; for the first time in his life he is faced with a major moral choice, and he cannot make it. Here is the way he puts it to himself.

"What has this convict done, this desperate man, whom I pursued even unto persecution, and who had me under his heel, and could have avenged himself, and owed it, both to his rancour and to his security to do so, — what has he done in leaving me my life, and showing me mercy? His duty? No. Something more. And what have I done in showing him mercy in my turn, — my duty? No. Something more. Is there, then, something higher than duty?"[37]

This is the question, utterly unprecedented in Javert's experience, before which he totters and quails, like a man on the edge of a precipice. Unable to move either forward or backward, and finding only one way to avoid the choice demanded of him, he takes this way. With a firm step he goes to the nearest police station; in a firm hand he writes a series of recommendations for the good of the service (none of them mentioning Jean Valjean); then, walking to the quay over the rapids of the Seine, he plunges into the water to his death.

It may seem a strange salvation that puts a man through intolerable torments of mind and drives him at last to suicide. But we have already seen that the second self as Saviour does not always succeed in saving the first self. Javert is not born anew out of his pain as Jean Valjean was, precisely because he is not Jean Valjean, but the other half of Jean Valjean. Nevertheless, just in the torments that his encounter with his other self has inflicted on him, just in the infection that proves fatal to him, a kind of salvation has been achieved, far more at least than in the case of the narrator of *Bartleby*. Both the relationship in *Bartleby* and that in *Les Misérables* end in death. But in *Bartleby* it is second self who dies, in disgust and despair at his failure ever effectively to touch the first self. "I know you, and I want nothing to say to you." In *Les Misérables* it is the first self who dies, and dies because he *has* been touched, beyond his powers of endurance. Bartleby's employer gets a glimmer of light, but it never really penetrates to anything deep within, because there is no longer anything deep within. Javert gets a blinding, bewildering flash that not only dazzles his eyes but floods through his whole angular, unresilient being, and bursts it asunder.

7

The Second Self As The Beloved

When Aristophanes, not as comic dramatist but as dramatis persona in Plato's *Symposium,*[1] finally gets rid of his hiccough and is able to take his turn discoursing in the honor of love, he gives a delightfully fanciful account of the way in which this emotion came into existence. Once upon a time, he informs the company, humans were fashioned very differently from those of today. They were rounded instead of one-sided creatures, with four hands and four feet, "back and sides forming a circle, one head with two faces, and the remainder to correspond."[2] This rounded-ness made them most formidable and presumptuous people, and to humble them Zeus proceeded to slice them into vertical halves, but with an attendant result which he seems not to have foreseen. For at once the two halves of the severed whole could think of nothing but of coming together again; they flung their arms around one another and clung desperately, seeking to grow back into one; and it is this quest which is the origin, and remains the essence, of the magical power of love.

This is a greatly simplified version of the fable as Plato's Aristophanes tells it. Aristophanes, as a good sophisticated Greek of the fourth century B. C., is making provision for homosexual as well as heterosexual love, and preferring the former (at least when it is between man and man) as the more noble. But in general, especially in the tradition of the Western world, it is the latter that has predominated: in Platonic terms the irresistible mutual attraction of the two halves of the original Androgyne,[3] the masculine *andros* and the feminine *gynē,* still by instinct one, though in physical fact now two.

Such is the Platonic account of the origin of love; and all readers are familiar with the similar account in Genesis, where God is again the divider, though not for the purpose of punishment.

> And the LORD GOD caused a deep sleep to fall upon Adam, and he slept; and He took one of his ribs, and closed up the flesh instead thereof;
>
> And the rib, which the LORD GOD had taken from man, made He a woman, and brought her unto the man.
>
> And Adam said, This is now bone of my bones, and flesh of my flesh; she shall be called Woman, because she was taken out of Man.
>
> Therefore shall a man leave his father and his mother, and shall cleave unto his wife: and they shall be one flesh.[4]

The parallel between these ancient myths is striking, but still more striking is the parallel between both of them and the modern scientific theory of how love came into being. The splitting into opposite sexes appears to have been a relatively recent event in the evolutionary cycle. Many forms of life are still bisexual; and such evidence as the breasts of the human male and the clitoris of the human female indicate that even in what we are pleased to call the highest form there linger vestiges of an original, prehuman, androgynous being. And not only does the same biological division of this being seem literally to have taken place, but it seems to have had much the same psychological results as those described by Plato and the Old Testament. "Ever since the sexes have been separated," writes a contemporary psychologist, "Man is restlessly searching for his Eve, the missing part of his self, and this view of the love-quest is confirmed by the marriage ceremony, which is supposed to make a woman one flesh and blood with a man and work the miracle of one soul in two bodies."[5] The fruit of the sexual act, the union of the masculine sperm with the feminine ovum, would appear to restore the original bisexuality; but at once the new being begins to take on the characteristics of one sex or the other; and so the division continues, and the hunger remains unappeased, and the search for the Beloved goes on.[6]

Now admittedly this hunger and this search to some extent characterize all cases of love between the sexes, as distinct from the love we considered in the last chapter or from sexual desire alone. The condition of what we call "being in love" always involves a certain mysterious "dividend" of emotion, a logically inexplicable sense of affinity, that resembles the mysterious affinity of the relationship between the selves. But this resemblance is a resemblance only, between things that are different in both degree and kind. For all the magic intoxication that attends it, love in most cases, whether in life or in fiction, is love between wholly separate people, who remain in all respects two no matter how much they may speak of becoming one. Nor is it enough, on the other hand, that the lovers should be complementary opposites in character; this, as we have seen, is one of the things that characterize a relationship between the selves, but it does not in the least constitute such a relationship.

What we must look for in this chapter is another and much rarer sort of love, in which the lovers do not merely attract each other, or merely complement each other, or even merely attract each other because they complement each other. The lovers we are looking for attract each other, if necessary from the ends of the earth, because they *are* each other; very much as though they had inherited in its full strength the nostalgic yearning for each other experienced by the two halves of one of those once-whole humans long ago bisected by Zeus, each utterly preoccupied with this yearning, yet equally unable to account for it or to satisfy it.

For the intense yearning which each of them has towards the other does not appear to be the desire of intercourse, but of something else which the soul desires and cannot tell, and of which she has only a dark and doubtful presentiment. Suppose Hephaestus, with his instruments, to come to the pair who are lying side by side and say to them, "What do you people want of one another?" They would be unable to explain. And suppose further, that when he saw their perplexity he said: "Do you desire to be wholly one; always day and night to be in one another's company? for if this is what you desire, I am ready to melt you into one and let you grow together, so that being two you shall become one, and while you live live a common life as if you were a single man, and after your death in the world below still be one departed soul instead of two — I ask whether this is what you lovingly desire, and whether you are satisfied to attain this?" — there is not a man among them when he heard this who would deny or who would not acknowledge that this meeting and melting in each other's arms, this becoming one instead of two, was the very expression of his ancient need.[7]

This is the special kind of mystery which distinguishes the love we are investigating from any other kind. In it we must expect no sense of proportion on either side, for save in regard to this love nothing else possesses any real significance, or any real existence. Yet it is no youthful fever of infatuation that will burn itself out or subside to a moderate glow; its flame is in the soul from birth, and we are often given the strong suggestion that it will not cease with death; nor can it ever be appeased, since what it longs for it cannot even clearly conceive of, let alone bring to pass. Furthermore, in order to be present in the soul from birth, it must have had its inception *before* birth; and because of the particularity of the love this inception cannot be anything so general as an original racial bisexuality, since by this time all that could be inherited from such a source would be the impulse to love, not the absolute and permanent concentration of all capacity to love upon a single person. The attraction between the lovers is that of opposite magnetized poles that apply to each other and to each other alone; and it draws them together, when the time for love is ripe, with an unmistakable little shock of recognition, the sense of love that has always been and has had its own plans as to the way it would unfold. It is this attraction, always a mutual one, though as usual we tend to know more about the first self's side of it, that is the special characteristic of the relationships involving the second self as the Beloved.

Obviously this category cuts across those which we have already considered, since the Beloved can be either evil or good. Nevertheless the evil Beloved and the good Beloved have far more in common with each other than either has with any of the second selves we have studied in the last four chapters. For one thing the second self as the Beloved differs from all other aspects in being always of the opposite sex from the first self — almost invariably female, perhaps since most literature has been written by males. This is an important difference, but still more important is the fact that the nature of the relationship makes it impossible for the second self as the Beloved ever to be evil or good in the same way, or in the same degree, as any of the others. This is particularly evident in cases of the evil second self in this category, which, far from being numerically preponderant (as we have found with second selves of the same sex), are in a very small minority, and which even in these cases can be called "evil" only in a qualified sense.

One of the clearest examples of such qualified evil is to be found in Poe's *Ligeia*.[8] Ligeia, the narrator's beloved and wife, is mysterious even in her beauty, a dark beauty of raven hair and large jet-black eyes under a high, pale forehead. And the origin of the owner is equally dark; the narrator has never known her paternal name, nor can he remember exactly when or where he first became acquainted with her. As is generally true of the second self, she is the first self's intellectual superior, in this case possessing an extraordinary knowledge of abstruse matters and acting as her husband's guide in them; and she is contrasted with the dependent and irresolute narrator in her fierce, gigantic power of will.

But this will is housed in a frail, if lovely, frame. Ligeia falls ill, becomes emaciated; soon it is evident that she must die. And only now does the narrator become aware of the true intensity of her reciprocal love for him. Her love *is* her life, and against the loss of it to the Conqueror Worm she puts all her great energy of volition. But her defiance does not save her, and the narrator, left alone, is utterly demoralized, becomes an opium addict, and at last as his crowning folly, "in a moment of mental alienation, I led from the altar as my bride — as successor of the unforgotten Ligeia — the fair-haired and blue-eyed Lady Rowena Trevanion, of Tremaine."

We find here the familiar color contrast, between the dark second self and the fair first self, but adapted to the relationship in which the second self is the Beloved. In such a relationship, while the second self tends to remain dark, the lightness usually given to the first self tends to be transferred to the second self's rival for the first self's affection. Actually, however, there is never any real rivalry, nor does the "rival" share identity with either of the selves, but offers to the first self at best the temporary appeal of safety, of withdrawal from his dark destiny which, of course, cannot be withdrawn from.[9] Such is the case in Poe's story. The marriage disintegrates; the narrator can think only of his lost love, and calls her name aloud at night as though in hope of summoning her back. Rowena (understandably) becomes ill, and in her illness she commences to fancy strange sounds and motions in the chamber in which she lies. Nor is she alone in fancying them. One night a faint shadow is visible on the carpet; a little later, when the narrator hands a goblet of wine to Rowena, he seems to see several drops of a brilliant red fluid fall into it. Immediately upon drinking the wine Rowena becomes worse, and soon dies. As the narrator sits alone beside her shrouded body, he hears all at once a low sob from the bed of death. Rowena's face shows color; apparently she still lives; but as he watches she stiffens once more into unmistakable death, and the narrator gives himself up to the visions of Ligeia that habitually fill his mind. But then again comes a sound from the bed, a sigh this time; again and more strongly than before there are distinct signs of life, only to fade again as he watches. Over and over through the night "this hideous drama of revivification" reenacts itself. At last comes the climactic struggle, at the peak of which the corpse actually rises from its bier and totters toward the middle of the room. It appears to be, it must be, the Rowena who died —

. . . but *had she grown taller since her malady?* What inexpressible madness seized me with that thought? One bound, and I had reached her feet! Shrinking from my touch, she let fall from her head, unloosened, the ghastly cerements which had confined it, and there streamed forth into the rushing atmosphere of the chamber huge masses of long and dishevelled hair; *it was blacker than the raven wings of midnight!* And now slowly opened *the eyes* of the figure which stood before me. "Here then, at least," I shrieked aloud, "can I never — can I never be mistaken — these are the full, and the black, and the wild eyes — of my lost love — of the Lady — of the LADY LIGEIA." [10]

Here the evil of the Beloved consists in defiance of natural law, and in healing the wound of separation from her other self not only by a return from death but by the murder of the woman who has taken her place. It is only in her relentlessness about accomplishing this return that Ligeia is evil. Far more unmistakably evil is the one example I know of where the Beloved is a man: a work which, interestingly enough, was written by a woman. The work is, of course, Emily Brontës *Wuthering Heights*. [11] In this novel we find a difficulty we have encountered before, that of not being given directly the viewpoint of either of the main characters; in fact here the difficulty is doubled by the real story's being transmitted to us through two layers of framework narration by exceedingly normal people: the pompous Lockwood, who tells the more recent events, and the pious Nelly Dean, who tells Lockwood the story within the story.

As compared with the two narrators, both lovers in the main story, Cathy Earnshaw and Heathcliff, are strange specimens. Nevertheless, of the two it is Heathcliff who possesses all the main attributes of the second self. Cathy is wild and proud, not infrequently cruel, but to the moment of her death these qualities are shown as the direct result of a spoiled childhood and a willful nature; her thoughts and impulses are always clear to us. Heathcliff is another matter. Even as a child he is surrounded by mystery. He enters the story as the alien intruder, picked up by old Mr. Earnshaw in the streets of Liverpool and brought back to Wuthering Heights; a dark little gypsy child, speaking his own dark incomprehensible tongue, homeless and of unknown origin. His initial encounter with his first self is a clash; for in bringing him back Mr. Earnshaw has lost the presents he promised his own children, and Cathy shows her resentment "by grinning and spitting at the stupid little thing," hating him as all the others save Mr. Earnshaw hate him. Heathcliff grows up a sullen, silent lad, full of calculating hardness and black temper, who from the first breeds bad feeling in the house; the invader from the dark who has brought with him, for the people who have taken him in, the darkness of their doom.

It is out of this background that there is born the love in which the story centers. Cathy and Heathcliff find in each other kindred spirits, wild and untamed, passionately fond of the wild moor that reflects their own wildness of nature; they become inseparable playmates. Both, however, are as proud as they are wild, and pride is always the enemy of love. When the young, wealthy Edgar Linton of nearby Thrushcross Grange begins to pay attention to Cathy, she becomes increasingly mindful of the fact that Heathcliff is nothing but a gypsy foundling, and when Linton proposes marriage she accepts. That is, her pride accepts, but in this concession to pride she becomes conscious for the first time of her love for Heathcliff, and of the special quality of this love, rising from the realization that "he's more myself than I am. Whatever our souls are made of, his and mine are the same; and Linton's is as different as a moonbeam from lightning, or frost from fire."[12]

But the contrast between the fair-haired Linton and the brown-haired Cathy, like the contrast between the fair Isabella Linton and the dark Heathcliff whom she later marries, and between the fair, placid world of Thrushcross Grange and the dark, tempestuous world of Wuthering Heights, while it plays an important part in the pattern of the novel, is not at all the kind of oppositeness that characterizes the relationship between the selves. Cathy's simile of frost and fire is not apt, for there is nothing in Linton so positive as frost; he is no more cold than he is hot; and the difference between their natures is largely one of irrelevancy. In fact Linton's part in this story, even in coloration, is strikingly like that of the fair-haired Rowena in Poe's *Ligeia*: the pallid, insignificant character who happens to come between lover and beloved, and who pays dearly for it. The real oppositeness is where we always find it in this literature, in the same place where we find the identity, and the coexistence of the two things creates the dynamic tension that gives the relationship between the selves its perilous excitement. Cathy and Heathcliff are the untamed creatures of the moor; Cathy feels herself to *be* Heathcliff, while Heathcliff speaks of her (and not figuratively) as his life, his soul. But within this sameness is also oppositeness: she, though spoiled and selfish, is by nature a warm, impulsive, vivacious, airy-light, ungrasping, understandable person; he is by nature just the reverse: sullen, withdrawn, heavy, malignant, miserly, mysterious.[13]

It is this oppositeness (not just difference) combined with this sameness (not just similarity) that is the central motivating force of the plot. It is this that causes Cathy, in her worldly pride, to desert Heathcliff. It is this that causes Heathcliff, after disappearing into his native darkness, to return from it again, drawn by a love which is inextricably bound up with hate, a love which leads him to torment Cathy and exposes him to torment by her, a love which not only brings the Linton household down in ruin but destroys his Beloved in the process. His very prayer to her, after her death, is half one of hatred: that she find no rest so long as he is alive, that she be forced to haunt him; and he curses her for a devil when she will not comply. Even when he does have the sense of his prayer's being answered, it does not in the least soften him, but moves him to his worst acts of violence, presumably murdering Cathy's brother, kidnapping and beating Cathy's daughter, murdering his own son by deliberate neglect. When he dies, in the conviction that he and Cathy are at last to be reunited, it is not with a peaceful smile on his lips, but with a sneer.

Thus while Ligeia is evil in one specific way only—that of defying the universe and killing her rival in order to return to her Beloved —Heathcliff is evil throughout. To be sure, he has a certain initial motivation, but when reviewed in the light of what follows, his motives seem to be much less the cause of his revenge upon humanity than an excuse for it.

I state the case this strongly (without, I think, exaggerating it) in order to emphasize the point I have already made: that even in such an instance the second self in this category is never evil for us in the same way or in the same degree as the other evil second selves we have studied. What makes this difference is what constitutes the lifeblood of all the relationships in this group, love instead of hate, the particular kind of love described by Plato, the all-in-all of love that by its nature must always be shared by both selves (though one or the other may pursue it more actively), the destined single love of their lives that yearns not simply for union but for a unity that can never be achieved. In all other categories what the evil second self wishes above all things is evil for the first self, but the second self as the Beloved and loving in turn, though willing evil for everyone else in the world, can never will it for the first self, any more than the first self can will it for the second; this despite the fact that in the excess of their love they may well destroy each oher. The love involved in these relationships is not the Christ-like love of the Bishop of D——; it is a love that may be experienced by extremely selfish people like Cathy and Heathcliff, and as a result it may lead to extremely evil actions. Nevertheless, the selfishness and the evil are not *in* the love, but *despite* the love; love of any kind is never selfish and is always the reverse of evil. Such figures as Ligeia and Heathcliff may pervert the love that seizes them, but they can never do so entirely, and the love in turn is bound to have its effect on them. Merely by touching them it to some extent ennobles them, transfigures them, lifts them above themselves: the murderess-revenant reaching back from the world beyond to the self she has left behind; Heathcliff standing outside the house of the dying Cathy, beating his head against the trees and howling like a dog. Such second selves invade with their darkness the world of light, but are always to some extent invaded by it as well.

This is why, in the category of the second self as the Beloved, the evil second self is comparatively rare, and even then refuses to be altogether classifiable as evil. Good second selves in this category, on the other hand, are far more numerous. Perhaps the clearest examples of such goodness are those in which the force that works from before their births to draw the lovers together operates through the medium of dream. What I am talking about, however, is not a mere dreaming *about* each other, but a dreaming *with* each other: the phenomenon of the shared dream, made possible by the sharing of the stuff which dreams, that is, the soul. Of such dream-sharing between the selves we have two famous examples, both products of late nineteenth-century English literature and almost exactly contemporaneous with each other.

One of these is Kipling's short story, *The Brushwood Boy*.[14] George Cottar, the first self, is hardly a person one would expect to have dealings with the mysterious in any form. A product of the English public school system, Sandhurst, and a military career in India, he is the very model of the most respectable and unimaginative mid-Victorian young John Bull. But in addition to his public life Georgie has also a secret nocturnal life, the life of dreams. All his dreams begin in the same way: at a pile of brushwood somewhere near a beach, around which he runs with other children, and from which further adventures begin. In these dreams there is from the start a little girl of his own age, to whom he gives his two favorite female names run together as "Annie*an*louise," and upon whose original appearance (borrowed from an illustration in Grimm's fairy tales) he superimposes that of a little girl, with a lisp and with her dark hair combed back off her forehead, who has taken his attention during a theatrical performance in Oxford.

He grows up, but the dream life does not come to an end. In the Indian hot weather his dreams are particularly vivid. Always he enters the dream-world by the same road, along a beach, near a pile of brushwood, with the sea on his right, and ahead of him, over a swell of rising ground, "valleys of wonder and unreason." Sometimes he is stopped on his way to the City of Sleep by Policeman Day, and then he knows he is in for a bad night. But other times he goes on, into remarkable and delightful adventures; by a small clockwork steamer across the level sea, past a stone lily labeled "Hong-Kong" and another labeled "Java," to a deep freshwater lock, with reeds arching above. "Some one moved among the reeds — some one whom Georgie knew he had travelled to this world's end to meet. Therefore everything was entirely well with him."[15] The person of the Lily Lock is, of course, the girl, the one-time Annie*an*louise, and she shows him the way across the world's fourth dimension in which he is lost, and flees with him hand-in-hand to the road which he understands (she does not need to tell him in words) to be the Thirty-Mile Ride, down which by pony he rushes back, menaced by "Them," whoever "They" are, between the dark-purple downs and the lashing sea, until he reaches the brushwood pile.

The years in India pass, and one night, when Georgie is on his way home for a leave, there comes a sudden change in the environment and personnel of his dream. For this night there is no panic, no pursuit; "They" either are friendly or have gone away, and he and Annie*an*louise flit together all over their country. But a far more significant change is in his companion, who all at once proves to be as grown-up as he, her black hair, still combed back from her forehead, growing now in a "widow's peak."

Georgie hurrries home, and while he is there his match-making mother invites to the house a Mrs. Lacy and her daughter Miriam, who plays and composes music. On the night the Lacys arrive, Georgie, returning late from the trout ponds, looks in the French windows of the drawing room and sees the girl at the piano, with her back to him. She commences to sing, and he listens in astonishment mixed with rising, incredulous excitement, for it is a song about the purple downs and the Sea of Dreams, the road that leads to the City of Sleep but is impeded by Policeman Day. Next morning at breakfast he meets her face to face for the first time — but of course it is not the first time, for here is the tall girl in black with the widow's peak and the combed-back hair, the grown-up version of the child of the Lily Lock.

But this is not merely a case of his meeting in "real life" the girl of his dreams; it is simultaneously a case of the girl's meeting the boy of *her* dreams; and most wondrous of all is the fact that the dreams of both have been, from the beginning, the same. Therefore not only does the dream-world impinge upon and extend into the reality-world in that these two young people, familiar to each other as dream figures, now encounter each other, wholly unchanged and recognizable, in "reality"; the dream-world itself is given one of the main dimensions of reality by being discovered to be the property of more than one person, becoming therefore verifiable in all its details, so real to them both that the task of now translating their dream-love into a formal betrothal in the reality-world is a nuisance and a bore. In the world's terms Miriam Lacy and Georgie Cottar have met and fallen in love; but in their own terms Annie*an*louise and the Brushwood Boy have known each other, and loved each other, all their lives, in the realm of stone lilies and other wonders that has now become continuous, for them, with the realm of waking life.

Much the same situation as the one used by Kipling, that of a dream-world shared as a private reality (and in ways a more real reality) by first and second selves as lovers, is given fuller and more serious treatment by George du Maurier in his novel *Peter Ibbetson*.[16] Here there is a much closer integration of the realms of dream and waking reality; the reality-world that *was,* in the earlier part of the story, becoming the dream-world that *is,* simultaneously for both the lovers, in the latter part.

The hero and first self we initially meet, as we meet Georgie Cottar, in his early childhood. He is then Pierre or "Gogo" Pasquier, child of a French father and an English mother, who live in a house in "The Street of the Pump," in Passy, in the outskirts of Paris. Like Georgie, Gogo is a normal and wholesome boy, but like Georgie, Gogo also dreams. Between dreams and play it is an idyllic life he leads, in the house with the lovely garden, adjacent to a large private park that seems to belong to nobody. On the way to Saint Cloud is a pond called "La Mare d' Auteuil," secluded, picturesque, and teeming with an endless variety of insects and reptiles.

Next to the Pasquiers live Dr. and Madame Seraskier, with their little daughter Mary or "Mimsey." Madame Seraskier is of Irish parentage, remarkably tall for a woman, and as beautiful as she is tall, and with her little Gogo falls madly in love. But it is Mimsey who becomes his playmate to the extent that she is able, poor little ailing Mimsey, the very reverse of beautiful, though clever and imaginative. For example, she has the fancy that a pair of invisible beings, "La Fée Tarapatapoum" and "Le Prince Charmant," are frequently present in the immediate vicinity of her and Gogo, and will watch over them through life; often she makes believe that she is conscious of their nearness; *"tout les deux — ils sont inseparables!"* At first when Gogo plays with Mimsey, carrying her pick-a-back when she is too weak to walk, he does so to please Mimsey's beautiful mother, but in time, growing attached to Mimsey, he does so to please himself.

But the happy childhood of Gogo and Mimsey comes to an abrupt end. Gogo's father is killed in an accident, his mother dies of grief, and he is removed to England by his mother's cousin, Colonel Ibbetson, where he grows up under the name of Peter Ibbetson. Meanwhile Madame Seraskier succumbs to cholera, and Mimsey goes to Russia with her father. For many years each supposes the other to be dead. Peter dislikes his uncle, dislikes school, dislikes the profession of architect in which he is apprenticed; his life is dull and lonely and empty.

At least with a single exception it is empty. One time, when he is in his late twenties, he is invited to a private concert, and sees a lady enter, the sight of whom arouses in him all the old love and rapture that he used to feel toward Madame Seraskier. Like Madame Seraskier she is very tall and very lovely, with dark hair and grey eyes and a smile that goes through him like a knife. Her name, he is told, is the Duchess of Towers. She on her side appears to notice him, and asks her hostess who he is.

She leaves, and the dreariness of his life closes back over him. He saves enough to make a pilgrimage back to the scenes of his childhood, but they are no longer the scenes of his childhood; even in these few years all has changed and cheapened, and he cannot summon up to memory the old familiar faces and forms. Unutterably homesick for a home that is no more, he catches sight of the Duchess of Towers, in a carriage with the French Empress, and is aware that she again takes special notice of him.

That night he has a dream that marks the beginning of his real, inward life, so different from his outward one. He is approaching his old school near the avenue gate, but in place of the school appears a prison, and the jailer and his wife, horrible little dwarfs, commence waltzing about him to an old familiar tune, and all at once he realizes that they are attempting to crowd him into the prison, to be hanged next morning. He rushes in terror to the avenue gate, and there meets the Duchess of Towers, who waves the dwarfs away. At the touch of her hand he feels that this is not a dream, but a new life to which he has awakened, incomparably more vivid than the daytime life he has been leading. The Duchess, who confesses that she cannot understand what business Mr. Ibbetson has in *her* dream, is nevertheless hospitable to him, instructs him in the technique of "dreaming true" (dreaming the things he wants to dream, bringing back to life the things he wants to recapture), and leaves him among the scenes of his past, looking over the garden wall and seeing, under the boughs of the old apple tree (of which a few hours earlier he was looking at the stump), his mother, Mimsey, and little Gogo Pasquier.

After returning to England he continues to "dream true" and thus revisit the old Passy. But in none of these dreams does he again meet the Duchess. His next encounter with her is in waking life, at the home of mutual friends, where being left alone together they discover not only that Peter Ibbetson and the Duchess of Towers are (of course) Gogo and Mimsey, but that on the occasion when she rescued him from the little dwarfs they were *both* revisiting their former selves in the same dream. She is deeply troubled, and says they must never so dream again, never meet again.

Then comes the great change in Peter Ibbetson's career, in which he begins to live, in his dream, what to him is his real life. Quarreling with his uncle, who has slandered the memory of his mother, he slays the elder man and is sentenced to death. While awaiting execution he "dreams true" again, and in the garden of the past once more meets the present Duchess of Towers. She tells him that his sentence is to be commuted to life imprisonment, that she is to be legally separated from her husband, and that she intends to devote to him, her lost and rediscovered Gogo, every hour that she can steal from her waking existence, in the realm of shared dream. So begins an extraordinary period of many years during which they pass eight or nine hours out of every twenty-four in each other's company, in a world which they are able to create at will out of the stuff of their own memories. In this world the people of the past are all alive for them, though not they for the people of the past, not even they for their earlier selves. Only little Mimsey is strangely conscious of invisible presences near her, and speaks to Gogo, sometimes when the elder, now-selves are standing by, of the Fairy Tarapatapoum and Prince Charming, the inseparable two who are watching over them.

At last comes the night when the duchess no longer joins Peter in dream, and he learns that she has died, and goes violently insane. Only after a long while does he dream true again, and, catching sight of his face in a mirror, finds that for the first time he has become old in the dream-world, as old and shabby as he has become in life (he is now confined permanently in an asylum for the criminally insane). He goes to the Mare d'Auteuil, intending to drown himself, but is stopped by the sight of a grey-haired woman on a bench, whom he suddenly recognizes as Mary Seraskier, come back to him, though only for a little while, from the dead. It is in her attempts to reconcile him to what is left of his life, and to explain to him what has brought her back on this last dream-visit, that we have one of the clearest expressions of that kind of love, that yearning for oneness which in earthly life can never be satisfied and must look beyond death, if anywhere, for fulfillment, which characterizes the relationship between the first self and the second self as the Beloved.

It is as though a long, invisible chain bound me still to the earth, and I was hung at the other end of it in a little transparent locket, a kind of cage, which lets me see and hear things all around, but keeps me from melting away.

And soon I found that this locket was made of that half of you that is still in me, so that I couldn't dissolve, because half of me wasn't dead at all; for the chain linked me to that half of myself I had left in you, so that half of me wasn't there to be dissolved . . .

I have come to tell you that we are inseparable forever, you and I, one double speck of spinal marrow — 'Philipschen!' — one little grain of salt, one drop. There is to be no parting for *us* — I can see that; but such extraordinary luck seems reserved for you and me alone up to now; and it is all our own doing.

But not till you join me shall you and I be complete, and free to melt away in that universal ocean, and take our part, as One, in all that is to be.[17]

In both Kipling's story and du Maurier's the female Beloved is the second self, not only because the mechanics of the situation place us further from her thoughts than from those of either Georgie or Gogo-called-Peter, but because she is throughout the person of greater mystery, more at home in the mysterious, able to act as guide and dragoman in the strange realm which she shares with the first self: thus Annie*an*louise showing Georgie the way out of the world of the fourth dimension, or the Duchess of Towers rescuing Peter Ibbetson from the evil dwarfs and leading him back to the garden of his heart's desire. And both are unquestionably good second selves, each cast in the role of Saviour. Yet it is true that both Annie*an*louise and the Duchess of Towers are very wholesome, "daylight" figures as compared with most other second selves we have met. As a result their goodness is rather plainly evident, and the element of opposition between them and their counterparts is largely absent. In the story to which we turn next, the second self as the Beloved is no less good, but is far stranger and somewhat sinister, welcomed initially by the first self, but bringing into his life confusion and even a kind of madness. A further difference between this story and the two we have just considered is the fact that here the selves do not grow up together, whether in dream or in waking life; they could not, since the Beloved is far younger than the first self, young enough to be his daughter, and this difference in age is of the utmost importance to the effect she has on him.

This story is Herman Hesse's novel *Steppenwolf*.[18] Harry Haller, the first self, is a middle-aged aesthete and philosopher, whose accumulation of years has brought him only frustration instead of fulfillment, isolating him within his own personality, and even there he can find no peace. He thinks of himself as only half man, the other half being a wolf of the steppes or "Steppenwolf," wild and shy and withdrawn from all human society. His Steppenwolf-nature, which makes it impossible for him to accept the values of the world around him (the world of post-War I Germany, with its cinemas and cafes and tinny jazz and other mass enjoyments), leads him not into hostility against this world so much as into the longing to escape from it at any price; it leads him into suicidal despair. And yet when he comes to the point of self-destruction the will to live reasserts itself. As he walks the streets one night he sees the letters of an electric sign playing across an alley wall: MAGIC THE-ATRE: ENTRANCE NOT FOR EVERYBODY: FOR MADMEN ONLY! and, by a man carrying a placard with a similar sign, is handed a little book which proves to be about someone named Harry, and is called *Treatise on the Steppenwolf*. Deeply curious he searches again for the sign, but in vain, and when he seems to find the man with the placard the latter denies all knowledge of any magic theater; if Harry wants a "show" let him go to the Black Eagle — though what the Black Eagle is he does not explain.

Now all this is very strange, and our tendency in this psychologically minded day is to explain it away as mental aberration. But the experience is not so presented to us; Harry's reality is undoubtedly colored by his state of mind and nerves, as are those of Ligeia's husband, but to what degree it is so colored is left an open question. This is most important to realize, for it is along the path of just such strange events that Harry makes his way to the Beloved. Deeply depressed by a quarrel he has got into he wanders through the streets at night, determined at last to cut his throat when he gets back to his lodgings, but because of that very determination he is unable to go back. Blindly he wanders on, until he comes to a public house in an unfamiliar part of town, and goes in, mechanically noting the sign over the entrance: "The Black Eagle." Inside there is no "show," only a crowd by which he is pushed forward until he reaches a table near the bar, at which a pale and pretty girl, with a curl at her temple and a withered camellia in her hair, smiles and makes room for him, almost as though she has been waiting for him. At once she takes him in hand, wipes his glasses, scolds him and orders him about like a child, mocking yet sympathetic, knowing just what is best for him, and also knowing just why it is he dreads to go home.

On the surface it is a most trivial incident. Harry does not even dance with the girl; nor does the girl, though she makes no secret of being a courtesan, sleep with him; since he is afraid to return home she arranges a room for him at the tavern, and goes off to another bar with another man. Yet we are left in no doubt that this is the moment of encounter between the soul-mates, even though neither consciously acknowledges it to be. Each claims that he is not in the least in love with the other, and perhaps this is true in any sense in which they have loved before. But we need not concern ourselves with the words they use. Once more there is that same mysterious "touching" of inward forces, that awareness of a kinship between them shared by no one else in the world, that sense of destinies permanently linked together, that special preoccupation with each other, that profound need for each other which as Plato pointed out long ago cannot be explained by either friendship or sexual desire. As usual, it is particularly on the part of the first self that we are aware of such reactions. Here is the mood in which Harry waits for his next meeting with the lady of the camellia.

... the importance of my relationship to this unknown girl had become alarmingly clear to me. I thought of nothing but her. I expected everything from her ... She was the one window, the one tiny crack in my black hole of dread. She was my release and my way to freedom. She had to teach me to live or teach me to die. She had to touch my deadened heart with her firm and pretty hand, and at the touch of life it would either leap again to flame or subside to ashes. I could not imagine whence she derived these powers, what the source of her magic was, in what secret soil this deep meaning she had for me had grown up; nor did it matter.[19]

Of her feelings toward him we know less; she appears at first to need him far less than he needs her. And yet we soon realize that for all her lightness of attitude, the relationship is no more a light matter to her than it is to Harry. She continues to order him about, to tease him, but for all that he has a place in her thoughts shared by no one else. She explains this to him quite frankly. She has singled him out because she intends to use him for a purpose: to make him fall in love with her, so much in love that when she bids him to he will kill her. She knows she is giving him the gift of life, and in return she wants of him her reward, which is to be the gift of death. This might seem a calculating sort of need, quite different from the need he feels for her. But in fact, though glazed over by the hard, bright surface of her everyday personality, it is quite as compelling, rooted in her special feeling of the bond of sameness which beneath their oppositeness links them together. Though they show it in contrary ways, they are both isolated and lost, dreamers of nobility and self-sacrifice in a world of jazz and beer, people with (as she puts it) "a dimension too many,"[20] both Steppenwolves, or rather both the same Steppenwolf, its masculine and feminine halves, held together by that mysterious affinity that serves as the bridge between them.

This affinity manifests itself in various ways. For example, there is the insight that dispenses with ordinary means of communication and enables the girl, at her first sight of Harry, to know all about what has brought him to the Black Eagle and what terrifies him about the idea of going home. Nor is this insight always on her side only. When Harry asks her name she tells him to guess it; and all at once she reminds him of a boy who was his friend in childhood, a boy named Herman. By this process, altering the name to its feminine form, he reaches the correct answer: Hermine. He is dumbfounded at his success, but she explains it readily.

Oh, you did all that yourself. Doesn't your learning reveal to you that the reason why I please you and mean so much to you is because I am a kind of looking-glass for you, because there's something in me that answers you and understands you?[21]

She is right, Harry knows; she has the faculty of being always right, the same faculty we have found in such different people as Ligeia, Annie-*an*louise, and the Duchess of Towers. Her face, so young and gay, now and again clouds over with dark seriousness, becoming indeed a kind of magic mirror of his elderly and careworn one. "Do you know," she asks him, "that we are both children of the devil?"[22] And so they are, not however of the Mephistophelean devil we met in Chapter 4, for such a devil is the God of the world of everyday despite its protestations to the contrary, but rather of the Faustian spirit of striving for a value and a vision in a world that does not even recognize the lack of these things. For such people as they there is nothing, nothing but death. And yet perhaps, she suggests, there *is* one other thing.

I say to myself: all we who ask too much and have a dimension too many could not contrive to live at all if there were not another air to breathe outside the air of this world, if there were not eternity at the back of time; and this is the kingdom of truth . . . Ah, Harry, we have to stumble through so much dirt and humbug before we reach home. And we have no one to guide us. Our only guide is our home-sickness.[23]

So deeply affected is he by these words which, as so often happens to the first self in his exchanges with the second, seem to come welling up from inside him at the same time he hears her speak them, that he wonders for a moment if she has not been reading his thoughts like a clairvoyant and giving them back to him as something new. So close are they in ideas and feelings that at such times it almost seems that she is hypnotizing him, at other times that he, like Ivan with Smerdyakov, may be hypnotizing her into hypnotizing him, and thus creating her into the Beloved other-self he so desperately needs.

Such things, however, are only a seeming and a suggestion, and are carefully kept from being more. To insist on such an interpretation of their relationship would be to take out of it just the quality that is its most important ingredient: the mystery. There are certain questions in certain kinds of fiction which it is legitimate to raise, but which it is not legitimate to answer, and this is one of them; while another is just where their relationship "really" takes them: whether the extraordinary *Walpurgisnacht*-scene in modern dress which brings the story to a close is reality, opium dream, or final mental collapse; whether Harry does in fact slay Hermine or only, as the public prosecutor of his fantasy puts it, stabs to death, with the reflection of a knife, the reflection of his Beloved.

In *Steppenwolf* the second self as the Beloved is indisputably benignant, though set beside Annie*an*louise and the Duchess she is a most uncanny, even unearthly figure. Yet if we examine these stories closely, we shall see that the difference is more one of degree than one of kind. The single story of the lot with a happy ending is *The Brushwood Boy,* but even here the tone is by no means all light; the dream world in which Georgie and the girl with the lisp have their adventures together is no cloudless child's paradise but a place of elemental terrors: the Sick Thing in the bed, the hostile "They" who menace from behind the purple downs, the wild and fierce pursuit down the Thirty-Mile Ride. In *Peter Ibbetson* the terrors of the dream world when one is not "dreaming true," like the ghastly little dwarfs waltzing outside the prison, are supplemented by the tragedy of Peter's waking life: the empty years after the death of his mother, the killing of his uncle, the years in prison, the lunatic asylum in which he dies. Few stories in the literature of the second self are happy in any usual sense of the word, but the least happy of all are those which we might expect to be the most, those in which the bond between the selves consists of love. It is as though some unfriendly, retributive force were always working upon this love; as though it were always a love forbidden, whether by an unknown "they" or by law or by shame or by death or by the will to death.

But why forbidden? Perhaps the very intensity of it, the all-engrossing preoccupation with and adoration of a fellow human being rather than a deity, always has a certain blasphemous quality. But without ruling out this possibility I should like also to suggest another, which seems to me to go deeper into the nature of the second self as the Beloved and into the guilt that tinges this love. Let us return for a moment to the Narcissus legend with which we began this study. So long as we consider the face that enchants the young man to be only the reflection of his own it is not, for modern readers at least, a true second self, for it lacks the element of objectivity that is one-half this figure's reality. But in a later version of the same legend, that reported by Pausanias, the face that gazes up at the down-gazing Narcissus, though the exact replica of his own, is not his own, but that of his recently deceased twin sister.[24]

We have already seen how strongly the Twin Brother of cult and myth and legend anticipates the second self of conscious literary creation: that is, the second self of the same sex. We have also seen the way in which this figure would seem to offer an explanation of the atmosphere of uncanniness that in one way or another always surrounds the second self. Now, of course, twins are not always of the same sex, and at first glance it may seem strange to find that the Twin Sister, at least the Twin Sister of a Twin Brother, plays so small a part in the famous Twin stories of the world. This may be due in part to the fact that she is so much less suited to participate in heroic exploits than someone like Enkidu. But an examination of primitive attitudes toward the Twin Sister suggests that her infrequency of appearance in later stories is caused by just the reverse of indifference to her. For if to the primitive mind the birth of twins of the same sex is looked on as a public misfortune, the birth of twins of opposite sexes is viewed as utter catastrophe. The official reason is not only that such twins are necessarily the product of adultery of the mother's part, but that the twins themselves have had sexual relationship in the womb they have shared.[25] Once more, however, as in the case of twins of the same sex, the official reason for revulsion would seem to be less the real than the readily understandable one, a justification for the brutality shown the twins rather than the cause of it. Here again, though greatly intensified, would seem to be working the fear of invasion by the spirit-world, in its most unnatural and insidious form, that of the seductress who is *nam-a-shoobra,* One of Twins, with the seduced.[26] It would therefore seem possible that the shadow which hangs over modern versions of the second self as the Beloved derives ultimately from the primitive gloom and hostility which once greeted, and in parts of the world still greets, the appearance of the Twin Sister.

For how else can the complementary opposites in the realm of sex be imagined, ultimately, save as Twin Brother and Twin Sister? True, they seldom take this form literally, just as seldom as the selves we have considered in earlier chapters take the form of literal Twin Brothers. Certainly they do not in any of the examples of this category that we have thus far studied. At the same time it is interesting to notice the prevailing overtone of twinship that is present in all of them. Ligeia, of unknown origin so that marriage with her is technically justified, is not so much the wife of the narrator as she is the mysterious wiser sister whose seeing guides his seeing. Heathcliff, also of unknown origin, grows up under the same roof with Cathy and actually if not legally is a member of the same family, the companion of all her games and pranks and thoughts, far more her "brother" than her literal brother Hindley ever is. When Georgie and Miriam meet in the former's drawing room it is for the first time; but in another sense, that of their shared dream world, they have grown up together no less than Cathy and Heathcliff; as the Brushwood Boy and Annie*an*louise, playmates and comrades, they constitute a twofold unity against all the threats that surround them. The same is true of Peter Ibbetson and the Duchess of Towers, except that the world they have shared as children is not a dream world but the real world that is to become their dream world, a world in which as Gogo and Mimsey they are so constantly together that they might well be, and grow up feeling themselves to be, brother and sister (indeed as they later discover they *are* related, the only living descendants of Gatienne Aubery). And while in *Steppenwolf* the first self is old enough to be the Beloved's father, his feeling toward her is not in the least paternal, or that of an elder man infatuated with a young girl; her capacity to stimulate him with her youth lies in her freshness of seeing and thinking, in her insight into his soul, as though despite their difference in years they had known each other all their lives. Repeatedly, indeed, Harry refers to Hermine not as his sweetheart but as his comrade *and sister*.[27]

A still more marked equivalence between the second self as the Beloved and the Twin Sister is to be found in Shelley's *Epipsychidion*. He does not claim that Emilia Viviani is actually his Twin, but wishes that she were, and feels that the relationship of Twin Brother to Twin Sister is the logical and fitting one for him to bear to "this soul out of my soul."

> Would we two had been twins of the same mother!
>   Or, that the name my heart lent to another
> Could be a sister's bond for her and thee,
>   Blending two beams of one eternity!
> Yet were one lawful and the other true,
>   These names, though dear, could paint not, as is due,
> How beyond refuge I am thine. Ah me!
>   I am not thine: I am a part of *thee*.[28]

Still the blending of the Beloved with the Twin Sister in *Epipsychidion* is merely something that is wished for, and even this wish is so idealized that there is no reason for either the shadow of guilt or the threat of retribution. It not infrequently happens, however, in the literature of the second self that the Beloved becomes literally the sister (and either literally or not also the Twin), in which case the shadow of doom deepens. This is least true, oddly enough, where the facts of twinship and incest are most clearly spelled out for us. An example of what I mean is to be found in Thomas Mann's short story, *The Blood of the Walsungs.*[29] The mutual attraction felt by those ultrasophisticated twentieth century twins, Siegmund and Sieglinde, is rooted in the same sense of oneness that is sinfully — and in the disdainful judgment of the modern pair most sentimentally — discovered by the Brother-Sister Twins of *Die Walküre,* the opera which the later Siegmund and Sieglinde attend together as a parting ceremony on the eve of Sieglinde's wedding. It is this sense, of belonging to each other because of being each other, of sharing in their twofoldness an identity far deeper than their likeness in outward appearance, which makes them rebel against the encroachment of the outer world (chiefly in the form of Sieglinde's betrothed Beckerath) upon their little closed partnership; which brings them together at last, in ignoble imitation of their Wagnerian antecedents, on the bear rug in Siegmund's room.

Nevertheless the prevailing mood of this story is one of social criticism rather than the exploration of mysterious states of mind and soul; the shadow that hangs over it is one of general social disease rather than personal guilt; and the only "doom" that threatens the two sinners is that of being the spoiled little degenerates they are. Far more effective, at least as examples of second-self literature, are those writings in which the literal act of incestuous love is not so rigidly insisted upon, and room is left for the indispensable element of wonder.

One such example is another of Poe's stories, *The Fall of the House of Usher.*[30] Here too we deal with a wealthy and degenerate family, in this case the time-honored but narrowly inbred proprietors of the House of Usher, the decay of which melancholy pile — an ancient structure with a barely perceptible fissure running vertically down its front wall —has proceeded step by step with their own. In this mansion live the only survivors of their name, Roderick and Madeline Usher. Roderick Usher is ill; he suffers inexplicably from a morbid acuteness of the senses, strange sensations the strangest of which is fear; not fear of anything he can identify but fear absolute. By degrees, however, we learn that his fear is not altogether without cause. The deepest of the things contributing to it — this he reveals last of all, and only with hesitation — appears to be his concern about the condition of his sister Madeline. For Madeline, his only remaining relative on earth, is also ill, even more seriously and inexplicably than he. Her illness baffles her physicians; she is wasting away before their eyes; and for all their efforts and her own struggles against it she plainly (so Roderick gives the narrator to understand) has no chance of recovery. " 'Her decease,' he said, with a bitterness which I can never forget, 'would leave him (him, the hopeless and the frail) the last of the ancient race of the Ushers.' " [31]

This extreme bitterness of Roderick seems a bit strange (grief, yes, but why bitterness?), and still more strange is what immediately follows. For at this moment Madeline herself passes slowly by and disappears again, and for this brief instant she is regarded by the narrator "with an utter astonishment not unmingled with dread." That same evening he learns that her condition has suddenly worsened, "that the glimpse I had obtained of her person would thus probably be the last I should obtain — that the lady, at least while living, would be seen by me no more." Within the next few days she dies. On the grounds that her doctors, in order to study her mysterious disease, might secretly exhume her body, Usher enlists the narrator's assistance in temporarily enclosing it in an underground vault beneath the building. Together they deposit it there, and turn back the lid of the coffin to take a last farewell. It is at this point that we are made to recall the strong impression exerted on the narrator by his one previous glimpse of Madeline.

A striking similitude between the brother and sister now first arrested my attention; and Usher, divining, perhaps, my thoughts, murmured out some few words from which I learned that the deceased and himself had been twins, and that sympathies of a scarcely intelligible nature had always existed between them.[32]

That phrase, "sympathies of a scarcely intelligible nature," could not be more vague, and partly because of its vagueness but also because of the context — the two men leaning alone together over the coffin in the torchlit underground vault that has been so strikingly anticipated by one of Usher's paintings — could not be more suggestive. It is the central phrase of the story, in the light of which the series of events that have led up to this moment begins to take on a different significance from that which Usher has tried to give it, and to form a coherent unity with the events that follow. These include the increasing agitation of Usher; the night of the great storm when the two friends sit together in the narrator's apartment; the sequence of noises — cracking, ripping, grating, clanging — which the narrator tries to dismiss as noises of the tempest, but of which Usher, frozen in terror, knows the real significance: the breaking forth of the girl from the coffin and the tomb in which they have placed her while still alive, her footsteps on the stair, the heavy beating of her heart, and now at last the swinging inward of the doors to reveal the shrouded blood-stained figure of Madeline, who, falling forward upon her brother, in her last agonies carries him with her into the death to which he has consigned her before her time. Rushing out into the storm the narrator casts back one final look at the scene of all these horrors, the mansion so closely identified throughout the story with the brother-sister pair who have been its last inhabitants. Rapidly, as he watches, the "barely perceptible fissure" running down the front wall widens, gapes open until the setting moon shines through; the old house splits in two just as the Roderick-Madeline "house" has been split by Madeline's apparent death and the sealing off of her body; but then with a sound "like the voice of a thousand waters" the two halves, exactly like the sundered halves of the inward house in the chamber above, sink together into ruin, "and the deep and dank tarn at my feet closed sullenly and silently over the fragments of the *'House of Usher.' "*[33]

I have said that it is in the light of those words murmured by Usher in the vault, "sympathies of a scarcely intelligible nature," a phrase evidently not meant to be understood by the narrator and evidently not understood, that the events of this story fall into a coherent whole. Let us go over them briefly. The summoning of the narrator by Usher after all these years could be simply an impulse on Usher's part. On the other hand, it does furnish him with a witness to the fact that Madeline was still alive at the narrator's arrival, was seriously ill and under medical care, and died of presumably natural causes, much to her brother's grief; it also furnishes him with an aide to effect the secret interment of her body. There is no proof of any such motivation; this is a story wholly without proofs, but alive with hints. For example, of the various "physicians" supposedly in attendance on Madeline, so fascinated with her mysterious disease that they might well (says Usher) exhume her in order to study it further, the narrator at no time sees more than one, who wears "a mingled expression of low cunning and perplexity," and who greets the narrator "with trepidation."[34] What these words describe is not a scientist sufficiently absorbed in his calling to risk a crime in order to increase his knowledge of it, but a quack who is stupid enough to be perplexed by the illness he is purporting to treat, of low enough cunning to be bribed into raising no questions, and struck with trepidation by the advent of a newcomer who might raise them. Both Roderick and Madeline are mysteriously ill, but in different ways. She is wasting away with some disease affecting the central nervous system ("frequent although transient affections of a cataleptical nature"), exactly what we would expect of someone being slowly poisoned; he is suffering from unbearable nervous strain and the threat of mental breakdown, exactly what we should expect of a sensitive person who has under-taken an enormity for which he is clever enough but not callous enough.

No sooner does the narrator get his first glimpse of Madeline (establishing the fact that she is alive) than she is whisked out of his sight for good. He is then informed that it just so happens her condition, on this particular evening, has suddenly and fatally worsened. In the days that follow, Usher's own condition of mental and nervous strain also worsens, approaching uncontrollable hysteria, during which time he improvises a a song about the approach of madness and paints a picture of a long, low underground vault. One evening he abruptly announces that Madeline is dead and that he intends to "protect" her body by hiding it under his own mansion. He persuades the narrator (without whom he could hardly have managed the task) to help him bear her encoffined body through a long archway to a low underground vault, differing from the one in the painting only in the fact that it has been carefully sheathed in copper and is equipped with a massive iron door. As the days pass Usher grows more and more feverish and distraught. "There were times, indeed, when I thought his increasingly agitated mind was laboring with some oppressive secret, to divulge which he struggled for the necessary courage."[35]

He never achieves the courage, but the secret divulges itself, forcing itself to the surface as the thought of the underground vault has forced itself, before Madeline's death, into the painting that mirrors the secret places of his mind, and as the contents of the vault now force themselves up out of the subterranean darkness in which he has tried to enclose them.

Such hints, taken together, make it almost certain that what we have here is a tale of terror containing strong elements of the tale of ratiocin-ation: a murder mystery with no Dupin to solve it, and with a narrator purposely made more obtuse than the reader is expected to be, but also made observant enough to pick up suggestions that the reader is expected to fit together. What these point to is that Roderick Usher is guilty of his twin sister's murder; furthermore that this murder is one of calculated strategy, that both the crime and the covering up of the crime have been in his mind for a considerable time and have caused profound disturbance there.

But why should Usher want to murder Madeline? This for our pur-poses is the far more important question, and regarding this we are given far less help. Indeed our only real hint is that last sight of Madeline's face, with its "mockery of a faint blush upon the bosom and the face, and that suspiciously lingering smile upon the lip which is so terrible in death" (though in fact neither blush nor smile *is* that of death); that last sight, and the little phrase murmured by Usher, about the "sympathies of a scarcely intelligible nature" which have always existed between brother and sister. What this little scene gives us, of course, is only further suggestion; still it is the only possible suggestion that fits all the facts: that the guilt of Usher, driving him beside himself as we see it do, is not simply the guilt of murder but the guilt behind this guilt: the guilt of an attachment in which he has also been "beside himself," the guilt of Usher's madness and Madeline's blush, the "sympathies of a scarcely intelligible nature" which have made the Twin Sister the Beloved, the victim, and (like the Black Cat) the irrepressible retribution from within the tomb.[36]

Even stranger than Poe's story is the last example we shall consider in this category: Melville's *Pierre, or The Ambiguities*.[37] Here the brother and sister are not literally twins, are not fully siblings, Isabel being only Pierre's illegitimate half-sister; the same relationship, except for difference in sex, borne by Count Victor to Brother Medardus, Smerdyakov to Ivan, and so on. But here again, as in the Twin-Brother stories we studied in Chapter 2, what is important is not so much the fact as the feeling about the fact, the feeling on the part of both the Twins and the reader that they are two of a pair, each belonging to the other quite as much as he belongs to himself, tied to the other by bonds of kinship and destiny that will defeat all efforts to keep them apart. It is in this sense that Isabel is quite as much the Twin Sister of Pierre as Sieglinde of Siegmund, or Madeline Usher of Roderick.

That it is Isabel and not Pierre who is the second self is made clear throughout. For though by the end of the book Pierre is no more rational than she, the source of his irrationality is the mysterious Isabel, and the beginning of his irrationality is the entrance of this wild shy creature, with raven tresses like Ligeia's, into the comfortable, well-ordered, daylit life of the young country squire-to-be. At the same time her entrance is not wholly unprepared for. Like the dreams of Gilgamesh, the gloom of Axel Heyst, the dissatisfaction of Faust, there is a hint of vulnerability in the wholesomeness of Pierre before he even knows of Isabel's existence, a tiny chink in the armor of wealth and health that surrounds him. Though again the sin of incest is not made explicit in this story (Pierre and Isabel live together nominally as man and wife, and it is implied that this relationship goes beyond the nominal, but only implied), the theme of incest runs through it from the beginning, even more prominently than through the story of the Ushers, and the roots of this theme go back to a sin which antedates the lives of both brother and sister, so that as in the case of

Brother Medardus and Aurelia their fateful attraction for each other follows a guilty pattern already established before they were born, by people they have never known.

These roots, however, we are not aware of at the opening, and the hint of vulnerability to which I have referred is so light and amiable that only in retrospect does it take on significance. It consists simply in the fact that Pierre Glendinning, the young heir-apparent of the Glendinning estate, and his widowed mother Mrs. Mary Glendinning, have fallen into the playful habit of calling each other "brother" and "sister." It is, of course, a game, and yet by degrees we begin to realize that like all games it has something behind it that is not entirely a game. Part of this something lies in the attitude of Pierre. For one thing, he considers himself to have a peculiarly lovely mother, who "still eclipsed far younger charms, and had she chosen to encourage them, would have been followed by a train of infatuated suitors little less young than her own son Pierre." Fortunately she does not encourage them, for Pierre has more than once sworn — playfully — that any man having the temerity to propose marriage to his mother would immediately disappear from the earth. For another thing, Pierre is deeply regretful that he has no sister; and to some extent the fictitious title that he bestows on his mother enables him to merge the two figures (the idolized mother and the longed-for sister) into one. And yet his behavior toward this mother-sister is not exactly that which is appropriate for either son or brother, but rather that of a young cavalier paying court; as when, tapping at the door of "Sister Mary's" chamber one morning, he gracefully passes a ribbon round her neck, and fastens it at her throat with a kiss.

But Pierre's attitude is not the only thing that makes the brother-sister game slightly more than a game. His mother's attitude, if more sedately revealed, is even less sedate in fact. It is to be sure "triumphant maternal pride" in this handsome son who bears such a striking personal resemblance to her, but it is pride that takes a peculiarly proprietary and jealous turn. She loves his nobility, so long as it is a docile nobility, and she proposes that it shall remain docile. For this reason she not only permits but decides to hasten Pierre's forthcoming marriage to Lucy Tartan, not because of anything remarkable about Lucy but just because of Lucy's lack of anything remarkable; "for she too is docile — beautiful," Mrs. Glendinning muses, "and reverential, and most docile"; little blue-eyed Lucy will do nothing, as "some dark-eyed haughtiness" might do, to challenge Sister Mary's vested rights in Brother Pierre.

In other words, though Mrs. Glendinning is not the second self of this story, she interestingly prepares the way for the latter, in that what Pierre loves in his mother at the outset is that as-yet-unknown but longed-for soul-mate whom his mother, also without knowing her, already fears as a rival. His attitude toward his fiancée Lucy, on the other hand, is that of brother toward sister in the completely innocuous sense, as it never is toward "Sister Mary" or his real sister Isabel. With Lucy he is gay and easy and detached; they get along swimmingly together; and the horizon of their future seems as cloudless as the glorious summer sky that arches over them as they drive through the clover-bloom of Sunset Meadows.

But in fact there already *is* a speck of cloud, not in the physical sky but in the figurative one: in the form of a female face, which has captured Pierre's imagination and intermittently haunts his thoughts; a face which could not have entered his life on a more improbable occasion. One evening Pierre accompanied his mother to a charity sewing; and no sooner did he enter and his name was announced than there came from the far corner of the room a sudden unearthly shriek that affected him as no human voice had ever done before, split through his heart and left in its wake a yearning gap. His mother was irritated by his reaction; obviously someone had fainted, and the well-bred thing was to take no notice of it. Pierre obeyed. Covertly, however, he did take notice of the girl who had screamed, and who was now quietly sewing again: a girl in black, with black hair and a dark olive face, in which wonderful loveliness combined with wonderful loneliness, beauty with anguish.

This is the face that has haunted Pierre, though with his marriage to Lucy almost upon him he has struggled to throw off its influence. But one evening as he approaches Lucy's home he is intercepted by a hooded stranger who thrusts a letter into his hand. It is from one Isabel Banford, who gives him the astonishing news that he is not the only child of his father, that she is the other child and therefore his sister; and who begs him to come to her the following night.

Astonishing news, but not incredible, much as Pierre thinks he would like it to be. Instantly it draws up out of his memory fragments of impressions that until now have only puzzled him a little, but that now, fitted together with this note, form a ton's weight upon his heart, and crush to dust the enshrined image of his dead father. Among other things there is the portrait of his father as a young man, a portrait which Pierre's mother has never been able to abide, preferring her own larger portrait of her husband in his dignified middle years. The smaller portrait, showing a much younger and gayer man, has been given Pierre by his great-aunt, who tells him of the way the picture happened to be painted, without the subject's knowledge, during a time when he was much interested in a beautiful young émigrée from revolution-torn France. Dissuaded by his friends from making so "unfortunate" a match, Pierre's father broke off his visits to her, and soon afterward the beautiful girl disappeared; only the portrait remains as a memento of those earlier times. Most remarkable about it, to Pierre, has been his mother's intense and wholly unaccountable dislike of it; and sometimes, studying it, Pierre has seemed to hear the smaller portrait warn him against taking the respectable larger one too seriously; suggest to him that the two paintings after all make one, the two sides of the same man, the youth that *is,* and the age that *seems.*[38]

And so it is that, when Pierre now visits Isabel, he sees again that dark, mysterious face that has haunted him since his first glimpse of it at the charity sewing; but in the same instant he sees in it another and equally familiar face: "not only the nameless touchingness of that of the sewing-girl, but also the subtler expression of the portrait of his then youthful father, strangely translated, and intermarryingly blended with some before unknown, foreign feminineness." Isabel, too, as a child, visited by a strange gentleman who has whispered the word "father" into her ear, has been struck with the likeness between his face and the reflection of her own. But on the night of the sewing, the night when she shrieked, her first sight of Pierre has shown her the same likeness between Pierre's face and that of their father, the first and only being whom until then she has loved. Thus through the media of the portrait and Isabel's early memories each finds in the other the face of the father he has loved, and each, like the Narcissus of the later legend, loves in the other the face that, transferred to a separate being and the opposite sex, is nevertheless his own.

That brother and sister should love each other is natural enough, and there is much in this love that is natural and praiseworthy. The shadow of sin that lies over all these stories goes back in this case, as I have said, to before the lovers were born, not so much to the guilty love of the elder Pierre and the French émigrée as to the inhumanity with which he has deserted her; and it is in the overwhelming sense of this inhumanity and the impulse to make amends for it that the younger Pierre now devotes himself to caring for the issue of that sin, Isabel. But to cast off the shadow of sin needs more than a generous impulse, and from its origination the impulse, without losing any of its generosity, is tinged with a sin far stranger than that of their father, a sin that leads them into steadily deepening shadow. On the face of it Pierre's plan has a certain logic; in order to take care of Isabel and to avoid betraying their father's memory he will pretend to have married her, and they will live together nominally as man and wife, though actually as brother and sister. But for all the tormented archaic verbiage in which Melville has chosen to tell his story he leaves no doubt that the motive behind the plan is not primarily logical (Pierre himself realizes that it makes no particular sense to spare his mother's feelings on one score by breaking her heart on another), and that the conversion of sister into wife is even less harmless than the earlier conversion of mother into sister. Here is the way Pierre proposes the plan to Isabel, and the way she receives it.

> He held her tremblingly; she bent over toward him; his mouth wet her ear; he whispered it.
> The girl moved not; was done with all her tremblings; leaned closer to him, with an inexpressible strangeness of an intense love, new and inexplicable. Over the face of Pierre there shot a terrible self-revelation; he imprinted burning kisses upon her; pressed hard her hand; would not let go her sweet and awful passiveness.
> Then they changed; they coiled together, and entangledly stood mute.[39]

But whether or not we are to understand that physical incest occurs, *Pierre* is no more primarily a story about this than is *The Fall of the House of Usher*. Primarily, like all the other writings we have considered in this chapter, it is a story in which the overtone of incest is an inevitable accompaniment to the central theme: the mutual attraction of the soulmates, the relationship of the first self with the second self as the Beloved. In this relationship Isabel is mostly passive, but it is a passiveness that, as in the passage just quoted, is not only sweet but awful; like all second selves, even the victimized Madeline Usher, she is the real aggressor, the Stronger. Out of the realm of the unknown and the buried she erupts into Pierre's life; the dark alien intruder into the world of safe comfortable reason; the night-side of the soul into the day-side. She is all these things; the darkness of her hair and eyes, like that of Ligeia's, is deliberately contrasted with the blond hair and blue eyes of the girl she displaces; as the daughter of the French émigrée she is literally half-alien; it is she who — both by coming to Saddle Meadows and by writing the letter — intrudes into Pierre's world, not he into hers.

And not only does she come into his world, captivating him with a strange magnetic power that is repeatedly alluded to; she takes him out of this world, utterly destroying it; takes him with her into hers. I do not mean simply that she takes him out of an environment of wealth into one of poverty, but that she takes him also out of happiness (however shallow a happiness it may have been) into misery, out of sanity into at least the first cousin of madness. For somewhere in Isabel's dark origin is a spot of special darkness, the years that she has lived, as a child, in a madhouse (we never know why), years that have left the stain of their darkness permanently on her mind, a dreaminess and bewilderment, an hysterical hypersensitiveness, a wildness and a mystery. And it is precisely such qualities that his association with Isabel imprints on the mind of Pierre.

This is not to say that she has any conscious wish for his destruction; it is her love for him, and the responsive love she awakens in Pierre, that march them down the path of their destiny to the destruction of each other. Partly it is their economic helplessness that pulls them down, but much more it is their shared sense of guilt, the knowledge that they are living a lie (the lie that they are man and wife), the vain struggle by Pierre to convince himself that this lie is of a more usual and more wholesome order than the one they are really living — in other words, that Isabel is not his sister after all. Both fall into despair, and the situation is not improved when Lucy Tartan, instead of marrying Pierre's successor to the Glendinning fortune, decides to follow them to the city, to live with them and to "serve" them. Here again we have the irony of Lucy, the intended wife, playing the role of sister in the conventional sense, while Isabel, the sister, becomes all the more conscious and jealous of *her* role as the wife. She can barely endure the thought of Lucy's earning money for them when she cannot; she is wounded when Pierre, who has been thinking of Lucy, involuntarily "started a little back from her self-proffering form"; she wishes that she instead of Lucy had the fairness of a good angel instead of her own somber colors; when Pierre at one point embraces her she flings open the door to Lucy's room, so that their visitor may see them locked together. And though it is Lucy who innocently brings the final catastrophe to them all (her brother and suitor follow her to the city and attack Pierre, who slays the latter), it is Isabel who again triumphs at the end, who brings to the prison cell, concealed in her breast, the poison for her Isabel-self and her brother-lover-self, and who in death once more claims him for her own.

"All's o'er, and ye know him not!" came gasping from the wall; and from the fingers of Isabel dropped an empty vial — as it had been a run-out sand-glass — and shivered upon the floor; and her whole form sloped sideways, and she fell upon Pierre's heart, and her long hair ran over him, and arbored him in ebon vines.[40]

This is not the first time Isabel has "arbored" and isolated the object of her guilty love with her long black hair;[41] and the darkness of Isabel, set off against the fairness of Lucy Tartan, constitutes, as we have seen, an important part of the imagery of the novel. But this contrast between the two girls should not be thought to indicate that they are in any way on the same level of importance, or that Pierre is at any time torn between them, like Faustus between his Good and Evil Angels. The relationship between the selves is always a matter of emotion rather than of mathematics, and from the viewpoint of emotion Lucy, while a sweet little thing, stands completely outside the relationship in which this story centers; she is no more an alternative second self of Pierre in his relationship with Isabel than is the fair-haired Rowena an alternative second self of Ligeia's bereaved husband, or the fair-haired Edgar Linton an alternative second self of Cathy Earnshaw. The way to make sure of this is to compare her effect on Pierre with Isabel's. There is nothing in the faintest degree mysterious about what he ever feels for Lucy, and there is nothing very intense; the closest approach to intensity is his remorse about breaking their engagement and, later on, a certain stirring of nostalgia not so much for Lucy as for the sunlit days before the shadow fell upon his life. But even at this point the real force working on Pierre is the caster of the shadow, the intruder from the realm of strangeness and guilt, who long before the scene in the prison cell brought him the poison that, with its forbidden sweetness, has united them in sin, and that unites them now in death.

8

The Second Self In Time

The aspects of the second self that we have thus far taken up, different from one another as they are — diabolical and saintly, death-bringing and life-giving, masculine and feminine, hated and beloved — have in common the fact that their relationship with the first self is exclusively a spatial twofoldness. The essential paradox of the relationship is achieved by the fact that the two participants in it are simultaneously separate from each other in Space and continuous with each other in personality. Now we come to what is surely the strangest form in which this always-strange figure is to be met with: the one in which he retains his separateness from the first self in Space (he must always do this), but adds to it separateness in another dimension, that of Time.

The human mind possesses a number of working concepts by which it regulates its daily affairs, but with which in its more thoughtful moments it is far from satisfied. Thus for everyday purposes it accepts both cause and chance, ignoring the fact that the two ideas completely contradict each other. Another such working concept is that of Time, according to which the events of life stream backward along a latitudinally trisected track, emerging out of an invisible future into the visible present and disappearing again into an invisible but recalled past. Not only are the

[161]

future and the past invisible; they are also, except as anticipations or recollections, nonexistent. All of us live by some such notion, but at intervals through the ages there has been the realization that it meets the test of neither experience nor logic. Fifteen hundred years ago Saint Augustine pointed out that, from the viewpoint of linear Time, since the future is that which does not yet exist and the past is that which no longer exists, and the present (the point where future cascades into past) is a knifeblade of incalculable fineness between them, it is scarcely possible to say that anything exists at all; it has no "time" to do so.[1] The same dissatisfaction has expressed itself in creative literature. The best of this, on the whole, has made its protest directly, without any forays into fantasy. Thus those two monumental works that appear at the beginning of the nineteenth and twentieth centuries respectively, Wordsworth's *Prelude* and Proust's *Remembrance of Things Past,* retain the viewpoint of linear Time even while struggling against it, struggling to blend Then and Now into some more meaningful synthesis.

In this study, however, we are dealing with literature that embodies its intimations in "as-if" fact, in fantasy. And it must be admitted that the attempts thus far made have not yielded very significant results. Doubtless one reason is the enormous difficulty which the human mind encounters in attempting to transcend our ordinary notion of Time, and above all in attempting to visualize this transcendence in terms of living experience. For example there is the simple matter (which C. S. Lewis among others has recognized[2]) of the unresiliency of other-Time, especially past Time. If we go backward in Time there is absolutely no effect that we can exert on the past scene we are visiting; the grass blades cannot bend by the slightest fraction beneath our feet, raindrops cannot be deflected by our bodies but must pass right through us; everything must behave exactly as it behaved then, since it is that Then which, for the duration of our visit, is our Now. Indeed to be entirely consistent we would have to say that it is absolutely impossible for us of the present (or, from the viewpoint of the past, for us of the future) to visit the past without altering it by the very fact of our being there, *unless we suppose that in the past we have already been there,* not only as features of the past scene but as visitants from the present. Du Maurier, the only writer of a Time fantasy I know who takes account of this problem, anticipates the return of Peter Ibbetson and the Duchess of Towers to their childhood by having Mimsey indulge in the fancy of a pair of invisible beings who watch over her and Gogo, Le Prince Charmant and La Fée Tarapatapoum. These, we realize later, are in fact the future selves of Gogo and Mimsey: Peter and the Duchess. But du Maurier still ignores the real issue, which is that Prince

Charming and Tarapatapoum are already there while Peter and the Duchess are still Gogo and Mimsey, and that to be entirely logical he would have to manipulate all *six* people on stage at once.

We could go on multiplying difficulties, but they are not really so relevant as they seem. What such objections overlook is the fact that to begin with they assume the validity of the linear-Time viewpoint, and are therefore bound to find contradictions in any effort to transcend it. To retain the notion of Time and simultaneously to deny its central implication, that only the present is "really real," can never genuinely give voice to our dissatisfaction with the concept of Time. For what this dissatisfaction points toward is, of course, the idea of eternity, in which, if we could get any firm grasp on it with our minds, the movement of events would be only a seeming, and therefore the fact that they had not yet entered the sphere of our experience, the "present," or had already left it, would in no way lessen their reality.

Of such an idea the human mind apparently can never have anything but intimations, yet it is such intimations that the writer of fantasy who wants seriously to respond to our dissatisfaction with Time must follow, throwing mechanical ingenuity to the winds. For after all the Timeless world is not absolutely unfamiliar to us. The human mind, though habitually thinking in terms of Time sequence, also habitually thinks in ways that to some extent violate the rules of Time. On the one hand it sweeps all past things into the grave of the "gone," but on the other hand it is constantly resuscitating these corpses, bringing them forward into the present, often with such warmth and vividness as to push the present moment into the far background of consciousness. Through the faculties of memory and anticipation every mind has had at least a faint taste of an existence beyond Time; if this were not the case there would be no intimations for the writer of fantasy to follow.

Similarly every mind has had a taste of the particular kind of Time-transcendence with which we shall deal in this chapter, in which the selves who are one are not only separate beings but inhabitants of different Time eras. Each of us is accustomed to referring to himself by means of the first-person singular pronoun. But it is unlikely that any reflective person has not sometimes wondered just what he meant by that glibly inclusive *I*. When one raises the question, "Will I, the spiritual I if there is one, live on after death?", exactly which *I* does one mean? The *I* at the instant of death, possibly mutilated beyond recognition, old, decayed, senile, demoralized by long suffering? Certainly not, and yet to what other *I*, since all prior *I*'s have been swallowed up by the past and ceased to exist, is one entitled? Suppose one were allowed one's choice from among all these *I*'s, which would one take? To ask the question is to answer it, for no one *I* would do; to make up the real *I* all *I*'s are necessary.

One's notion of oneself, in other words, is like a vastly more complicated version of Duchamp's painting, *Nude Descending the Stairs,* in which the nude is at no one stage of the descent but at all. Something like this is the picture in man's mind of his own identity: not any stage in the descent of the staircase of life, not the infant on the top step nor the oldster on the bottom, but the whole series of minute alterations that have cooperated in making the journey. Through me, at any moment, speak all the selves that I have been, and only in a less direct way all the selves that I shall be. Nor do I mean this in a figurative sense; I mean that these countless selves literally constitute what I am. From the viewpoint of Time, such a simultaneity of existence is impossible. But by the same token, from the viewpoint of man's idea (conscious or unconscious) of his own identity, Time is impossible.

It is this latter sense of impossibility that lies behind all the pieces of writing we shall consider in this chapter. In them is presented a counter-impossibility, but one that at least gropes toward a notion of identity more comprehensive than that which is restricted to the immediate instant. It is only a groping, for since literature is the most articulate of the arts, and the one most directly expressive of human consciousness, it is the one for which the transgression of Time barriers is by far the hardest. It cannot present its parts all at once as can be done by the Space-medium of painting; it has no way of unfolding, really no way of visualizing anything, save in the form of event, which is itself a temporal phenomenon. Yet there is one kind of event which can contrive both to observe the laws of Time and to defy the laws of Time, to fold Time backward or forward upon itself and yield a glimpse of that sort of Timeless identity of which we all have a sense, faint and confused as it may be. This event is the relationship between the selves in a new form, the first self being presented as the Now-self, the second as the Then-self. It is the latter who is referred to, in the title of this chapter, as the second self in Time.

I have spoken of the difficulty of visualizing such a relationship at all. It is not too much to say that in order to do so the imagination must re-create its universe into one in which every phase of every happening, every stage of every growth, possesses permanent existence. The flow of life must be thought of as having neither beginning nor end, but as resembling the flow of traffic along a busy thoroughfare, that which has gone past the onlooker and that which is approaching him being simply outside the range of his particular view. Really to imagine such a universe rather than merely to say the words is a most formidable task, and the serious efforts that have been made at it in creative literature are few indeed. In this category, for the first time, we are faced with just the reverse of the embarrassment of riches we have encountered up to now. The majority of examples are not full-fledged examples at all, but only approaches of one kind or another to incorporating a true second self in Time.

In one of these approaches, Henry James' *The Jolly Corner*,[3] what we have, instead of a relationship between a Now-self and a Then-self, is a relationship between two Now-selves, but Now-selves who are separate from each other in a way we have not met with in any of the earlier categories. The expansion of Time that occurs is not an expansion of the present to include past or future, but an expansion of the Time that *is,* the upper layer of existence which we normally consider the only one, to include a strange lower layer, contemporaneous with the upper and in all respects the reverse correspondent of it: the Time that *might be.* To use the subjunctive, however, is to deprive the might-be of reality, and in this story the dark underworld layer of existence, in the form of a second self who has lived exactly the life that the first self has not lived (though he might have), comes to life, and for a terrifying moment breaks through the thin integument that separates it from the layer above.

In a way this can be said of all second selves, especially the evil ones. But in this story the element of Time is involved in the protagonist's sense of having, sometime in the past, parted company with the self he might have been, the self who he comes increasingly to feel is no mere figure of speech but an alternative being in a different dimension, whose secret and so different development has at every step kept pace with his own. This protagonist, the middle-aged Spencer Brydon, has returned to his native New York after thirty-three years in Europe, to look over the property on the income from which he has managed to keep it, and America in general, at a comfortable distance. He is initially repelled by all the modernization and mechanization that surround him. Yet at the same time, in turning his attention now to his property, he finds to his surprise that he possesses something of a talent for practical matters, so much so that his friend Alice Staverton suggests (with some irony) that for all these years he has neglected a real gift for business and construction; if instead of living as a dilettante among the fine things of the elder hemisphere he had remained at home and given his native genius its head, he might have been one of the builders of twentieth-century America.

— If he had stayed at home; if he had taken the road not taken.

But in a sense the very fact that it was not taken, that it forms so clearly the alternative of the road that *was* taken, gives it in his mind a kind of substance. And it is a tempting substance to dwell on, this might-have-been self that went by the lower road, for with the self that took the upper one Spencer Brydon, for all his insistence that money is not everything, is far from satisfied. He has lived — he says it jokingly, but it is not entirely a joke — "a selfish frivolous scandalous life," and it is this knowledge that makes him so growingly curious about the more purposeful, powerful life he has just missed living.

It comes over me that I had then [at that moment in the past when the two roads parted] a strange *alter ego* deep down somewhere within me, as the full-grown flower is in the small tight bud, and that I just took the course, I just transferred him to the climate, that blighted him for once and forever.[4]

But in saying this Spencer Brydon is assuming that his second self of the moment of decision was a subjective phenomenon, and that by going abroad he necessarily transferred the other self to an unfriendly climate and destroyed him. What he overlooks in this assumption, but what he is beginning to realize, is that this "just so totally other person," just in his total otherness, would have had a will of his own and would not have concurred in the first self's decision, would have remained here in his own favorable climate, flourished here, and with his hammered hardness of soul hammered his own way to wealth and power, and would be here now. But where, exactly? Where but in the old family house in which they have both been born, the house on the Jolly Corner, about which Brydon's profits from his new commercial project enable him to be sentimental and protective?

More than half playfully entertained at first, this notion takes increasing hold of Brydon's mind. Again and again, arriving at dusk and remaining until the small hours of the morning, he goes alone to the old house, in search of something that is not there but almost-there, and drawing steadily closer. He feels it closer still as he makes his nocturnal prowls from room to room, experiencing a secret pleasure in the excitement of a chase such as no man before has ever undertaken. Nor is it all a one-way chase, for by degrees, especially in the upper rooms, he realizes that in his pursuit, if as yet very unobtrusively, he is also being pursued. At last one night he knows that the preliminaries are over, and that his victim is ready to make a stand.

It is what he has been after, yet it is a little too much what he has been after, and he prowls that night not only with excitement but with a growing reluctance. At last he pauses before the door of an upper room with no other entrance or egress. The door of this room is closed, which in itself is nothing remarkable — if only it were not for his certainty that when last he passed it, fifteen minutes eariier, it was open. He stands on his side of the partition, not touching it, convincing himself that his not doing so is a free and reasonable and even charitable choice. "If you won't then — good. I spare you and I give up. . . . I retire, I renounce — never, on my honour, to try again. So rest for ever — and let me!"[5]

But the covenant between them has been all his own; he has spoken for both, and from behind the door comes no word of confirmation. He turns, makes his way to the staircase and descends, feeling better as he approaches the hallway, but suddenly realizing that the faint light of dawn is filtering straight in through the high fan-tracery of the entrance. For the hinged halves of the inner door, which he has closed on coming in, stand as open as the door above, which he left open, stood closed. And now in the uncertain glimmer he sees it take shape: a man in evening dress, with dangling double eye-glass, but with grizzled head bent and face hidden by raised masking hands, which despite the fact that one of them has lost two of its fingers effectually conceal the lowered features. His other self, Brydon concludes, cannot, dares not, face him. But the very thought, with its flash of triumph, seems to produce a little stir in the figure opposite; the hands open, lower, and Brydon is looking into the face that can only be his own, but that at his first glimpse of it he utterly rejects as his own.

Such an identity fitted his at *no* point, made its alternative monstrous. A thousand times yes, it came upon him nearer now — the face was the face of a stranger. It came upon him nearer now, quite as one of those expanding fantastic images projected by the magic lantern of his childhood; for the stranger, whoever he might be, evil, odious, blatant, vulgar, had advanced as for aggression, and he knew himself give ground. Then harder pressed still, sick with the force of his shock, and falling back as under the hot breath and the roused passion of a life larger than his own, a rage of personality before which his own collapsed, he felt the whole vision turn to darkness and his very feet give way.[6]

Whether this confrontation, when Brydon is awakened from his faint, has constituted a defeat or a victory for him (and in his assumption that it has been the latter there are strong suggestions that it has been the former), the second self in the hallway obviously has many things in common with the second self as Vision of Horror: the unacceptable but undeniable other side of the soul. But in the case of Spencer Brydon this horrifying other side does not appear out of the blue; it is deliberately sought out in the ancestral home because it is known to be there, because thirty-three years earlier it was left there, to go its own way along the other street of Time; it is simultaneously not only both Spencer Brydon and the opposite of Spencer Brydon, but also a past memory and a present reality.

Nevertheless it is true that the second self who appears in *The Jolly Corner* appears as the contemporary of the first self, and that this story therefore does not give us any of that buckling or telescoping of Time which, in collapsing our ordinary concept of it, also dizzyingly enhances it, forces our minds to clutch at the notion of a Time without segmentation, without progression, without temporality.

The second self who appears in stories embodying this latter attack on Time takes either of two main forms. One is the second self from outside the period of the first self's personal life. In such stories we are dealing in one way or another with the phenomenon of palingenesis, the rebirth of a self from the past in the self of the present. The trouble with such an idea for our purposes is that it is very difficult for the first or present self to encounter the alien intruder except in the form of memories, sensations, impulses and the like, which seem at first not to belong to him, but which nevertheless appear within him. As a result what we tend to have in such cases is rather a version of the psychological or subjective second self than a true second self in Time.

Thus in Poe's story, *A Tale of the Ragged Mountains,*[7] the present self, whose name is Bedloe, has a strange visionary experience while walking in the Ragged Mountains of Virginia. All at once he hears the beating of a drum; a half-naked man dashes past him, pursued by a hyena; he sits in the shade of a tree, which proves to be a palm tree. He is in India, and suddenly becomes involved in a wild melee with natives, is struck in the temple by a poisoned arrow and is killed. Yet he rises from his own corpse and returns home, where he learns that many years earlier, before his own birth, a British officer named Oldeb, exactly resembling the present Bedloe in features, was killed at Calcutta in exactly this fashion; that Bedloe has not only visualized but in every detail lived through the events of Oldeb's death without ever having heard before of the latter's existence. Here Bedloe would appear to be the first self and Oldeb the second.[8] But in fact Bedloe never encounters Oldeb; he merely finds himself increasingly "possessed" by the earlier figure, who, however, has no objective existence within the story. A true second self can never merely repeat himself in a counterpart from another Time-segment; he must in his own living person come forward from the past or backward from the future to meet the first self of the present.

In Walter de la Mare's novel, *The Return,*[9] we get a closer approach to this sort of meeting. Lawford, the first self, a mild, unimaginative man of middle age, wanders one day through a cemetery, on the outskirts of which he seems to have a heart attack, and in his weakness to become possessed by the soul of someone buried there: one Nicholas Sabathier, a seventeenth-century French émigré, who (so the weathered inscription says) died by his own hand. Lawford retains his own consciousness and sense of identity, though his tastes and the workings of his mind are influenced by those of the revenant. The most direct change brought about in him, however, is not mental but physical, to reveal which de la Mare takes advantage of that device which has had such varied use in the literature of the second self, the mirror. As Lawford, arriving home from the cemetery, goes upstairs to shave, he glances at himself in the mirror; and to his inexpressible astonishment and horror sees instead of his own broadish blond-haired countenance a completely unfamiliar face, long and swarthy and saturnine, with black hair and slanted eyes: the Latin face of the intruder, the possessor.

Unlike most stories of possession, then, *The Return* does involve for the moment a sort of meeting between the selves, as the second self from the past stares back at the first self of the present. But it is still not a real meeting. Lawford perceives with shock the changes wrought on him by Sabathier, but despite these changes he remains Lawford; there is never a real twoness, but only a somewhat altered and confused oneness.

In only one of the writings that I know in which the second self belongs to a period of Time outside that of the first self's life is there a genuine second self in the sense in which I am using the term in this study, both identical with and separate from the first. This is another of the "ghostly tales" of Henry James, the remarkable fragmentary novel called *The Sense of the Past*,[10] out of which James, in his own words, "filched" the idea for *The Jolly Corner*.[11] But in fact the two stories are very different from each other. The situation of the hero, Ralph Pendrel, is exactly the reverse of Spencer Brydon's. Instead of the middle-aged American who has spent most of his life abroad we have here the young American who has never been abroad at all, though he has dearly longed to go, and though his temperament has so peculiarly fitted him to go. For he has by instinct an extraordinarily vivid sense of the Old World, the sense of the past, and even has written a little book about it.

Suddenly two events occur which give his sense of the past the chance to indulge itself. One is the death of his invalid mother, setting him free to travel; the other is the death of an elderly relative in England, who has been impressed with the young man's book and has bequeathed to him the old family house, Number Nine Mansfield Square, London.

Number Nine Mansfield Square is an old house not only in years but also in preference. It has its real roots in the past, and seems to face the future with hostile reserve; it is therefore Ralph's task, *as* its future, to make it "speak" to him. But as he visits it and roams through its rooms and hallways, he wonders if such an idea does not reverse the process that must take place: if it is not the house that must make *him* speak, not by coming forward into his present but by demanding that he go backward into *its* present, to hear in his presently living ear "the very tick of the old stopped clocks." It is not for him to awaken the old ghosts, he feels. "It was for the old ghosts to take him for one of themselves."

And so the old ghosts do, in perhaps the most extraordinary Time fantasy (or rather anti-Time fantasy) in fiction, in which Ralph Pendrel, entering through a door which on the outside belongs to his own day, finds himself on the inside in the world of 1820, paying his initial visit to his cousin and betrothed, Molly Midmore. But of special interest to us is what immediately precedes this visit and makes it possible. For the present Ralph Pendrel's penetration into the past is only part of a reciprocal agreement, the other half consisting of the penetration by a past Ralph Pendrel into the present. This past Ralph Pendrel is a young man of exactly the same age as the present one (meaning that in the 1820s out of which he has stepped, he *was,* and in stepping out he continues to be, the same age), of exactly the same appearance, and also newly arrived in London: the protagonist's second self of nearly a century before.

The encounter between the two takes place during one of the first self's lonely nocturnal prowls through his newly acquired home. He looks over the portraits of the dead that follow him with their painted eyes, and finds himself particularly struck with one, a portrait remarkable for the fact that its subject is shown with his back turned, and so skillfully that more and more, as the present Ralph studies the work, he gets the feeling that it has *just* been turned; that this turning away takes place each time Ralph's footsteps approach, and lasts only for as long as he is there in the room.

Increasingly this sense grows upon Ralph, and one gloomy evening, as dusk thickens into darkness, and he strikes a match to light his candle, he finds his hand shaking with excitement. Once more he approaches the room that holds the painting, and seems to catch, there ahead of him through the doorway, the reflection of his candleflame on some polished surface — except that the light he sees, he realizes suddenly, comes not *through* the doorway but from *within* the doorway, where someone is standing, facing him. He raises his candle to be sure, and the figure in the doorway, the figure in the portrait that is no longer in the portrait, raises its own in an answering movement, and they stand gazing at each other almost as though with brandished weapons.

He was staring at the answer to the riddle that had been his obsession, but this answer was a wonder of wonders. The young man above the mantel, the young man brown-haired, pale, erect, with the high-collared dark blue coat, the young man revealed, responsible, conscious, quite shining out of the darkness, presented him the face he had prayed to reward his vigil; but the face — miracle of miracles, yes — confounded him as his own.[12]

Unfortunately for our purposes, the Ralph Pendrel of the portrait drops out of the story almost as soon as he enters it; we never see him again, but only hear about him, and only briefly. The upshot of the encounter is that the present Ralph pays a visit to the American ambassador, and reveals not only the fact of the meeting, but the further fact that strictly speaking he is no longer himself; he is someone else, while someone else is he. For his earlier self and he have agreed to take advantage of their resemblance to each other in order to exchange identities: the other to come forward into the present, Ralph to go backward into the past. Already the first part of the exchange has been accomplished; the earlier Ralph Pendrel has managed to "come over," to such an extent that the two of them — young men now of the same age, for all the fact that one lived nearly a century before the other — have driven together to the Ambassador's, and the man of 1820 is waiting downstairs in the cab. But when the first-self Ralph and the Ambassador go down, the second self is gone, having apparently become impatient and walked off into the future-become-present. With the Ambassador the first-self Ralph returns to Number Nine Mansfield Square, mounts the steps with the whole world he has thus far known sinking out of existence below him, and enters through the door into a world that had ceased to be before he himself was born.

Certainly *The Sense of the Past* gives us a second self and presents him in a most dramatically effective fashion. The trouble with him *as* a second self is that even if the mechanics of the plot had not required his disappearance, it seems unlikely that James would have attempted to do anything further with the relationship between the two Ralph Pendrels. The idea of a basic identity that spans separate lifetimes is simple enough to put into words, but not to visualize in fact. Strain our imagination as we will, the elder Ralph Pendrel for us has already lived and died as an independent being. Imaginatively we can bring him to life again, even bring him forward into a later era; but to give him the same unity-in-separation with the later Ralph Pendrel that we have seen established between the selves in earlier chapters seems almost impossible.

More readily imaginable is the second self who represents a certain stage of development, but not the present stage, *within* the first self's own lifetime: either a stage not yet reached, in which case he is known or felt as an anticipation, or a stage already experienced, in which case he is consciously or unconsciously recognized by memory. Naturally the self one will be tends to be a less vivid image than the self one has been. In Hawthorne's little tale, *The Prophetic Pictures,*[13] we have a case in point. Here, as in *The Sense of the Past* and *The Picture of Dorian Gray,* we find that old device of Gothic Romance: the portrait that is more than a mere reproduction of its subject and therefore possesses a life of its own. Walter Ludlow and his fiancée Elinor have their portraits painted by an artist who has the faculty of looking not only upon his subject's features, but also into their minds and hearts, and thus seeing not only what they are at the moment, but also what they will be. In the pictures as they are finished the features are entirely accurate, but the expressions are most unlike their accustomed ones; they are expressions that cause wonder to their acquaintances and deep uneasiness to themselves, for on Elinor's face is a look of anguished terror, on Walter's one of dark wild menace. Walter and Elinor are married, and time wears on, until one day the painter visits the Ludlows and finds them standing before the portraits, wearing the same expressions that the painter has summoned out of the shrouded future into "that narrow strip of sunlight, which we call Now." By the sight of his own ferocity mirrored before him Walter is kindled to action; he draws a knife to plunge it into Elinor's breast, while she sinks beside him in horror, and their resemblance to their painted selves is at this instant complete. Thus the destiny which the pictures have prophesied is carried out, and does not require the consummation of the murder, which the painter manages to prevent.

But the pictures of this story, for all their prophetic expressions, remain only pictures; they show none of the living purposiveness that marks the picture of Dorian Gray or that of the earlier Ralph Pendrel. In a play by Ferdinand Raimund, *The Spendthrift,*[14] we have a figure that similarly represents a warning of future developments in the protagonist's career, but one that possesses independent objective existence. *The Spendthrift* is a charming fairy tale in modern dress, in which the fairy

Cheristane, on a mission to earth, has fallen in love with the young hero, Julius Flotwell, and enormously enriched him. Worried, however, by his lavish and headstrong generosity, she arranges a warning of the disaster which his future holds in store for him.

It is the nature of this warning, rather than the way in which Flotwell is eventually saved, that is of interest to us. For as Flotwell emerges from his castle one day he is confronted by a Beggar, somewhat like the Beggar of Strindberg's play but much older than the protagonist; a man whom Flotwell seems to have seen somewhere before but cannot place, who looks as though he wanted to sing the funeral song of Flotwell's happiness. Three times the Beggar appears to the young man; and then all at once Flotwell is no longer a young man; twenty years have passed; his fortune and castle are lost as were those of the Beggar before him; and we see him sitting before what was once his own castle, in exactly the same spot where the Beggar has sat in the earlier scene, in all respects exactly resembling the Beggar.

In other words, what we appear to have here is the bringing together on stage, in living relationship with each other, of two separate phases of a single life. But it all proves to have been only an appearance. The Beggar of the earlier part of the play, presumably the Flotwell of the future who has invaded the present as the second self of the younger Flotwell, proves in fact to have been Azur, a spirit in disguise, delegated by Cheristane to save her young protégé from the consequences of his spendthrift behavior. Instead of a true second self, therefore, we have merely one of the "mistakes" that have been discussed in Chapter 1, in this case one of the objective kind.

But the self that one will become, as I have said, is always less easily visualized than the self one has already been; not in an earlier existence, but in this one. In Heine's moving little poem, *Silent is the Night,*[15] the poet visits again, in the silence of night, the house where his sweetheart once lived. She is no longer there; she has long since left this city of quiet streets and unhappy memories; yet someone is there: a man who stands and stares upward at the deserted house, and who wrings his hands in anguish. The moon falls on the other's face, and in horror the poet recognizes his own; not that of his remembering first self, but that of his remembered second self become for the moment a presence and not a mere memory, the pale, romantic, posturing mooncalf of old who mocks his old sorrow by aping the gestures of it.

A far fuller and more ingenious treatment of the idea of a second self out of (or rather in this case visited in) the past is found in a novel that has already been discussed in another connection, du Maurier's *Peter Ibbetson*. This story is unique in the literature of the second self in that it contains two quite separate but equally unmistakable second selves, of different kinds and sexes, both sharing identity with the same first self, Peter Ibbetson. The second self as the Beloved, Mimsey Seraskier who becomes the Duchess of Towers, we have discussed in the last chapter. The other second self of Peter, the second self in Time, is little Gogo Pasquier: not the Gogo whom we meet in the first part of the book, for he is then, as the character whose viewpoint we share, the first self; but rather the unchanged Gogo whom the matured Gogo, now Peter Ibbetson, encounters in his strange revisits to the scenes where as first self he once lived, but where as second self in Time he forever lives.

This is without doubt the main artistic achievement of the novel. The fact that Peter's return to the Gogo-World can take place only in dream (Peter's dream, not Gogo's) in no way diminishes its convincingness, for from the moment this dreaming begins we have it impressed on us that there is nothing in the least unreal about it. Not only do Peter and the Duchess meet in such dreams, but later in waking life they are able to discuss such meetings, just as in dreams they are able to tell each other of things they will do next day in waking life. Furthermore, the return of the adult Peter to the Gogo-world is beautifully prepared for, early in the book, while we are still *in* the Gogo-world, by hints later explained for us when we revisit this world with Peter. These hints I have already spoken of: the half-joking fancies of little Mimsey about Prince Charming and the Fairy Tarapatapoum; only fancies, of course; and yet many years later, as we look on the children from outside with the grown-up Peter, we realize that the invisible watchers *were* there then because they *are* there now; and that their true names are Peter Ibbetson and the Duchess of Towers. Once the Peter Ibbetson who does not yet exist from the Gogo-viewpoint, looking over the garden wall at the Gogo Pasquier who has long since ceased to exist from the Peter-viewpoint, leans down and puts his hand to the nose of his long-dead dog Medor, which whimpers in its sleep; whereupon Mimsey says to Gogo: *"C'est le Prince Charmant qui lui chatouielle le bout du nez."* [16]

It is chiefly in these revisits and the careful preparation for them that *Peter Ibbetson,* for all its sentimentalism and frequent sloppy craftsmanship, is such a remarkable imaginative feat. It voices a universal hunger, to double back upon one's earlier life in a way more intimate than by mere memories, to cheat if only for a little the remorseless progress to decay and dissolution; and it visualizes the satisfaction of this hunger more successfully than any other piece of writing I know. There is no mere momentary glimpse of the past self, but a proximity and even an association (if a one-sided one) that go on for many years. Nor does the fact that after the death of his Beloved the Peter Ibbetson of dream becomes old and worn and gray, like the Peter Ibbetson of the prison cell, in any way signify the intrusion of Time into the world of Time-transcendence; to the contrary it widens Peter's perspective, enables him to see, as a unity rather than as a sequence, the whole span of his life. Making his way over the dream-fields to the Mare d'Auteuil of long ago he inspects the famous brand-new fortifications that have been put up with confidence to keep the French capital of 1840 intact; and he, the Peter Ibbetson of 1890, "smiled to think how little those brick and granite walls would avail to keep the Germans out of Paris thirty years later (twenty years ago)."[17] Time, the Mary Seraskier who has come back from the dead explains to him, has no real meaning; "there is so little difference, *là-bas*, between a year and a day"; but these are only words; what is much more effective is the situation in which she speaks them; for there are Peter Ibbetson, the elderly criminal lunatic of the "present," and Mary Seraskier of the day of her death years before, together beside the Mare d'Auteuil of half a century before that.

It is this meeting, as we saw in the last chapter, that reconciles Peter Ibbetson to separation from his Beloved; but what makes this reconcilement possible is another effect which their meeting, and parting again, have upon him: the final confirmation of his long-growing sense of a disbelief in Time. It simply will not "wash," and as Saint Augustine demonstrates the fact with logic, so Peter Ibbetson, as he approaches what from the Time viewpoint will be his end, demonstrates it with a series of playful juxtapositions. The Duchess of Towers never returns to the Mare d'Auteuil, but she has left her gloves behind, and he lays them side by side, palms upward, on the bench, and watches the youthful Madame Seraskier whom he worshipped come sometimes to the water's edge and sit (though without ever flattening them) upon the gloves of her middle-aged daughter. He watches the Pasquier family; loves his beautiful mother, no longer as his mother but now, himself more than twice her age, as his own daughter; loves her tall, handsome husband, who slings stones into the water and sings with a divine voice, as he might love his own son; loves them both for having presented him with so singularly comely a grandson: the little Gogo Pasquier who both was and is himself.

And yet for all its remarkable achievement in the telescoping of Time, Peter Ibbetson's encounter with his earlier self leaves one thing wanting, and that is the duality of reciprocity. For except to the extent that Mimsey's notion of Le Prince Charmant transmits itself to Gogo, the experience is entirely one-sided. It is only Peter and the Duchess who are "dreaming true," that is, have transcended the world of Time; all the people of the past whom they visit, including Gogo, are awake only in the Time world, that is, in their *present*. Therefore, though they are visible to the visitors from their future, the latter remain always invisible to them; invisible, inaudible, and intangible. Peter is acutely aware of Gogo, but Gogo is almost heartlessly unaware of Peter; looks through him, throws a snowball through him, walks or runs through him at will.

To produce a real encounter between the selves of different Time periods, in other words, there must be not only the spanning of Time that brings them together, but also the phenomenon of *mutual impact*. The difficulty of achieving such an impact I have already pointed out. That the later self, especially when he is the viewpoint character, should be affected by the earlier self is conceivable enough, for the later self at least appears to be having his experience for the first time, and therefore all things seem possible. But that the earlier self should be affected by the later self, in however minute a way, means a tampering with something which has already taken place; something which, from the Time viewpoint, is "fixed" for all ages to come. It is just from this difficulty, of any real intervention by present or future in the events of the past, that fiction about self-meeting in Time tends to shy away.

Perhaps the most famous example of such intervention comes not from creative literature itself but from the autobiographical account of a creative writer. This is the episode in *Dichtung und Wahrheit*[18] in which Goethe tells of what happened to him after one of his visits to Fredrike Brion.

In such oppression and confusion I nevertheless could not keep from seeing Fredrike again. They were painful days, the remembrance of which has not remained with me. When I extended my hand to her from horseback, tears stood in her eyes, and I was very sick at heart. Now I rode on the footpath towards Drusenheim, and there I experienced the most extraordinary presentiment. I saw, not with the eyes of the body but with those of the spirit, my own self returning again on horseback along the same path, and indeed in clothes such as I had never worn: they were light grey with some gold. As soon as I had aroused myself from this dream, the shape had entirely disappeared. Nevertheless it is strange that eight years later, in the same clothes which I had seen in my dream, and which I wore not by choice but by chance, I found myself on the same path, going again to meet Fredrike.[19]

Though very little is made of the episode by Goethe, it contributes to the idea of self-encounter in Time two features that we have not met with in any of the examples we have yet studied. One is the fact that, as must inevitably happen to one living in Time-sequence, the first self shifts his role from the younger self leaving Fredrike to the elder self returning to Fredrike, the elder self who eight years earlier was the second self; while the second self on the later occasion, though not met in Goethe's account but only recalled, is (or would be if he appeared) the younger self. The other feature is the fact that, unlike the relationship between Peter Ibbetson and Gogo Pasquier, a definite effect is exerted by each of these Goethes upon the counterpart-Goethe, especially by the elder man upon the younger, who from the viewpoint of the elder has already been and therefore cannot be affected, living as he does in the fixed intactness of the past.

This is not an example from creative literature, nor is there enough done with it to make it of much significance for our purpose. It can serve, however, as the taking-off point for a modern novel which constitutes, so far as I know, the only fictional effort to take full account of the necessary twofoldness of a self-meeting in Time: necessarily consisting in *two* such meetings which, just as the two selves who meet are at the same time one self, must be at the same time *one* meeting; and necessarily entailing a shift of first-selfhood from younger self to elder as the former grows into the latter.

The work in question is Osbert Sitwell's *The Man Who Lost Himself*,[20] the title of which (abandoned because another work had already used it) was originally to have been *The Man Who Found Himself*. It tells the story of Tristram Orlander, a young Irish writer who seems to have had showered on him all the gifts of the gods but one, that of wealth or of the capacity for accumulating it. This comparative poverty, always a worry, becomes a disaster when all at once he falls in love with someone he has known for years as an intimate friend and by whom he has never until now been stirred, the beauteous and emancipated Ursula Rypton. To Lady Ursula this change is most unwelcome; Tristram is valued as a friend, but because of his lack of means he is impossible as a suitor and becomes a positive menace when she finds that, despite all her intentions to the contrary, she is beginning to return his love. Fear makes her cruel, and without a word of warning to Tristram she agrees to marry a financially more eligible suitor.

The breakdown in Tristram's health that follows this blow forces him to go abroad, and after traveling for a while in Spain he settles down in Granada. It proves to be not exactly a cheerful town for him. For one thing, there is a pair of beggars who constantly accost him, a black-clad

Frenchwoman leading by the hand a little emaciated boy ("Merely to look at him, was to suffer"), murmuring to herself as well as to others of the cruelty of this land and of this old, dead, terrible town in which her destiny has placed her. For another thing he is worried and dejected by his expenditures; bitterly he reflects that "if he had only chosen to write badly and vulgarly, he would by now be rich, surrounded by every kind of luxury, universally beloved and respected. His whole life would have been different." [21]

But if Granada does not cheer Tristram Orlander, it holds him with peculiar power, despite the inanities of the tourists, the faked local color, the offensiveness of such monuments of vulgarity as the Boabdil Palace Hotel, with its pretentiously painted concierge's booth in the lobby, out of which the torso of a shifty-eyed porter pops into view from time to time, jerky and grotesque as a figure of Punch. With the heat of summer the tourists depart, but Tristram stays on. The heat becomes insupportable, and, joining forces with it, a black fog broods close in the breezeless air, fortifying everything within Tristram that is in tune with darkness. One night he dreams that he is walking in a valley, the puppet-like concierge from the Boabdil Palace Hotel running along in front of him, beckoning him forward. The Frenchwoman with her son appears, whereupon the concierge, dancing up to Tristram, bids him particularly to notice the child, never to forget the child. As Tristram studies the child's features, the shrouded figure of Ursula turns her head toward him, parting her veil as though to kiss him, her lovely face approaching him, but turning as it comes into a death's head, a skull with a lipless and snarling grin. He turns to run, but the Frenchwoman's child blocks his way: the emaciated child who suddenly grows up and becomes the concierge, dressed in the latter's uniform.

As he awakes and lies there in the black silence, it comes over him how utterly he has wasted his life, giving it up to useless things like the quest for truth or the pursuit of beauty, when he could so easily have bent his talents to the things that mattered: happiness, wealth, success, the world's respect and adulation. Like a drowning man he sees his whole career pass before him, and with especial vividness he sees the image of the Ursula he would have won instead of lost — had he, like Spencer Brydon, not failed to take the road not taken.

Next day he finds himself intolerably lonely, and goes to the Hotel Boabdil to find out if anyone he knows is staying there. He will think of some fictitious name, and when the owner of it proves not to be there he will ask to look at the list of guests in order to make sure. He approaches the concierge, but is distracted by hearing the latter speak to him in exactly the voice of his dream. He has the dizzied sense of having been through all this before, though he cannot recall when. Nor can he recall the name he has invented, and therefore asks for the one name he is sure cannot be on the register: his own. To his astonishment the concierge, smiling almost as though in readiness, replies in the affirmative, darts ahead down a passage to the lobby of a private suite, knocks at the inner door and throws it open, and disappears. A voice from within bids him enter, and Tristram, going in, finds himself face to face with an elderly, bearded stranger who has put down a book and rises now to meet his young visitor. The stranger's voice sounds in Tristram's ears as one he has heard before, indeed heard constantly, every day. And now he looks full into the bearded face, and the world reels around him.

It was then, only then, that the feeling that he had indeed come in contact with this man before, firmly established itself as the truth: only then that he recognized in this elderly, elegant figure — his own figure; in the handsome, lined face, rather spoilt by the fleshy pouches sagging beneath the eyes, his own face; in the hard, stubborn, insensitive old mouth — his own mouth; in the dead, cold eyes, his own eyes and himself. In those eyes, which matched though they distorted, his own, in those eyes into which he was compelled to stare, so that he could not even make any movement of escape, nor any effort at pretence, was to be seen, in spite of their frigid suavity, a hatred at once intimate and intense. And, during the words that had been spoken, Tristram, too, had felt this same bitter personal antagonism that he read there opposite him. At this very moment, he could have flung himself on this jaunty, old figure, killed him then and there, such was the force of this almost physical enmity. Indeed, the elder man appeared to understand what emotion was at work, for he stepped back suddenly, and put up his hands as though to shield his head. "We shall meet later," he said. And this was the last thing that Tristram remembered. [22]

He comes to himself lying on the floor of the hotel lobby, the concierge bending over him, telling him that he fainted while attempting to ask for someone. The experience seems to have had no ill effect on him. He returns to London and plunges again into life and work. These, however, are altogether different from the life and work of his earlier years. His devoted friends and his own brilliant talents are all thrown aside; he writes no more of the difficult and demanding literature that has entranced his small audience. Instead there flows from his hand, year after year, a a torrent of "muddy fiction," imitative, empty, undistinguished, and increasingly welcome to the wider public that has hitherto ignored him. In the words of one critic, "Mr. Orlander has found himself at last." He becomes wealthy and marries a wealthy woman; he is knighted; he is the hero of the lending libraries and for forty years remains the darling of the British public.

Then, in Tristram's old age, comes another and equally unpredictable change. He becomes dissatisfied with his success, is troubled with nerves and insomnia. He sees again some of his old friends; he looks up Ursula, now a withered and ancient walking corpse, and is outraged at the thought that this is the woman who once broke and cast away his genius. "The tree was beginning to bear blossom once more, but just before the first frost was due. But as he looked back down the years, and saw how, as a young man, he had thrown away his gifts, a great hatred for that other, younger self entered into him."[23]

He is working on a novel that is to be his masterpiece and redeem him as an artist, but somehow it will not shape itself in his hands. He becomes ill and revisits Granada, some inner censorship having apparently erased all memory of the incident at the Hotel Boabdil. Indeed it is to this same pretentious pseudo-palace that he goes. His suite is comfortable, and equipped with a special edition of his own Spanish romances. On the second evening of his stay he finds beneath these vacuous books a copy of one of his earliest and best, *Ring Down;* opening it he becomes so absorbed in this work that seems now so far from him that he loses all track of time. All at once there comes an abrupt rapping at his door, and he hears his voice, as though from a long way off, shout, "Come in." The door is thrown open, and the first person to enter is the concierge, and with a sensation of nausea Tristram recognizes him: the whining, piteous, emaciated beggar-son of the French beggar-woman, the child grown up and clad in the concierge's uniform. The concierge, announcing, "The gentleman to see you, sir," retires, and a stranger advances into the light.

But who could be coming to see him at this hour, and in this place? Who could it be? He looked up, and saw standing there a tall, young figure, his gold hair shining under the light, the narrowing, upward-slanting and deep blue eyes fixed upon his and flashing out a whole fire of contempt and hatred; a tall young figure, every line instinct with beauty, pride and genius. The prosperous, famous, elderly man sat there not stirring, without a movement, though the book he had been reading fell from his hand with a clatter down upon the floor; sat there, gazing at this apparition. What actually took place, who will ever know? But certainly into those moments was concentrated a lifetime of terror and mystery, and of a growing materialism that had been shattered at a blow. The past came toward him as might a charging bull, in one overwhelming rush. And it was in that familiar welter of years and deeds that Tristram Orlander went down; went down, perhaps, too, in circumstances which he, in his young days, would have been the only writer to understand and appreciate. [24]

In the eyes of the outside world at least there is one major difference between this episode and the one that preceded it nearly a half-century before. On the second occasion there is no talk of the caller's having fainted in the hall. To the contrary, the concierge and other people as well testify to the fact that they saw the young visitor enter the old novelist's suite just before the latter fell dead of a stroke, but did not see him leave again. This, of course, raises the question of just how the two meetings which are really one could differ from each other at all, let alone in so obvious a way. With this question we get no help, and one suspects that the problem has not been thought through. Nevertheless *The Man Who Lost Himself* remains the one work of creative literature I am familiar with that takes account of, and attempts to render in fictional form, the necessary twofoldness of the self-encounter in Time.

True, it is only an encounter, as brief as that of Spencer Brydon with his counterpart of the massive income and the mutilated hand. By the time of the later meeting we as readers know both the younger Tristram and the elder, but they know each other only by anticipation or memory, along with instinctive, unreasoning mutual hatred. In none of the writings that we have taken up in this chapter is there the developed relationship that we have found in the earlier categories, the cases of spatial but not temporal twofoldness. And perhaps it is too much to expect that there should be. To deal with any sort of paradox in fiction — that is, to embody it in imagined experience — is a difficult task enough; but to deal with this particular paradox, the simultaneous independence and identity of the Now and the Then, puts an enormous strain on the mind of the artist, requires of him that he live at once in two worlds, the latter of which is utterly inconceivable to the former: the worlds of Time and of Beyond-Time. Perhaps the best we can expect, this side of madness or the grave, is glimpses of the latter, fleeting and fragmentary and always frankly partaking of the supernatural rather than merely balancing on the edge of it as in most of the earlier examples we have studied. To the self-meetings in Time a certain amount of artificiality, even of trickery, attaches itself as it does not to the self-meetings that confine themselves to Space.

I do not believe, however, that these differences necessarily indicate that the second self in Time is any less genuine or important an aspect of the second self than the others. They arise from the peculiar difficulties which this aspect presents to both writer and reader. And as we turn now to the question of what the second self means, we shall discover to what extent such difficulties, of seeing with any clarity this face that looks at us out of a past or future that is also the present, make it in one respect, if the most elusive of the faces, the most informative and even the most representative of all.

9

The Meaning of the Second Self

The main purpose of this work has been not to interpret the second self in psychological or any other terms, but to accomplish the essential preliminary to such an interpretation: that of understanding what he is and of becoming familiar with him in the various forms in which he has appeared.

What remains is to fit together the discoveries that we have made, to try to see the second self as a coherent whole. To do so naturally takes us into the question of how it is possible that a single figure should wear so many and such different faces, should be not only the Pursuer who drives but the Tempter who entices and the Horror who chills the blood, should be malignant devil and benignant saint and bewitching enchantress, should be both death-dealing and life-bringing, male and female, Now and Then. And this question takes us into another, the question of what he means; of why so strange and generally sinister a creature, even at his simplest so hard to conceive of, should have come into existence in the first place, and should for so long have played such an important role in the imaginative products of the human mind.

This is not the first time such questions have been asked; indeed the problem of meaning is the one on which most of the few works that have been written on the subject have concentrated. Before undertaking any analysis, therefore, let us notice briefly what main theories have thus far been advanced.

The earliest work I know that deals specifically with the second self is Max Dessoir's *The Double-I*.[1] Actually this has little bearing on our subject, since what Dessoir is interested in is primarily the second self or *Unterbewusstsein* (lower consciousness) of experimental psychology, a purely subjective phenomenon. The reason for mentioning it is that Dessoir does at one point refer to the second self of creative literature, explaining the emergence of this make-believe second self, out of what he considers to be the real one (the subpersonality or *condition seconde* that lies below the threshold of consciousness), as due to the fact "that we incline to convert all 'inward' into an 'outward' ";[2] and drawing a parallel in this respect, very similar to that drawn by Theseus in *A Midsummer Night's Dream,* between the author (*Dichter*), the dreamer, the neurotic, and the hypnotic. But obviously this sort of explanation does not take us very far toward what we are after. It is possible that an author may be these other things as well as being an author, but in his role of author he is quite distinct from them, and he most certainly does not "live with his own images as with actual persons,"[3] as Dessoir holds. Like anyone else, he experiences to one degree or another the sense of an inward division or twofoldness, but this is not at all the same thing as self-encounter; and to say that the literature of the second self is an imaginative elaboration of the sense of inward twofoldness is merely to restate the problem in other terms. Why does the artist choose to make such an imaginative elaboration, to convert this particular inward into an outward, and why has he done so with such remarkable frequency?

An answer of sorts is offered by Emil Lucka in *Doublings of the I*,[4] a study which is more psychological than literary, but which does make specific reference to literary examples, including *William Wilson, The Picture of Dorian Gray,* and the Gottfried von Strassburg version of *Tristan and Iseult.* In any moral person, Lucka holds, there is bound to be a certain *Zwiespalt* or discord between the "empirical I" of factual experience, that is, the "I" he has found himself to be, and the "pure I" representing his idea of moral perfection; and there is bound also to be a strong sense of guilt at the degree to which the lower will of the former has been able to prevail against the ethical aspiration of the latter.

Such a person tends to embody the empirical "I" or lower self in the image of his *Doppelgänger*,[5] a figure of shame and fear, as well as a living admonition: To thine own self be true. It is the "conditioned" or unfree part of the psyche, the part which can be recognized only by its own moral consciousness, that is personified in the second self, the hated alien power that, as though from without, negates the autonomous (ethical) will, in the form of a symbol of one's own self-enslavement, the ape in the soul of man. And as it is with the individual, so with the race. "The outstanding personification of individual fear is the *Doppelgänger;* the personification of human fear is the Devil."[6] But just what relationship fear has to guilt (they are quite different emotions), what it is fear of, and why either fear or guilt should stimulate the artist to create the figure of the second self: these are questions that are neither answered nor asked.

A far more searching and detailed work, without much doubt the most important that has concentrated specifically on the subject of the second self, is Otto Rank's monograph, *The Double*.[7] Though written by a psychoanalyst and dealing centrally with the psychogenic origin of the second self, Rank's work is of special interest to us because it uses for its main evidence not psychoanalytical case histories but examples from creative literature and legendary-traditional material, to which it applies the theories of Freud and others. Rank stresses particularly what he finds to be the unfailing ambivalence of the second-self figure: the interweaving, in all treatments of him, of the themes of love and death, as in the story of Dorian Gray, who first loves his own portrait, but as the latter grows old and ugly gradually turns to hatred of it, shifting the love to his own ageless person. In all cases, in other words, an erotic component is concealed within the first self's hatred for the second, eroticism which is really auto-eroticism, infantile narcissism carried forward into adult life. Heroes of *Doppelgänger*-stories, like the authors who create them, are capable of love only for themselves — and by this Rank means not a mere self-cherishing but a sexual attachment. But this self-love is a secret and guilty love, and hence one that tends to disguise itself in a murderous hate; that is, to shift its burden of guilt to another, diabolical "I," a creature threatening death and in turn meriting death.

This is the first stage of Rank's argument, really a theory in itself. To it he adds a second and far more complicated theory, which attempts to explain the emergence of a genuine death-wish toward the second self out of the original, and always central, motivation of auto-eroticism. Rejection or evasion of the guilt is never by itself an adequate explanation for the murderous hate, for the narcissism is always stronger than either fear of blame or stirring of conscience, much too strong to permit the obliteration of the beloved "I" for anything but selfish reasons. And the selfish reason that makes this obliteration so often the climax of the relationship between the selves is, strangely enough, just the fact of self-love: love, however, fixed on the self in a certain stage of its development, the stage of youth and beauty which enchants Dorian Gray. The inevitable process of decay, which will rob him of the object of his love, is unbearable to him, and can be forestalled only by suicide. But to the true narcissist, slaying the treasured self is as unthinkable as watching the decay is unbearable. Hence, the preliminary condition of suicide is the splitting off from the "I" of a second self that threatens the first self and must in self-protection be destroyed.[8]

Thus Rank offers not one answer to the problem but two, reconcilable with each other in the sense that the second supplements the first, but by no means identical with each other. The fact is interesting to note, because even this twofold argument is not his final word on the subject. In a much later essay, *The Double as Immortal Self*,[9] he drops the idea of guilt-evasion and devotes himself to a further development of the idea of the death-wish, and in the course of doing so swings all the way from the Freudian view, which sees the mainspring of the human soul as repressed sexual desire, to the Jungian view, which sees it as the desire for rebirth.[10] Like Jung, Rank here takes the position that modern man has deceived himself in supposing that he is a purely rational being, and in rejecting the "irrational life forces" of his primitive ancestors, among which was the need for an assurance of survival beyond physical death. The result of this need, originally, was the emergence of the idea of the second self, symbol for primitive and archaic man of the *ka*, the self that will survive, the immortal soul. Such was the "animated inanimate duplicate" like the shadow or mirror image;[11] such also, says Rank, turning to a body of evidence not touched on in his earlier work,[12] was the Twin, "the earliest personification of the Double-soul."

The twin-traditions are particularly important as the transitional link between the primitive conception of the Double as immortal self and its creative self-expression in works of art. For the twins through their unusual birth have evinced in a concrete manner the dualistic conception of the soul and thereby given proof of the immortality of certain individuals singled out by destiny. [13]

Out of this "spirit of twinship" evolved the figure of the primitive hero, "constituted by a fusion of the two separate selves, the mortal and the immortal, in one and the same personality; he has, so to speak . . . two lives to spare." [14]

But such fusion as this, Rank concludes — such "integration of the personality," as Jung would call it — is impossible for the overcivilized ego-consciousness of modern man to accept; he will have none of such irrationalities. As a result, the figure of the second self, once a symbol of hope and reassurance, has become in the mind of modern man, and in the literature that expresses his mind, a symbol of exactly the opposite value: of menace and doom; "a reminder of the individual's mortality, indeed, of death itself."[15]

A more recent work than either of Rank's is *The Double in Literature,* by Robert Rogers.[16] It is also, in its coverage, the most comprehensive work on the subject that has yet appeared, dealing with or touching on numerous selections that have been used as examples in the present study. Its interest is chiefly in the "latent double" rather than the "manifest double," a distinction apparently somewhat similar to the one that I have made between psychic dualism and physical dualism, except that Mr. Rogers includes in the category of manifest double all cases of physical dualism even when, as in *William Wilson,* there are profound roots of psychic dualism going down beneath the manifest surface. But whether manifest or latent, according to Mr. Rogers, the literary double is the result of the decomposition or fragmentation of the author's psyche, and this process of decomposition is analyzed from a strictly or "classically" Freudian viewpoint. *The Double in Literature,* therefore, is not a work of criticism that explores the literature of the second self in an effort to understand it, but a work of psychoanalytic theory that uses selections from literature to support an already familiar, and to its author already established, doctrine regarding the nature of the human psyche. Since it begins, not with the question that here concerns us, but with the answer to this question, it becomes less an investigation than a series of demonstrations: of the fact that the second selves or doubles of creative literature, like all other human products, are psychosexual manifestations, reflecting suppressed because shameful sexual desire, always of an incestuous or perverted nature.[17] Such doubles (and frequently all the characters of a piece of fiction are found by Mr. Rogers to be "doubles") are ultimately projections of their creator, who through them expresses and attempts to deal with his own internal conflicts.

All of these are primarily psychological approaches to the subject. The approach of Wilhelmine Krauss, in *The Double-Motif in Romantic*

Literature,[18] is primarily that of the literary scholar and historian of ideas. The literature of the second self, according to Miss Krauss, is a product of the writers of the German Romantic Movement, with Tieck and Jean Paul forming the terminus a quo and the early Heine the terminus ad quem. The "psychic-historic groundwork" of the second self in creative literature is the subjective idealism so typical of the thinking of the German Romantic Movement, expressed in philosophy by the solipsism of Fichte and Schelling, in aesthetics by Schlegel's theory of romantic irony, and in creative literature by the figure of the second self. Though in each writer the figure takes a different form, nevertheless behind and beneath all these forms, as behind and beneath the metaphysical and aesthetic theories, can be seen that "yearning after the infinite" (*Sehnsucht nach dem Unendlichen*) which is of the essence of subjective idealism, the struggle of the "I" to extend itself beyond its mortal, finite limits. But only the *will* of the "I" is infinite, and it is bound to conflict with the *fact* of its finite limitations (here we have, of course, a parallel to Lucka's conflict between the "pure I" and the "empirical I," as well as to Rank's conflict between the unconscious yearning for immortality and the conscious rejection of irrationality). The result is a dualistic splitting of the world into whatever satisfies the yearning on the one hand and whatever opposes it on the other: infinite versus finite, ideal versus real, soul versus body, irrational versus rational; and it is this split as well as this struggle that the "I" embodies in the imaginary conflict between the hero (the Ideal) and his Double (the Real), or (in the terminology we have adopted) the first self and the second self.

Also approaching the subject from the viewpoint of the literary scholar rather than the psychologist is Ralph Tymms' *Doubles in Literary Psychology.* Like Miss Krauss, Mr. Tymms concentrates his study centrally on the writers of the German *Romantik,* assuming as she does that it is in the products of this school that the theme finds its most characteristic and important expression. He does carry his consideration forward into the twentieth century, and adds several examples from literatures other than the German, making his study a more comprehensive one than that of Miss Krauss.

As a whole, however, Mr. Tymms' work is mainly a historical survey. To the extent that it reaches any conclusion it agrees substantially with Miss Krauss, that the second self is primarily a product of Romantic literature — by which, like Miss Krauss, Mr. Tymms means primarily German Romantic literature. Specifically, the figure emerges from the "subjective realism" of romantic writers: "the paradoxical attitude that insists on the faithful and realistic reproduction of mental processes, even when they seem to have a purely subjective validity; such fantasies as hallucinations or derangement may suggest to the imagination are then treated with the objectivity of a psychiater's case-book."[19] Alternating with this "psychological double," the subconscious self imaginatively projected into the objective world, is the "allegorical double," who plays his part in the struggle between good and evil within the soul of man. "These two aspects, then, together determine the evolution of the double; the one a product of the unconscious, and the other of the conscious mind, they appropriately present the twin faces of its Janus-head."[20]

Like Miss Krauss and Mr. Tymms, Marianne Wain concentrates on German examples of the second self.[21] The second self of "Romantic narrative," by which is meant purely the fiction of the German *Romantik,* she considers to be the result of three unwholesome symptoms of the Romantic temperament: a moral uncertainty, an affinity with madness, and above all a disturbance of the sense of reality caused by the philosophical speculations of the time, particularly the solipsism of Fichte. In emphasizing the effect of contemporary philosophy on Romantic creative literature Miss Wain follows the lead of Miss Krauss, but her conclusion has less to do with the meaning of the second self per se than with the psychological and sociological implications of the literature in which he appears, all of it a manifestation of the Romantic disease of hyper-subjectivity, of withdrawal from the healthy objective world. Indeed she holds that this literature was being used by such writers as Schlegel and Jean Paul to warn readers against the dangers of the unbridled imagination.

Claire Rosenfield, on the other hand, has given us the first general study of the subject that gets away from German Romanticism and concentrates mainly on examples from English and American literature.[22] In both the material treated and the conclusion reached her study tends to anticipate that of Mr. Rogers. For while her specific thesis is that writers have become increasingly aware of what they have been doing in their exploitation of the second self, her more general (and for our purposes more important) thesis is that this exploitation has been the reflection of psychological pressures within themselves: of "the conflict between the conscious and the unconscious life, the constant menace of personal disintegration which apparently threatens us all and the loss of identity consequent both upon mental disorder and the necessity that the character mask his internal life by creating roles to play."[23]

A much broader work of literary criticism than either of these, Masao Myoshi's *The Divided Self,*[24] is also in considerable part sociological and psychological in its interest. Though it deals with various examples of the second self in creative literature, it does so only in the course of developing its point that nineteenth-century English literature in general gives expression to the profound self-division experienced by the writers of this period: division between rationality and irrationality, self-control and passion, intellect and imagination, morality and art, civilization and eros, action and imitation — generally speaking, the lawful and the unlawful. Mr. Myoshi is certainly right in pointing out that interest in the mystery of self expresses itself in many ways other than the figure of the *Doppelgänger,* and that all these expressions, especially those that appear in imaginative literature, are closely related to one another. His book is in this respect pertinent to our subject, implicitly explaining the second self as one manifestation of "the confusion, the perplexity, the deep unease of the English nineteenth century":[25] a condition which he seems to look on as simultaneously a personal and a social illness, however productive its results in a literary way.

These, then, are the important works, so far as I have been able to unearth them, that bear on the question of what the second self means. [26] It will readily be seen that despite the widely different approaches and attitudes and terminologies of these works, the explanations that they offer are basically in agreement with one another. Their common theory can be reduced in very general terms to this: that the figure of the second self is created by its author, either consciously or unconsciously, to express in fictional form the division within his own psyche, whether caused by purely personal problems or by the wider problems of his culture or by both. This figure usually embodies the author's own shortcomings, his "darker side," the self which he really is: the empirical I, the narcissistic I, the mortal I, the finite I, the rejected primitive irrational I (Rank), the restricting earth-bound rational I (Krauss), the homosexual father-hating mother-desiring I (Rogers), the I that reflects the impossible complexity and contradiction of his age (Myoshi) — embodies this self that he really is as against the self that he would like to be, or at least would like to be thought to be: "pure," outgoing, ageless, immortal, infinite, enlightenedly rational, transcendently irrational, wholesome, and whole. As a result, though occasionally the roles of the hero and his *Doppelgänger* may be reversed, in which case the latter becomes the *Schützgeist* or Voice of Conscience or some wish-fulfillment character, predominantly the second self is a figure of menace and loathing, who arouses shame, fear, and often murderous hatred in his counterpart, the first self, with whom the author tends to identify himself.[27] In other words this figure is never simply a technical device; he is a symptom (or collection of symptoms) of the writer's own inward disorder. But he is a symptom in peculiarly devious form, which by being expressed in this fashion is also disavowed; he is a trick whereby the writer contrives to put the undesirable aspect of his character outside himself and so to disown it. In the very broad sense of the word he is a scapegoat, upon whom the writer has unloaded his own limitations and poisons, and whom the writer frequently punishes with death.

Now I have no wish to discredit any of these analyses for the sake of justifying my own. They are all interesting works, and valuable to any student of the subject. Nevertheless I can scarcely ask the reader to bear with me in the formulation of yet another theory about the second self without explaining briefly why I feel such a formulation to be necessary.

One reason I have already discussed: the failure of the studies that have thus far been made to decide just what the second self is. The result has been a treating as interchangeable three things that are very different from one another: (a) the objective second self, a case of mistaken identity; (b) the subjective second self, a mental content mistaken for external fact; (c) the genuine second self, always simultaneously both objective and subjective, and never explainable as a mistake. Such vagueness has made impossible any systematic analysis of the last figure, any study of the variety of his forms and of the relationship between them. Nor has there been any attempt to differentiate between the first self and the second, with the result that each of them may be referred to, at different times in the same study, as "the Double."[28]

The other reason is the failure of these studies to base their conclusions on a wide enough body of evidence, or to examine this evidence in sufficient detail. In part this failure follows inevitably from the first, since many of the examples considered, by all these writers, at best merely skirt the edges of the second-self theme. The result of this inadequacy of scope has been the missing of another paradox about the second self, no less important than his combined objectivity and subjectivity, a paradox that has gradually become apparent as our picture of him has unfolded. This is the presence, along with the evil side of his nature on which these studies have largely concentrated, of a side exactly the opposite of evil. True, there has been mention of an occasional reversal of roles which makes the second self the *Schützgeist* or protective spirit of the first, a reversal seldom explained save implicitly as the exception that proves the rule. But to dismiss this latter side in such a way is to do considerable damage to the facts that have been uncovered in the foregoing chapters. For one thing, the second self as Saviour is not a protective spirit; his function is to save even if he must destroy in the process; his role therefore is quite as positive and important a one as that of the evil second self, though he works toward the opposite end. For another thing, he cannot be explained as a mere exception to the rule. Though examples of him may be somewhat less plentiful, he is fully developed as the reverse side of the evil second self, even corresponding in his three main aspects to those of the latter: Pursuer, Tempter, and Vision of Horror. Nor is the second self as Saviour the only kind of good second self. The second self as the Beloved, though on rare occasions evil, is even in these cases prevented by the nature of the relationship from being evil in intent toward the first self; and for the most part, despite all the guilt and suffering the relationship may bring, stands clearly on the good side of the line rather than on the bad.

But in addition to the quantitative argument for the view of the second self as essentially evil there is a qualitative one, much more perceptive and difficult to meet. This grants the existence of the good second self as well as the bad, but points to the undeniable fact that the goodness of the former is always to some extent penetrated by, and always partakes of, the badness of the latter. And this fact might well suggest that the latter is the more basic of the two, the former having grown up as a façade to conceal him, or as a kind of placatory euphemism for him, much like the name *Eumenides,* "the Gracious Ones," for the terrible Erinyes.

It might suggest this, if it were not that the bad second self is no less invariably, if less obviously, penetrated by an element of the good. We see signs of this penetration from the beginning. Plainly the Great Fear that constitutes the most primitive reaction to the spirit-Twin is not the fear inspired by such an alien intruder as the ravening wolf or tiger. It could hardly be, for there is nothing in fact menacing about the birth of twins. Before the feeling of the fear, therefore, must come the working of the imagination; and the menace of the Twin Brother (or Sister) must be one with which he has been invested by those who consider themselves menaced by him. He has not merely intruded into the tribal world; he has been, however unconsciously and for whatever reason, *invited* to intrude.

In the evil second self of modern and recent literature we find this element of implicit invitation to be even stronger. Here the fear is felt not by the tribe as a whole but by a particular member of it, the first self; but actually the latter is always more or less representative of the "tribe view," of "us." Here, also, there is usually a very understandable reason for the fear; the threat offered by the second self is often very definable and tangible indeed. But as we have seen, such threats are never what make the threatener chiefly fearful to the threatened. They do not reveal to the first self the malignity of the second, but simply support the first self's intuitive, prior knowledge of this malignity. Such knowledge is very difficult to reconcile with the theory that sees the second self as scapegoat. If he were the embodiment of those qualities which his creator wanted to renounce, surely the last thing the author-first-self would do would be that which in all the many examples we have considered he never fails to do; to emphasize above all else the *linkage* between the self he supposedly wants to divorce himself from and the self he wants to be. Even more clearly than in the case of the Twin Brother, in other words, the intruder from the dark seems to have been invited to intrude, invited by the imagination that has shaped him.

But this is not at all the same thing as saying that he has been invented, or that his power over the first self is in any way unreal; for as second self he must to some extent, in exercising his own will, exercise that of his counterpart as well. It is to this extent that the evil second self is not evil, that is, is not the worker-against the first self, but the worker-with and the worker-for. And what gives the evil second self his core of goodness is the same thing that gives the good second self his aura of evil. That sense of mysterious and unwilled affinity which always characterizes the relationship between the selves is one side, the hither and recognizable side, of the second self's uncanniness.

For of course uncanniness, etymology to the contrary, does not mean for any of us merely that which is beyond our ken.[29] In none of the examples we have studied is the second self someone wholly unknown to the first self, nor could he be, for that which is simply unknown to us leaves us simply indifferent. It is that which enfolds the familiar within the unfamiliar, presents us with the known obscured and loomingly amplified by the unknown, or with the unknown into which we find we have unaccountable glimpses of insight or almost of memory: that is the truly uncanny; that is what cuts the ground from under our feet, because we can neither own it nor disown it, and cannot be sure where we stand.

Therefore the same quality of uncanniness that is the barrier between the selves is also the bond between them; the same quality that makes the intruder at his best alien and suspect makes him at his worst the reverse of alien, the unbidden interloper who is also the bidden guest. This Janus-faced duality of the second self, this interpenetration of his evil side and his good, should not really surprise us. It is all the same figure we have been studying, and though one or another aspect is more prominent depending on the angle from which he is seen, all aspects are bound to be present at all times: the Tempter in the Pursuer, the Horror in the Tempter, the saint in the sinner, the male in the female and vice versa. To try to excise one aspect and discount or ignore the rest is like the task imposed on Shylock: to excise the flesh and shed no drop of blood.

But what about the effect which this invited intruder exerts on the life of the first self? This after all is the heart of the matter. As has been pointed out earlier, we are interested in what the second self *does,* but centrally we are interested in the results of this doing: in what happens to, and especially what happens within, the first self. And, as we have seen, what happens to the first self as the result of his relationship with the second seldom brings sweetness and light into his life; it is far more likely to bring turmoil and disaster. Nor is this destructiveness in effect confined to the second self in his evil aspects. For all the saintliness of Jean Valjean and the kindness of Hermine and the devotion of Isabel, Javert and Harry Haller and Pierre Glendinning are no less destroyed by them than are Heyst, Ivan Karamazov, or Lord Jim by their malignant counterparts. Would this fact at least seem to lend support to the view that the second self is always essentially evil?

I think the answer must be, only if we consider that the effects he brings — emotional upset, suffering in body and soul, loss, and death — are necessarily evil. To question whether they are is not to suggest that they are necessarily good, either. But if they are necessarily bad then we must conclude that life itself is necessarily bad, for all these things are the lot of the living. There are no happy endings save in fairy tales; for all of us there is only one ending, and it could not be more destructive. If we are to raise any question about these things at all, it must not be whether they will happen; it must be how they happen, what they seem to lead to, and what if anything they seem to yield beyond their own dark reality.

And when we ask the question this way we come, I believe, to the strongest evidence we have yet uncovered that the view of the second self as essentially evil is an inadequate one. We have just seen that the primitive fear of the Twin Brother is a fear not so much of concrete danger as of the uncanniness itself: the same uncanniness that causes him, in tribes of slightly more advanced culture, to be uneasily reverenced as the potential bringer of good; in other words, there is a strong kinship between the fear of harm and the hope of benefit. In the more archaic but culturally far more sophisticated versions of the Twin Brother that occur in world religion and legend, this kinship becomes stronger still. Thus Judas-Satanaël, the betrayer-persecutor of Christ, unintentionally heightens the glory of his victim by the very victimization. Thus Kamatha-Samvara by repeated slayings of Marubhuti-Parsva unintentionally shapes the latter's soul and steers it to its ascension as Tirthankara; and the shaping of the persecuted brother is accompanied by, and really indistinguishable from, the shaping of his persecutor, so that the ascension of the former is simultaneous with the redemption of the latter. Thus the wild, shaggy Enkidu, though he does come out of the unknown, though he does cross the will and violently oppose the person of Gilgamesh, and though he does by his death cause lasting anguish in the latter's soul, nevertheless in the course of these things brings into being a better Gilgamesh, tempering him in his arrogance, broadening him by comradeship, deepening him through suffering and sympathy.

Again, furthermore, as we come forward to the literature that has served as the main subject of this study, we find the point far more fully illustrated than in primitive and archaic examples. As I have said, we must look not only at the harm done to the first self by the second, but at all the reverberations it sets in motion, at what, if anything, the experience is made to yield. And if we compare the first self before his experience of the second with the same first self after the experience, even in the moment of despair or death, we will see that in most cases we have studied, especially the major examples, it has yielded a great deal. We have only to compare the Brother Medardus who returns in penance to the monastery and ends his life in peace; the Billy Budd who at the instant of death calls God's blessing on the man who has condemned him; the grief-stricken Heyst who immolates himself on Lena's pyre; the Ivan who, though he cannot make amends in external action, tortures himself into madness in expiation of the crime into which he has willed another; the Mr. Thompson who places the shotgun muzzle beneath his own chin; the Lord Jim who presents himself for execution at the hands of Doramin; the Raskolnikov who turns himself over to the police; the Javert who hurls himself into the Seine — we have only to compare such people with the people they were when we first met them, not only to see the difference, but also to understand the extent and nature of it. In the vast majority of cases the harm done to the first self by the second is harm as catastrophic as harm can be. But also in the vast majority of cases it is not a harm that narrows the first self or limits him or causes him to shrink in stature; it may and usually does kill him at last, but it does not lessen him. To the contrary, it is a harm that stirs awake, that lances through the comfortable shell of self-complacency or self-protection, that strips away all masks of self-deception, that compels self-awareness and in the agony of the process brings self-enlargement.

This is not, of course, to say that harm is necessarily beneficial and suffering its own reward; any fool knows better from his own experience. It is simply to say that in the particular imaginative product that we are studying the outward destruction tends, so regularly that there can be no mistaking the fact, to be inwardly constructive. Every second-self story, so far as the first self is concerned, is to one degree or another a story of shaping, a *Bildungsroman*. Indeed in one of the major examples we have taken up, one of the cases where the evil second self is the Evil One in person, this *Bildung* of the first self by the second not only is implicit throughout but is explicitly stated for us as the central theme. The Lord in *Faust* feels no hatred toward the Spirit of Evil, for the latter despite himself serves the cause of God, in a way in which no one else could serve it.

> Man's active nature, flagging, seeks too soon the level;
> Unqualified repose he learns to crave;
> Whence, willingly, the comrade him I gave,
> Who works, excites, and must create, as Devil.[30]

This creativity of function is entirely unintentional on the part of the evil second self, and in most cases on the part of the good second self as well. The second self may achieve his conscious purpose, but it is very seldom that this particular conscious purpose is directly responsible for the main result that he brings about: the growth of the first self. Furthermore, failure by the second self to achieve his conscious purpose seems to be just as effective as success in bringing about this growth. What then does bring it about, or, to assume as little as possible in the question, why does it come about? The easiest answer is coincidence or chance. But the main characteristic of chance, to the extent that it means anything, is that its dice are always completely unloaded, and considered over a reasonably wide area the results of its throws should be pretty well distributed over the entire range of possibilities. Obviously then we do not seem to be dealing with chance, since almost all literature of the second self, by however complex a network of routes, comes to the same end. And if we resort to the alternative of chance − cause − we are in equal trouble, for the end that we are talking about, as we have just noted, seldom results from the will of the second self, and even more seldom from that of the first self, the only two parties whose will to cause the end could have any bearing on the matter.

But what other alternative is there? For our answer we must go back to something mentioned at the beginning of this study as one of the distinguishing features of the relationship between the selves. The second self, we are always made to feel, not only does create, but in the words of the Lord *must* create, and not haphazardly but in just that way, in just that context, and within just that "other" who is affected by him. What we feel, then, is not really an alternative to chance or cause, but a force that reduces them to only apparent forces, mere instruments of this real one that uses both of them; uses them interchangeably, indifferent to the fact that they are completely contradictory to each other; transcends both concepts and unites them in the larger and infinitely more difficult concept of fate.

Naturally I am not asking the reader to believe in this concept, or in any other concept. I am asking him to understand what it means, and how vital a role it plays in the literature of the second self. "Fate" is a word that has been used no less loosely than "Double." Fate is never the same thing as chance. Chance refers to that which comes about in a particular way but might just as easily have come about in any other way or not come about at all; fate refers to that which comes about as and when and how it does because it must so come about and would defeat any effort in the universe to prevent its so coming about. Chance is the purely fortuitous, fate the absolutely inexorable. Nor is fate any closer to cause. Cause refers to that which comes about in accordance with definite, determinable, logical rules, and therefore can always be hypothetically averted by counter-causation. Fate is that which supersedes all logic and all rules, either known or knowable; not all the "if's" in the world can alter it by a fraction.[31]

It is this which is always the central controlling force in the literature of the second self. As every second-self story is a story of growth in the first self, so every second-self story is likewise a story of fate, the fate that demands this growth. The second self is the being who comes to the first self, through an accident which is always felt to be the reverse of accident, at a moment of special vulnerability or need on the first self's part, vulnerability to and need for the influence that only the second self can bring; he comes into the first self's life at exactly that juncture at which the first self, however reluctantly, is ready for him. Count Victor "happening" to visit the particular monastery in which Brother Medardus is serving as keeper of the holy relics, Mr. Hatch "happening" to arrive at the Thompson ranch on that particular blazing brain-inflaming afternoon, Gentleman Brown and Mr. Jones "happening" to come across the sea to the sanctuaries of Lord Jim and Axel Heyst, John Claggart "happening" to walk by at the moment of the spilling of the soup, Svidrigaïlov "happening" to pass within arm's length of Raskolnikov at the moment when the latter is giving his address. Bartleby "happening" to appear in answer to that particular advertisement, Hermine "happening" to be in the Black Eagle at the time when Harry Haller comes stumbling in out of the rain, Peter Ibbetson "happening" to go to the same concert attended by the Duchess of Towers — we could endlessly extend the list of those "moments of encounter" the very apparent casualness of which underscores the implicit purpose behind them. It is never simply the purpose of either of the selves involved, but a more inclusive and completely irresistible purpose; yet at the same time this larger purpose is not felt to be simply apart from those of the selves, either; the sense of fate always includes the sense of a certain participation, consciously unwilled or even unwilling though it may be, by the fated. This is achieved, in the encounter between the selves, by the paradox of their being simultaneously one and not-one. Objectively separate from each other, they may know nothing of each other's existence up to the moment of meeting; subjectively continuous with each other, they have not only a wordless knowledge of each other but a wordless power of communication with each other, and so also the power of summoning and responding, the inward necessity that underlies the outward. Nor is the sense of fate by any means confined to the moment of encounter; all that follows, and above all the resolution of the relationship, is pervaded by the same sense of inscrutable inevitability.

I am not by this trying to explain fate; I am trying to describe it, at least the role that it plays in the literature of the second self. And certainly one thing that must be included in such a description is something that has already been discussed as particularly characteristic of the category I have called the second self in Time, but that I think we are now in a position to see as characteristic in only somewhat lesser degree of all other categories as well. I have said that the concept of Time is a one-way street, all traffic moving out of unseen (and therefore really nonexistent) future into seen present into unseen (and therefore "gone") past. The same one-way street is envisaged by both the chance-concept and the cause-concept; chance and cause are the dynamisms that move the traffic, and we who live in Time think and order our actions in accordance with a not very logical alternation between the two ideas. Now fate is to cause and chance as Timelessness is to Time. It sees chance as meaningful and never fortuitous, in other words as only the visible fragment of a larger entity. It sees as no less possible than the cause that produces an effect the effect that *elicits* its cause. It transcends the divisions between chance and cause, cause and effect, just as Timelessness transcends the divisions of Time; indeed it can do so only by thinking (so far as the human mind can think) in Timeless terms: by thinking of the events of life not as a lineal sequence but as an "all-at-onceness," all parts of which are always equally vibrant and alive. The sense of fate is probably the nearest approach to the concept of Timelessness that we can expect to achieve. This is why I have called the second self in Time, despite the little that has been done with it, in one way at least the most important and even the most characteristic of all.

In all these ways we see the inadequacy of the view that holds the second self to be exclusively or predominantly evil, and of the interpretation that makes him a scapegoat of any of the various sorts that have been suggested, a device to "cover up" for his creator. This whole tendency to assume that the critic is engaged in a game of wits with the author, that the phenomenon of artistic creation must be explained by ulterior motivation whether conscious or unconscious, seems to me a most unfortunate one.[32] Ulterior motivations when applied to artistic products give us only ulterior explanations; the artist is always trying to escape from something: his guilty sexual desire, his knowledge of his own finiteness, his sense of the inevitability of decay and death, and so forth. And somehow it is not quite convincing to think of *King Lear* or the *Missa Solemnis* or the *Last Supper* as a means of running away from, rather than as a running, or a mighty toiling, toward.

So it is with the theories that have been advanced to account for the figure of the second self. Even if we granted the highly questionable thesis that all authors of such literature have been psychologically maladjusted people with a tendency to personality dissociation, we would be no closer to understanding why such maladjustment should have shaped and tortured itself into art. Between neurotic symptoms and artistic creation lies a chasm which very little has yet been done to bridge. Nor is there really any need to bridge it. The literature of the second self makes perfectly good sense in what it says, provided we remember that it says this in terms of direct living experience rather than of general concepts. Such experience, of course, is of the imagination; in everyday life there is no second self in the sense in which we have been using the term. Nevertheless there is evidently within us a dissatisfaction with our normally strict division between the objective and subjective worlds (the literature we have been discussing is one strong indication of the fact), as well as a deep-seated need to fuse them together while still keeping them apart, to preserve the twoness but to expand it with a simultaneous oneness; and such dissatisfaction is therefore the first thing that the student of this literature must try to understand.

It is a dissatisfaction similar to our dissatisfaction with Time, and like this or any other deeply rooted dissatisfaction it would seem to be rooted in something: in intimations, hints, fragmentary almost-glimpses, of a synthesis which the "real-life" view rejects as impossible. Even our attitude in "real life" toward the purely objective and the purely subjective second selves is colored by such intimations. While the objective fact of twinship has been explained, in the sense of being described and named, by biology, and the subjective fact of personality dissociation has been similarly explained by psychology, actually both these phenomena are as extraordinary to us, beneath our habituation to names, as they have ever been. At this moment over the greater part of the earth twins are regarded with much the same uneasy awe as was felt by our most remote ancestors; and the profoundly mysterious mutual preoccupation of twins, the influence they exert (especially in the case of identical twins) on each other's lives, the way in which they tend to respond to each other's states of mind and health, remain as mysterious to us as they have been for thousands of years.[33] The other phenomenon, of internal division, is no less widespread, and no less mysterious. We may use such words as *Unterbewusststein* or repressed unconscious contents or autonomous partial-systems, but like twinship the phenomenon itself remains as extraordinary, and captures our imagination as powerfully, as it has ever done.

These things capture our imagination because they represent in however elementary a form that paradoxical twofoldness of which we have intimations, intimations which leave us dissatisfied with the either-or version of what we are. Such intimations are bound to be rather frightening at first. But if they were only or even primarily frightening, there would be no reason for the perennial impulse to incorporate the figure of the second self in creative literature. Along with the negative reaction of fear to such an idea there is a positive reaction that has gradually outweighed (though it has never replaced) the negative one: the will at whatever risk to become acquainted with this strange, expanded version of what and who one is, to know the Other who is also the I.

In a literal sense such an effort at self-exploration can never take us very far. To use general concepts about the unknown realms of one's mind is only to deceive ourselves, for what we want to describe is not a world of concepts but a world of the most poignant experience, yet not at all the kind we are used to. About the only way we have found to talk about it is through the use of "symbols": familiar images that have taken on unfamiliar coloration, like familiar voices that have taken on strange echoes and reverberations intensifying and deepening the sense of what they say.[34] A symbol has no equivalent that can be identified as its "real" meaning; its sole reason for existence is that there is no equivalent. Such a symbol is the figure of the second self.

If we understand this we will understand much better why the effort to translate the literature of the second self into something else is to miss the whole point of its existence. It is a struggle not to cover up anything but to reveal as vividly as possible an essential though buried truth. Furthermore, if we understand this symbolic function of the second self, we will understand more clearly the main points about him that have emerged from our study as a whole. His possession of combined objectivity and subjectivity is what makes him unmistakably representative of the irrational-unexplored and a link with it. His possession of so many and so widely varied aspects is a reflection of the varied states of self-dissatisfaction that arouse the need for self-knowledge and set in motion the adventure of self-meeting. Probably when one's conscious view of oneself is comparatively simple and complacent one is comparatively apprehensive of change, and the fearful potentialities of the second self are emphasized. When dissatisfaction is stronger, need overshadows fear, and the vision of the second self is altered accordingly. In all cases fear and need are both present, but in varying degrees. Sometimes the result of this mixture is a figure of malice from which one shrinks or of depravity before which one stands appalled. Sometimes he has resources of wisdom and benignity so different from what one is used to in oneself that he may seem evil because of his very goodness. Sometimes he, or more usually she, presents a vision of loveliness not easily distinguishable from one's own unrecognized capacity to love, a vision which makes demands so strange and high that one is liable to respond to them with the wrong (because inadequate) answer of physical desire, a vision which perhaps for this reason so often evokes guilt along with love. Sometimes he may afford a glimpse, however difficult, of an identity that combines with what one is at the moment all one ever has been or will be.

This Other who is likewise the self is always felt to be more formidable than the familiar foreground personality, and to be gifted with powers of an almost supernatural sort, which enable the second self regularly to dominate the first. But there is also a more important reason for his dominance: that the point of the relationship between them is the adventure of the first self, the expanding of his horizon, the second self serving as the hammer to beat the metal of the first into new shape. He is not, however, an independent hammer, for if the first self were merely a passive recipient there could be no adventure at all. Hence the sense of fate in this adventure, the sense of a working together of which neither is aware, the sense that the searching by the one and the shaping by the other are parts of a larger force that is guiding them both to an end so necessary that in a way it has already come about before the process leading to it has started.

It is this end which is the goal of the adventure of self-meeting. If we ask why it should be sought, when the seeking is so often unpleasant and even fatal, we can only answer that there appears to be in living creatures generally the urge to do a thing which can never be justified in practical terms: to see the unseen, to sail beyond the sunset, to cross the mountains of the moon. And when the uncrossed mountains are within instead of without, or rather within as well as without (for, as I shall shortly explain, one's relationship with oneself is not wholly distinguishable from one's relationship with other selves) — when this is the case there seems to be a special urgency, arising out of a sense of incompleteness, even of self-deception and self-deprivation. For to live as only half oneself is to live a kind of lie, and to live a kind of lie is to live a kind of death.

This interpretation has certain things in common with those that have already been advanced. It agrees with Miss Krauss and Mr. Tymms that the subject of the second self is a romantic one. But it would use the word "romantic" in a much broader sense than they do, not restricting it to a particular literary movement or period but applying it to a tendency of mind at least as old as any literature, that which prefers to explore the unknown rather than record and analyze the familiar. This tendency is interested, of course, in exploring the objectively unknown, but the latter is a comparatively limited field; much more inviting, in part because much more forbidding, is the subjectively unknown, combined with and seen through, in other words symbolized by, the objectively unknown. This romantic appetite for wonder is always synthetical rather than analytical, since analysis tends to categorize and systemize and so put an end to exploration. When the romantic mind uses analysis it does so in order to polarize opposites, and then undertakes the endless because logically impossible task of reconciling these irreconcilables: Now and Then, Here and There, Chance and Cause, Light and Dark, Heaven and Hell, Self and Not-Self. Nothing has been more misunderstood than the phrase "Romantic self-assertion." The true romantic always asserts his individuality, insists on his wonderful uniqueness, but if he stops with the uniqueness he soon kills the wonder and ceases to be a romantic. The deeper he follows this wonder the more infallibly it takes him, not away from other selves, but toward them; he commences to find himself in them and them in him — just as he learns to see a world in a grain of sand, or the whole mystery of life and death in the meanest flower that blows, or all of wronged creation in a slain albatross.

This interpretation also agrees with Dessoir and Lucka and Rank that writers of second-self literature are unconsciously telling us something about themselves. But it strongly disagrees with the notion that the second self has been created as a scapegoat on which to unload shameful psychic contents, or that the artist is "disturbed" and his art a symptom of the fact. Certainly artists are "disturbed" and out of their disturbance comes their art; but for that matter everyone else is also disturbed; life itself is a disturbance on the tranquil plain of nonexistence. Therefore to say that the literature of the second self has a psychological explanation is not to say that it has a pathological one. To the contrary, if we consider disease to be a retreat from the normal unfolding process of life, the psychological explanation that has been arrived at here would have just the opposite meaning.

Actually the thesis that has emerged from this study has much more in common with the theories of two writers who have not yet been mentioned because so far as I know they have not dealt directly with the subject of the second self in creative literature, but who indirectly have done much to shed light on it.

One is the psychoanalyst C. C. Jung.[35] As most readers will know, the basic theme of Jung's work is the need for "integration of the personality": a process which is not a mere pulling together but a coming to know and accept and assimilate elements of the psyche of which one is not consciously aware, but by the emotional pressures of which one is strongly affected. To this extent Jung's concept of the psyche is similar to Freud's, and indebted to Freud's. But Jung's theory of the unconscious is more complex than Freud's.[36] The latter Jung calls the "personal unconscious," containing things which have either slipped down out of the conscious area or not yet worked their way up into it, though they are perfectly adapted to doing so. Such a personal unconscious Jung believes to be only the upper layer of unconsciousness, beneath which we must infer the existence of another and much deeper layer which he calls the *impersonal,* or *transpersonal,* or *collective* unconscious. It is impersonal or transpersonal because in its contents the sense of individual ego seems to disappear; it is collective because its contents seem to be not peculiar to anyone but common to all, and to recall a primitive state of mind that might be called "pre-individuality," *participation mystique,* in which the boundaries between I and Thou, Now and Then, Here and There, are not sharply defined.

I shall not go into Jung's theory of the collective unconscious as a whole. I wish only to mention certain major denizens of that darkness, which Jung calls the "archetypes" or "archetypal symbols," and which one tends to meet with as one descends into the lower depths of one's own mind. Outstanding among them are three fearsome and uncanny beings, uncanny by reason of that fusion of known and unknown that I have already described. The one that is most readily accessible and most unqualifiedly unpleasant is the "shadow," not a physical shadow but the personified sum of all the inferior, less respectable, even criminal potentialities of one's own psyche, potentialities that have not been relegated to the unconscious but have never been allowed to emerge from the unconscious, that is, have never been acknowledged as one's own potentialities at all, and therefore are not so recognized when they are met with, in the form of this "dark brother," the dark counterpart of the conscious ego.

The other two main archtypes of the collective unconscious are more deeply buried and more mysterious, and in order to clarify the point I am trying to make I shall reverse the order in which Jung usually speaks of them. One is the figure called variously the pointer of the ways, the old magician, and the wise old man: the personification of the accumulated wisdom of the human soul, the pointer of the way into the *Unbetretene* where there is no way, the old binder of spells. The other is the figure called the anima, a creature peculiar to the masculine psyche and embodying all that is feminine within it.[37] She too has unaccountable knowledge of hidden truths, but primarily, as her name implies, she is man's image of his own resources of spirit; not the mother, but that within the male which gives the mother-image its often dangerous power, born anew in every male child.[38]

Both the wise old man and the anima are benignant figures compared with the shadow, but because they are more deeply buried in the psyche they are stranger and at least initially often more fearsome than the shadow himself. The wise old man knows too much for comfort, and therefore has about him at first something eerie and sinister, the crafty weaver of plots, the Archimago, who only by degrees is recognized by the seeker as the one who not only knows better than he but wills better, better for his sake.[39] The anima is the point of flame that aspires upward in the reluctant fleshliness (psychical as well as physical) of man; but flame burns and hurts and so the anima too is often seen at first as hostile: enchanting but deadly in her enchantment, perhaps the lamia, the vampire, the succuba.[40] And indeed she *is* destructive in a sense, for her role is to mock and tease and torment the somnolent flesh toward spiritual life. Both the wise old man and the anima tend ultimately to be recognized as benignant, unlike the shadow. But in a larger sense all three figures are benignant, if not intentionally so, in that the recognition and acceptance of them make possible the integration of the personality, the healing growth of the soul.[41]

I have spoken of the "intentions" of these figures as though they were real, in part to underscore the fact that in their special sense they *are* real. Naturally they are part of the whole psyche, but this does not mean that they are "imaginary" in the way in which we generally use the word. They are, in Jung's words, "autonomous partial-systems," given their independence, ironically, by the very effort of the conscious ego to be independent of them. They are not subject to conscious control; to the contrary, they tend to control or at least strongly to influence the consciousness.[42] I have referred to the *descent* of the ego-consciousness into its own depths, and this is the image repeatedly used in fairy tale and legend, but modern man in his encounters with these figures is more likely to experience them as rising to him, as invaders of his self-sufficiency and peace of mind, as alien intruders out of the Great Dark. In other words each as it is met with (and each meeting is a separate experience, since each of these archetypes inhabits a different level of the collective unconscious) constitutes the second self of the conscious ego, and each corresponds strikingly to one of the main categories of second self that we have studied. The shadow, as Pursuer or Tempter or Vision of Horror, corresponds to the evil second self; the wise old man to the second self as Saviour; the anima (animus in the case of Heathcliff) to the second self as the Beloved. All three are ageless figures, and in this respect transcend the limits of Time, so that their relations with the conscious mind have the fateful quality that I have described as characteristic of all relationships between the selves.

The other writer I wish to mention is the existential philosopher Martin Buber,[43] and I realize that at first glance Jung could hardly be given a stranger-seeming bedfellow, for Buber is interested not in the relationship between conscious and unconscious but in that between man and man. According to Buber man lives in a twofold world, made so by his own twofold attitude, which in turn determines his relationship to the world. One attitude is expressed by the phrase *I-It* (or *I-He, I-She*), in which *I* is separated from *It, It* being looked on or felt toward by the *I* as an object, secondary to and serving the purpose of *I*. The other attitude is expressed by the phrase *I-Thou*, in which there is no separation, though neither is there simple identity, but rather the only true reciprocity, "the real twofold entity *I* and *Thou*."[44]

In the *I-It* world, with which we are generally familiar, we are in the realm of experience; only in the *I-Thou* world do we know the realm of relation, a paradoxical condition, one being that is shared by two participants.[45] The realm of relation is characterized by "a bold swinging — demanding the most intensive stirring of one's being — into the life of the other."[46] As Buber points out, his idea of the *I-Thou* relation is similar to Kant's ideal of the Kingdom of Ends: the principle of thinking of one's fellow men not as things but as persons, not as means to an end but as ends in themselves; though it differs in its emphasis on "the interhuman," the "vital reciprocity" in which *I* and *Thou* become one, a twofold one.[47] Through entering the realm of the interhuman we have intimations of the suprahuman; "we look out toward the fringe of the eternal Thou . . .; in each *Thou* we address the eternal *Thou*."[48] But for all this the world of relation as distinct from the world of experience is both forbidding and fearsome to enter. The world of *I-It* is the comfortable world of daylight, the world of activity and knowledge. The world of *I-Thou* is a disturbing world, known to us in "strange lyric and dramatic episodes, seductive and magical, but tearing us away to dangerous extremes, loosening the well-tried context, leaving more questions than satisfaction behind them, shattering security — in short, uncanny moments we can well dispense with."[49]

In two main respects, then — the paradox of the twofold entity with the resultant special closeness between the *I* and the *Thou,* and at the same time the resistance to this closeness in the sense of uncanniness it evokes —, the *I-Thou* relation is similar to the relation between the conscious ego and its archetypes, as well as to the relation between the first and second selves of creative literature. Furthermore, as in these other relations, that between *I* and *Thou* transcends Time differentiations and has a fateful, suprarational quality. "The world of *It* is set in the context of space and time. The world of *Thou* is not set in the context of either of these."[50] Therefore the world of *I-Thou,* unlike the world of *I-It,* is free from the domination of casualty;[51] it is the world of destiny; and the man who knows this world "believes in destiny, and believes that it stands in need of him. . . . He must sacrifice his puny, unfree will, that is controlled by things and instincts, to his grand will, which quits defined for destined being."[52]

I am not maintaining that Jung and Buber have said the same thing; plainly they have not, and in many respects they could hardly be more different from each other.[53] But on one subject, the central subject in each case, they have come closer to saying the same thing than may be at first apparent, and in their very different ways of saying it interestingly complement each other. From their opposite angles of approach both have been preoccupied with a problem which, though doubtless as old as humanity, is peculiarly the problem of modern man: Who am I? — a problem which involves the additional one: How am I related to the Not-I? Jung has studied the way in which one finds other people, other personalities (not just hidden forces or suppressed desires), within oneself. Buber has studied the way in which one finds oneself within other people, does not just find he has things in common with them but "shares in a reality, that is, in a being that neither belongs to him nor merely lies outside him."[54]

In both cases the *I* proves both less (less independent) and more (more inclusive) than it seemed as the ego-consciousness or the *I* experiencing *It;* and though the process of change works from within in the one case and from without in the other it is essentially the same process and works toward the same end. For the unconscious into which the *I* must descend, according to Jung, is not the personal but the collective unconscious, communal and anonymous; so that descent into it does not isolate the *I* from others but just the reverse; it is just these depths one is exploring that one shares with the rest of the human race. By the same token it is through the *I-Thou* relation that man discovers himself and the depths within him, learns decision and freedom, learns to address the eternal *Thou,* "becomes conscious of himself as sharing in being, as co-existing, and thus as being."[55] In other words, the two discoveries are the two sides of the one mystery: that the *I* one ordinarily supposes oneself to be in the everyday world is not the only tenant in the house of self, and that this house is far larger than one has imagined, full of shadowy recesses and corridors, but full of wonder as well.

Perhaps the most striking parallel between the two theories is their explanation of the need for this change and this discovery. Very briefly summarized, Jung's position is that the development of civilized man, out of what we infer to have been primitive human mentality, has been dominated by the principle of differentiation, the separation of an *I* or ego-consciousness from the unconscious and from the rest of the world, an *I* which then enters into its infinitely varied relationship with this outside world. This principle of differentiation emerges from and sloughs away as dead skin the older principle, the principle of participation, which seems to have been so comparatively strong in the psyche of early man, to the extent of a blurring of any sharp line of demarcation between separate identities, times, and places. This process of *I*-realization through a sharpening of consciousness (and with it of self-consciousness) is inevitable, and is not in itself bad; all the achievements that man has made have been due to it. What *is* bad is the tendency to do it in too easy and limited a way, to stop with an *I* that is only a fraction of the whole rich potentiality of the self, to let consciousness of identity degenerate into ego-centricism and ego-cherishing, a closed preoccupation with one's own welfare and one's own importance. When this happens (and apparently it always happens to some extent), the sharpened consciousness brings not expansion of horizon but limitation of it, and there can be only one remedy: to go back and try again, to try to do the job more searchingly, more painfully, more humbly, more genuinely.[56]

Almost exactly the same explanation is given in his own terms by Buber. The *I-Thou* relation, a state of participation in which the *I* is not conscious of itself as a separate being, can be seen in the earliest years of life. "In the beginning is relation — as category of being, readiness, grasping form, mould for the soul; it is the *a priori* of relation, the *inborn Thou*."[57] This is the "blood-stirring *Thou*," recognized as the Other but not separated from the *I*, for at this stage there is no strict consciousness of the *I*.[58] By degrees the wondrous and stable *Thou* of relation becomes the changing *Thou* of experience; in other words it slowly ceases to be a *Thou* and is transformed into an object, an *It*. In the course of this change there emerges the self-conscious *I*, recognized as separate: the *I* of the experience *I-It*. This change is not bad; it is inevitable, and necessary to human progress. "Every response binds up the *Thou* in the world of *It*. That is the melancholy of man, and his greatness. For that is how knowledge comes about, a work is achieved, and image and symbol made, in the midst of living things."[59] Only through the converting of relation into experience, wonder into usefulness, can life be made feasible. But it is done at a price: "without *It* man cannot live. But he who lives with *It* alone is not a man." In the depths of his being he yearns for, and — despite all the uneasiness and disturbance it means for him — struggles to recapture, the world of relation; for "that which has been so changed into *It*, hardened into a thing among things, has had the nature and disposition put into it to change back again and again. This was the meaning in that hour of the spirit when spirit was joined to man and bred the response in him — again and again that which has the status of object must blaze up into presentness and enter the elemental state from which it came, to be looked on and lived in the present by man."[60]

Above all what is important to us about these two theories, however, is less their relevancy to each other than their joint relevancy to the subject of the second self. We have seen earlier in this chapter that the specific interpretations of the second self which have been advanced so far have concentrated primarily on the evil second self, what Jung would call the shadow. It has been my contention that the material studied by the present work affords ample evidence that evil and darkness characterize only one side of the second self, which is counterbalanced by the side of goodness and light. I have also explained why I feel that this larger view of the second self shows him to be far more a sign of health than a symptom of disease, and the very reverse of an instrument of self-concealment and self-deception; that to the contrary, whether evil or good, he appears to be an instrument of self-exploration, self-realization, of expanded rather than contracted being.

It is such expansion of being that is the central interest of both Jung and Buber. And the process by which it is to be achieved, whether by uniting oneself with unrecognized resources of the collective unconscious or by entering into relation with a fellow creature, is basically the same. It is the process of reconciling the opposites of the principle of differentiation, which has given us the conscious ego and all the tangible accomplishments of the world of *I-It,* and the older principle of participation which it is all too ready to cast aside as outmoded, but which is never outmoded, for it is the wellspring of both our vitality and our humanity. There is nothing very strange about the idea of such a reconciliation; it is precisely this that modern psychology, sociology, and the other social sciences are gropingly in search of at the moment, though whether or not they will be in time remains to be seen; in any event it has been only within the last century or so that man has commenced particularly to feel what might be called the dilemma of barren individuality, and has commenced to reach out with increasing exigency for some means of retaining the individuality while overcoming the barrenness.

What he seems to want, in other words, is to have his cake and eat it too, to retain his differentiated selfhood while at the same time sacrificing it to participation in shared selfhood; and it is just this paradox of which Jung and Buber, through their theories of the collective unconscious and the *I-Thou* relation, assert the possibility. Nor are they by any means the only ones who have done so. It is this same concept, of a basic interconnection of selves, that is given such eloquent expression by Emerson's doctrine of the Over-Soul, "within which every man's particular being is contained and made one with all other; . . . the soul of the whole; the wise silence; the universal beauty, to which every part and particle is equally related; the eternal ONE."[61] It is the same concept that, though emerging from a very different process of reasoning, is the "better knowledge" of Schopenhauer, man's only weapon against the ruthless will-to-live which enslaves him and degrades him and sets him into conflict with others: the knowledge that in being "others" his enemies are also himself, that all are no more separate from one another than the limbs of the same body; the knowledge therefore that always "the inflicter of the suffering and the sufferer are one." [62] It is only in such living knowledge of our true nature, concludes Schopenhauer, that we can rise above our jungle-nature, can quiet the will, can find peace at last; it is only in such transcending of our individuality, concludes Emerson, that "this bitterness of *His* and *Mine* ceases. His is Mine. I am my brother and my brother is me." [63] Nor should it surprise us that these so different thinkers, the great American optimist and the great German pessimist, are not only saying the same thing but saying it in almost the same words; for both, of course, are drawing upon the same source: the ancient Vedic notion of the Atman or World-Soul, of which Emerson's term "Over-Soul" is simply another rendering; and the necessary inference from this notion, to Schopenhauer the very kernel of the fruit of supreme wisdom, that in order to know oneself one must look upon every other creature in the world, living or lifeless, and say to oneself from the depths of one's being, *Tat twam asi:* "This thou art." [64]

The reader, I hope, will understand that just as he was not asked to believe in fate so he is not asked to believe in a World-Soul, whether it be called that or the Over-Soul or the collective unconscious or the *I-Thou* relation. Let it be called whatever one likes: an intimation, a superstition, an impossible hunger for the best of two mutually exclusive worlds. What I am trying to do is make clear how powerfully this idea has caught the imagination of mankind and how very widespread and age-old it is: this idea of simultaneous differentiation and participation, rendered by this paradox of simultaneous objectivity and subjectivity, which we have encountered over and over and in such variegated form throughout the foregoing chapters.

Granted, we have not encountered it in a relationship existing between one and all, but only in relationships between one and one, between first self and second self. That the theme should be treated more narrowly in fiction than in philosophy, however, is not difficult to understand. Philosophy at its most poetic deals with abstract concepts, fiction with concrete if always imaginary realizations. To realize this concept in its fullest degree would mean that every other would become my second self, that in every other creature I encountered I would find, in one of the main manifestations we have examined, my complementary and counterbalancing other half, as infinite in his variety of aspects as I. But even to form the concept of such an all-inclusive interconnection is difficult. To realize it would be vastly more so, and it is doubtless for this reason that writers of fiction have tended to express their sense of it by the specific case and the individual relationship, that of one to one or one-half to one-half (actually it is always both): by the image of the single second self and the paradox of unity in duality. Nevertheless, in just this sense, that such a relationship can be known with one fellow being, is implied the sense that it can be known with all.

It is as the expression of this sense that I believe, on the basis of the foregoing study, the figure of the second self in creative literature is most convincingly explained. It is on the one hand the quailing before the demand (which this sense always entails) to surrender the small, familiar security of self-sovereignty — of the point of ego-consciousness or the *I* of *I-It* or the dweller in a world of Space and Time — that accounts for the terror of this symbol, which even at its most saintly or enchanting has something terrible about it. But on the other hand, and more powerful than the quailing, is the demand itself, the hunger for the adventure, of losing the self that one may find it, of reconciling the opposites of two-ness and oneness, the principle of differentiation with that of participation. The adventure of such a reconciliation, imaginatively symbolized by the adventure of encountering the second self, is of the essence of all the examples we have considered. It fits the facts just as the scapegoat-theory, in any of its various forms, fails to fit them.

For the scapegoat-theory begins and ends in fear, and we have seen how little fear, by itself, is able to account for the literature we have been studying. The literature of the second self makes use of fear, but for a purpose entirely different from that of the fear alone. From the earliest and crudest beginnings this seems to have been true: that behind the Great Fear lies the Great Fascination, that within the darkness from which the alien intruder comes is felt to lie some invisible seed of light that touches him and causes his coming to be not just permitted but insisted on. Insisted on only to be violently rejected at the beginning, and even after all these centuries, even in his most winning forms, still in one way or another always contended with, for the sense of danger in this adventure remains strong; yet still insisted on, for the sense of need is always stronger. It is the struggle to satisfy this need, the imaginative straining after self-realization and self-fulfillment, that is embodied in the literature of the second self.

Notes

Preface

¹ My reason for not using either of these terms, but for using "second self" instead, is explained in Chapter 1, *infra*.

² I do not at all mean that it is disregarded in this study, or treated as a matter of secondary importance. It is of the utmost interest to any student of the subject, and it is given full attention in its proper place: after the evidence is in.

³ I have tried to keep any one author from dominating this study at the expense of others. Poe, because his stories are such clear as well as compact examples and can therefore be discussed with comparative brevity, is represented by five selections; Dostoyevsky, whose treatments of the subject are much longer and more complicated, is represented by three. It is for this reason, for example, that I have omitted the relationship between Myshkin and Rogozhin in Dostoyevsky's *The Idiot*.

⁴ This is essentially the position taken by W. K. Wimsatt, Jr., and M. C. Beardsley in "The Intentional Fallacy," *Sewanee Review* 59 (1946), 468-88, though of course not first enunciated there. Half a century earlier, for example, Nowell Smith had pointed out that "literary history" in the sense of literary biography is all too often neither literature nor history, but a branch of scandal. See "Coleridge and His Critics," *Fortnightly Review* 64 (July 1895), 342. Naturally the writer is the writing, and a complete knowledge of the former, if we could come by it, would give us a complete understanding of the latter. But what actually have we ever known about the personal life of any writer, even a living one, or perhaps most of all a living one? A few dozen or hundred snippets of information pasted together into an impression that changes every few years with added snippets or the fashion of the day. Take for example such "well-known facts" as the alcoholism and drug addiction of Poe, on which so many critical inferences have been based: facts that in recent years have misted away into insubstantial fables, and may in the

course of time condense into facts again. Or take the case of Whitman, of whose character, since his death, at least three separate versions have flourished, each completely incompatible with the other two.

But there is more to the difficulty than this. For even if our "facts" about a writer were dependable, and even if we had some way of knowing that they were, we would still be talking only about the man of everyday, from whom we would have a very wide gap to bridge (with no equipment to do the bridging) to this man as artist, from whom we would have yet another wide gap, involving all the unfathomed mysteries of the process of artistic creation, before we could get to the work itself. Until our knowledge of these matters is enormously increased it would seem that biographical data can be applied to literary interpretation only in a supplementary fashion and only with the utmost caution, for their tendency is rather to draw us away from the literature we are studying than to take us deeper into it.

[5] *Das Doppelgängermotiv in der Romantik*. Studien zum Romantischen Idealismus: Germanische Studien, Heft 99 (Berlin: Verlag von Emil Ebering, 1930).

Chapter 1

[1] This point is also made by Albert J. Guerard in "Concepts of the Double," *Stories of the Double,* edited by Albert J. Guerard (Philadelphia and New York: J. B. Lippincott Company, 1967), pp. 1-2.

[2] In *Werke,* herausgegeben von Gustav Lohmann (München: Carl Hanser Verlag, 1959), II, 42. In dealing with works written in foreign languages, I shall wherever possible refer the reader to translations that are readily available and (so far as I am competent to judge the matter) reasonably accurate. Where I have been unable to find such translations, or where (as in the case of most writings that deal in a general way with the subject of *Doppelgänger*) I have been unable to find any translations, the translations on which I am dependent are my own. In references to fiction, since so many examples are to be used, I shall give specific page numbers only for particularly important points or for comparatively extended direct quotations.

[3] "The word *double,*" says Mr. Guerard (*op. cit.,* p. 3), "is embarrassingly vague, as used in literary criticism." This is to put the matter very mildly indeed. The result of such vagueness has not been embarrassment, but that wholesale talking at cross purposes which is the inevitable consequence of a failure to agree on what is being talked about or even (Mr. Guerard is an exception in this respect) to recognize that there is no such agreement.

[4] Ralph Tymms, in *German Romantic Literature* (London: Methuen & Company, Ltd., 1955), makes but does not further use a distinction between the "Other Self" and the "first, habitual self." See p. 94.

[5] The main ones will be discussed in Chapter 9, *infra.*

[6] Translated by Arthur Waley (London: G. Allen and Unwin Ltd., 1942).

[7] "Compensation," *Essays: First Series,* in *The Complete Works of Ralph Waldo Emerson* (Boston and New York: Houghton Mifflin Company, 1903-21), II, 97.

[8] Cf. C. G. Jung, *The Integration of the Personality,* translated by Stanley Dell (New York and Toronto: Farrar & Rinehart, 1939), p. 20.

[9] Cf. Thoreau's discussion of this point in *Walden. The Writings of Henry David Thoreau* (Boston: Houghton Mifflin Company, 1893), II, 211.

[10] Margaret Goldsmith, *Franz Anton Mesmer* (New York: Doubleday Doran, 1934).

[11] Morton Prince, *The Dissociation of a Personality* (New York: Longmans Green and Company, 1905), pp. 45, 47n, 48.

[12] Though the word "psycho-analysis" properly belongs to Freud, I shall for convenience use it in its broader sense, to cover also all schools of thought that derive and differ from Freud's, including Adler's "individual psychology" and Jung's "analytical psychology."

[13] The distinction I am making is similar in part to that made by Morton Zabel, in his Introduction to Conrad's *Lord Jim* (Boston: Houghton Mifflin Company, 1958), p. xix. Mr. Zabel uses the term "double self" for the subjective component and the term "other self" (if I properly understand him) for the figure of combined objectivity and subjectivity, the one that we shall be concerned with in this study. I am not belittling the importance or the interest of either external duplication alone or internal division alone; I am not calling fiction about them "bad"; I am not calling critics who have applied the word "Double" to them "wrong." I am pointing out that these two phenomena are different from each other, furthermore that both are different from still a third phenomenon, the only really mysterious one of the three, and the one that I refer to as the genuine second self of creative literature: genuine because, as I shall explain later in this chapter, it really is, rather than merely seeming to be, both second *and* self.

[14] Adelbert von Chamisso, *"Peter Schlemihls Wundersame Geschichte," Chamissos Gesammelte Werke,* herausgegeben von Max Koch (Stuttgart und Berlin: J. G. Cotta'sche Buchhandlung Nachfolger, n.d.), II, 275-339.

[15] E. T. A. Hoffmann, *"Die Geschichte vom Verlornen Spiegelbilde," Dichtungen und Schriften* (Weimar: bei Erich Lichtenstein, 1924), VI, 27-48. This little story, for some reason, has been a particular stumbling block to psychologically minded critics. Lawrence Kohlberg, in "Psychological Analysis and Literary Form: A Study of the Doubles in Dostoevsky," *Daedalus* 92 (Spring 1963), 345-62, has Spikher's mirror image become a "devil-figure," which "takes on a life of its own and persecutes its former owner until the victim attempts to kill it and so kills himself." See p. 359. Robert Rogers, in *The Double in Literature,* makes the same mistake, and suggests that this ending was borrowed by Poe for that of *William Wilson.* See p. 25. Actually there is nothing remotely resembling such a conclusion in Hoffmann's story, and it is just the lack of such a real confrontation that keeps the latter out of the category of second-self literature. So far as I know Erasmus Spikher is still wandering the earth in company with Peter Schlemihl, the two economically sharing between them the former's shadow and the latter's mirror image.

[16] As in Longfellow's "The Sicilian's Tale," *Tales of a Wayside Inn* (Boston: Ticknor and Fields, 1863), pp. 55-68.

[17] This story will be discussed in Chapter 6, *infra.*

[18] Cambridge, Mass.: The Riverside Press, 1891.

[19] *Ibid.,* p. 445.

[20] Fyodor Dostoevsky, *Stavrogin's Confession,* translated by Virginia Woolf and S. S. Koteliansky (New York: Lear Publishers, 1947). Except when (as here) quoting others who follow different versions, I shall use the spelling *Dostoyevsky.*

[21] Cf. Ralph Tymms, *Doubles in Literary Psychology* (Cambridge: Bowes & Bowes, 1949), pp. 15-27.

[22] In *The Works of Robert Louis Stevenson* (New York: The Davos Press, 1906), V, 229-307.

[23] William Morris, "The Lady of the Land," *The Earthly Paradise* (New York: Longmans Green, 1900), I, Part II, 164-84.

[24] George du Maurier, *Trilby* (New York: Harper & Brothers, 1874). For Gecko's explanation see pp. 457-59. Among other examples of the purely subjective self I would include Vladimir Nabokov's *Pale Fire.* The relationship between the poet Shade as second self and the narrator Kinbote as first self exists only within the latter's deranged mind, of which the novel is a brilliant study.

[25] In *Xingu and Other Stories* (New York: Charles Scribner's Sons, 1916), pp. 241-80.

[26] Since there has been so much misunderstanding on this point, let me emphasize the fact that the true second self is separate from the first self not only in his body but also in the self which inhabits this body. At the same time the separateness must be of such nature as always to suggest a mutual complementing and indispensability. It is the separateness between the two halves of a single being which together they make up.

[27]I realize that it is difficult for most modern readers not to conclude that any such mutual preoccupation, any mysterious affinity, between two people of the same sex can be explained only by repressed and unconscious homosexual attachment. But such an analysis sounds much more meaningful than it is. Repressed and unconscious homosexuality is simply what constitutes normal heterosexuality; elements of both sexes are present in everyone, and one grows into what one becomes by emphasizing certain things at the expense of other things, which, however, do not disappear but retire into the background, repressed and unconscious. Unless we have something more positive to work with than such "homosexual overtones," we really have nothing at all. Actually the evidence seems to me overwhelming, in all the categories we shall examine, that sexual attachment of either kind is one thing and the affinity between first and second selves quite another.

Readers may also wonder whether there cannot be more than two selves involved in the latter relationship: a situation corresponding to the condition of so-called "multiple personality." Theoretically there is no reason why not; and as we shall see it *is* possible for the first self of one relationship to become the second self of another, and vice versa. But in fiction, if not in psychology, even such complications are rare. Whether because the relationship between consciousness and unconsciousness is felt to be always basically twofold, or for some other reason, the second self of fiction has not tended to fragment or splinter into sub-identities, as does the second self in certain cases of personality dissociation. For a further discussion of this point see Chapter 9, *infra.*

Chapter 2

[1]J. Rendel Harris, *Boanerges* (Cambridge: Cambridge University Press, 1913), pp. 15-48. As will be evident, I am indebted to Mr. Harris' work throughout this chapter. An excellent brief discussion of the subject is E. Sidney Hartland's article, "Twins" in *Encyclopaedia of Religion and Ethics,* edited by James Hastings (Edinburgh: T. & T. Clark, 1911-58), XII, 491-500.

[2]For a discussion of the shadow, the mirror image, and the portrait as primitive "doubles" or sharers of the individual's life, see Sir James George Frazer, *Taboo and the Perils of the Soul,* Vol. III, *The Golden Bough* (New York: Macmillan, 1935), pp. 77-100. "For if it [the shadow or reflection] is trampled upon, struck, or stabbed, he will feel the injury as if it were done to his person; and if it is detached from him entirely (as he believes that it may be) he will die" (p. 78). In *Adonis Attis Osiris* II, 169-70, and in *Balder the Beautiful* II, 163, constituting Volumes VI and XI respectively of *The Golden Bough,* Frazer tells of the belief that "every person has a double, namely, the afterbirth or placenta, which is born immediately after him and is regarded by the people as a second child. Now that double has a ghost of its own, which adheres to the navel-string [of the first child]; and if the person is to remain healthy, it is essential that the ghost of his double should be carefully preserved" (*Adonis Attis Osiris* II, 169-70). Similar to these notions is the Egyptian one of the *ka,* the soul which is a man's exact counterpart, born with him, following him through life, declining with him; see *Taboo and the Perils of the Soul,* pp. 28-29. Obviously such things are closely related to our subject and represent approaches to the figure we are studying, but are not sufficiently developed into independent though participant beings, possessed of individual personalities and wills, capable of entering into what I have called "important and counterbalancing relationship" with their originals, to constitute second selves in the sense in which I am using the term.

[3]The will or spirit, in some form other than the body of the owner, sent forth (usually for malignant purposes) from this body.

[4]For a full discussion of such figures, see A. E. Crawley. "Doubles," *Encyclopaedia of Religion and Ethics,* edited by James Hastings (Edinburgh: T. & T. Clark, 1911-58), IV (1911), 853-60. See also Ralph Tymms, *Doubles in Literary Psychology,* (Cambridge: Bowes and Bowes, 1949) pp. 15-27. For the reader's convenience I will give full bibliographic information about each reference the first time it is cited in each chapter.

[5] Harris, *op. cit.,* pp. 75, 275; also Alfred Métraux, "Twin Heroes in South American Mythology," *Journal of American Folklore* 59 (April-June 1946), 114.

[6] Harris, *op. cit.,* pp. 49-53.

[7] *Ibid.,* p. 113.

[8] *Ibid.,* pp. 81, 86, 159.

[9] *Ibid.,* p. 167.

[10] *Ibid.,* p. 306.

[11] In most myths Horus and Seth are nephew and uncle, as in "The Contest of Horus and Seth for the Rule," translated by John A. Wilson, in *Ancient Near Eastern Texts,* edited by James B. Pritchard (Princeton, N. J.: Princeton University Press, 1950), pp. 14-17. Here the two are contesting for the power of Horus' father Osiris. Jung, however, speaks of one Heru-ur, the "elder Horus," as the Twin Brother of Set (C. G. Jung, *Aion: Researches into the Phenomenology of the Self,* translated by R. F. C. Hull [New York: Pantheon Books, 1959], Bollingen Series XX, Vol. IX, Part II, p. 78).

[12] Harris, *op. cit.,* pp. 275-80.

[13] *Ibid.,* pp. 307-9.

[14] For discussion of this difficulty see Harris, pp. 9, 61-65, 97, 276-79.

[15] *Ibid.,* pp. 9, 306-8. See also the distinction made between Monster-Slayer and Child-of-the-Water, the Twin Heroes of Navajo myth, as recounted by Gladys A. Reichard, *Navaho Religion* (New York: Pantheon Books, 1950), Bollingen Series XVIII, II, 192, 418, 449-51.

[16] Harris, *op. cit.,* pp. 305-8.

[17] *Ibid.,* pp. 159, 336-37.

[18] *Ibid.,* pp. 61-64.

[19] *Ibid.,* p. 86. Not infrequently, in Twin stories, one Twin does literally slay the other.

[20] *Ibid.,* p. 162.

[21] *Ibid.,* p. 382.

[22] *Ibid.,* p. 5.

[23] *Ibid.,* pp. 276-79. See Harris' analysis of the significance of Esau's sale of his birthright.

[24] *Ibid.,* p. 275.

[25] I am following the version of the Parsva story given by Heinrich Zimmer in *Philosophies of India* (New York: Pantheon Books, 1951), Bollingen Series XXVI, pp. 181-204. Joseph Campbell, editor of this work which was left unfinished at the author's death, explains that Zimmer's exact source is not known, though it agrees in the main with the version in Bhavadevasvi's *Parsvanatha Carita,* summarized by Maurice Bloomfield, *The Life and Stories of the Jaina Savior, Parçvanatha* (Baltimore: Johns Hopkins Press, 1919). See Zimmer, p. 181n.

Because of the difficulty of reproducing the diacritical marks on Indian names, I am following a rather general modern practice in omitting them throughout this study, although they are retained by both Zimmer and Bloomfield.

[26] "The Acts of Thomas." pp. 364-437, *The Apocryphal New Testament,* translated by Montague Rhodes James (Oxford: Oxford University Press, 1924). See for example Act III, "The Serpent," in which the serpent says to Thomas: ". . . for I know that thou art the twin-brother of the Christ and always abolishest our nature," p. 379 (this quote is from the Greek text, which James believes preceded the Syriac). See also such passages as those on pp. 431-32, where Thomas is referred to simply as "Judas." For a full discussion of this point see Harris, *op. cit.,* pp. xvi-xvii, 245-49.

[27] Matthew 13:55; Mark 6:3.

[28] John 14:22.

[29] I am only inferring that it is a result; I have no proof of the fact.

[30] Zimmer, *op. cit.*, p. 187n: "Judas, indeed, is represented in a number of mediaeval legends as the elder brother of Jesus." As I have explained, this work was left incomplete at Zimmer's death, and he has not specified the legends to which he refers. But the combination of the fact that Judas is identified in the Apocrypha with Satan, and the fact that in Gnostic legend Satan becomes the elder Twin of Jesus (see n. 32 *infra*), necessarily gives support to this statement. It is interesting to note that by tradition, at least into the Renaissance, Judas Iscariot was thought of as red-haired. Cf. Celia's remark about Orlando's hair, "Something browner than Judas's," *As You Like It*, III, iv. 9. In many cases the second self as Twin Brother is the Red Man, for example, the red Cain, the red Esau. Frequently, as in the red robes of the Dioscuri, the color of the spirit Twin becomes that of the human Twin as well. In origin, however, it is clearly the mark of the spirit parent: the red lightning of the Thunder God, or the red head of King Woodpecker, perhaps the earliest of all examples. Cf. Harris, *op. cit.*, pp. 5, 31-48.

[31] John 6:70. See also John 17:12, also John 13.27: "And after the sop Satan entered into him [Judas]."

[32] James, "The Arabic Gospel of the Infancy," *op. cit.*, pp. 80-82. A summary only is given by James. For a fuller account see Aurelio de Santos Otero, *Los Evangelios Apocrifos* (Madrid: Biblioteca de Autores Cristianos, 1926), pp. 347-48.

[33] *"Duos, ut iam dixi, a deo constitutos asserunt, Cristum et diabolum."* Sanctus Epiphanii Episcopi Constantiensis Panariorum, Liber Primus, Tomus Secundus Corporis Haereseologici, edidit Franciscus Oehler (Berolini: apud A. Asher et Socios., 1859), p. 267. Saint Epiphanius is here referring to the beliefs of the Ebionites. For a full discussion of this point — the Gnostic belief that Satan was the elder brother of Jesus — see C. G. Jung, *Aion*, pp. 42-44, 52, 56-57, 61, 77-78, 81; also Jung, *The Spirit Mercury*, translated by Gladys Phelan and Hildegard Nagel (New York: The Analytical Psychology Club of New York Incorporated, 1953), pp. 26, 33-34, 40. See also Gertrude Jobes, *Dictionary of Mythology, Folklore, and Symbols* (New York: The Scarecrow Press, 1961), II, 1,402, for reference to a Bulgarian sect (unidentified) which likewise believes Satanaël to be the elder, and Christ the younger, of God's two sons.

[34] Métraux, *op. cit.*, p. 121.

[35] I shall follow the translation of E. A. Speiser, "The Epic of Gilgamesh," in *Ancient Near Eastern Texts*, pp. 72-99. This agrees in the main with Alexander Heidel's earlier translation, *The Gilgamesh Epic and Old Testament Parallels* (Chicago: University of Chicago Press, 1946).

[36] Speiser, *op. cit.*, pp. 81, 85.

[37] *Ibid.*, p. 76.

[38] *Ibid.*, p. 78.

[39] Cf. Heidel, *op. cit.*, p. 6.

[40] S. Langdon, who first published the text of the Pennsylvania Tablet, which includes the account of this combat, gives the victory to Enkidu. See his "The Epic of Gilgamish," *The Museum Journal* 8 (January 1917), 35-36. The same position is taken by E. A. Wallis Budge, *The Babylonian Story of the Deluge and the Epic of Gilgamish* (London: British Museum, 1920), p. 43. Heidel (*op. cit.*, p. 32, n. 57) holds that Gilgamesh is the winner. Speiser's translation, p. 76, changes Heidel's "Gilgamesh bent over" to "Gilgamesh bent the knee," which sounds rather like an acknowledgement of defeat (Langdon reads, "Gilgamish bowed to the ground at his feet"). The matter is of no real consequence to us. It is the total effect *on Gilgamesh* of this encounter with his "equal," and of his subsequent friendship with and loss of Enkidu, that brings about the change I am describing and accomplishes the purpose of the gods. Heidel, *op cit.*, p. 6, reaches the same conclusion.

[41] Speiser, *op. cit.*, p. 88.

[42] *Ibid.*, pp. 98-99.

[43] Heidel, *op. cit.*, p. 4.

[44] Speiser, *op. cit.*, p. 74; Heidel, *op. cit.*, p. 19.

Chapter 3

[1] In *The Complete Works of Edgar Allan Poe* (New York: Plymouth Publishing Company, n.d.), Sec. I, Part III, pp. 136-51.

[2] *Ibid.*, p. 138.

[3] *Ibid.*, p. 139.

[4] *Ibid.*, pp. 144-45.

[5] *Ibid.*, p. 146.

[6] "The Horla," *The Life Work of Henri René Guy de Maupassant* (New York and London: M. Walter Dunne, 1903), II, 1-35. Translator's name not given.

[7] *Ibid.*, p. 28.

[8] Albert J. Guerard, "Concepts of the Double," *Stories of the Double,* edited by Albert J. Guerard (Philadelphia and New York: J. B. Lippincott Company, 1967), p. 8, refers to the way in which the invisible persecutor interposes itself between the narrator and the mirror and thus for the moment robs him (as Erasmus Spikher in Hoffmann's story is robbed by Giulietta) of his mirror image. The *Spiegel-Ich* itself, however, plays no part in this story.

[9] In *The Complete Andersen,* translated by Jean Hersholt (New York: The Heritage Press, 1942), Sec. III, pp. 50-62. Much the same situation is exploited in "The Penman," Sec. II, pp. 449-54.

[10] The scenario in question has not been available to me for this study, and I am following the very detailed summary given by Otto Rank in *Der Doppelgänger: Psychoanalytische Studie* (Leipzig, Wien, & Zürich: Internationaler Psychoanalytischer Verlag, 1925), pp. 8-10. This work was originally published in Rank's *Psychoanalytische Beiträge zur Mythenforschung* (Leipzig and Wien: Internationaler Psychoanalytischer Verlag, 1919), pp. 267-354. The film *The Student of Prague,* as revised and directed by Henrik Galeen, was produced in Germany in 1926.

[11] Boston and New York: Houghton Mifflin, 1883.

[12] In a twentieth-century German story — Wilhelm Schmidtbonn's *Der Doppelgänger* (Berlin: Deutsche Buch-Gemeinschaft, G.m.b.H., 1928), pp. 7-60 — we have another objective approach to the second self as Pursuer, though here the pursuit is as comic as that of *The Scarlet Letter* is tragic. The physical duplicate of the actor Heynemann, who appears so inexplicably on the street before him, who insists on accompanying him, who victimizes him with such remorseless insight and such apparently motiveless persistency, is in fact the outlaw, the dark Gottlieb, playing an elaborate joke on his more respectable counterpart.

[13] Translated by George Bird (Bloomington, Indiana: Indiana University Press, 1958).

[14] In "The Theme of the Double in Dostoevsky," translated by René Wellek, included in *Dostoevsky: a Collection of Critical Essays,* edited by René Wellek (Englewood Cliffs, N. J.: Prentice-Hall, 1962), pp. 112-29. Mr. Chizevsky, however, accepts Golyadkin junior as a "Double," without explaining what he means by the word. Of course I do not say that psychic disease on the part of the first self necessarily prevents the second self from being real. But when there is *nothing but* psychic disease, when it is a disease that deceives instead of revealing, and when we the readers are given to understand that the first self is deceived, then there can be no true second self, but only another mistake. This is generally the case with Golyadkin senior in his relationship with Golyadkin junior. It is not in the least true of Ivan Karamazov, who gradually goes insane, in his relationship with Smerdyakov. For a discussion of the latter relationship see Chapter 4, *infra.*

[15] Translated by Ronald Taylor (London: John Calder, 1963).

[16] *Ibid.*, p. 226.

[17] *Ibid.*, pp. 227-28.

[18] But not, I think, quite to the extent suggested by Tymms, *Doubles in Literary Psychology* (Cambridge: Bowes and Bowes, 1949), pp. 56-62. Victor's supposedly dead body is not buried, but disappears before burial, and after the murder of Aurelia vanishes without a trace. Cf. Hoffmann, *op. cit.,* pp. 305, 315, 317, 321.

[19] In *Billy Budd and Other Prose Pieces* Vol. XIII of *The Works of Herman Melville* (London, etc.: Constable and Company, 1924) pp. 5-114.

[20] *Ibid.,* p. 46. Cf. Poe's doctrine of the "Imp of the Perverse." Poe, *op. cit.,* Sec. I, Part IV, pp. 27-36.

[21] *Ibid.,* p. 60.

[22] Vol. XVI of the *Collected Works of Joseph Conrad* (Garden City, New York: Doubleday, Page and Company, 1925.) With an introduction by Bliss Perry.

[23] *Ibid.,* pp. 175, 219.

[24] In both my interpretation and my evaluation of this novel I am wholly at odds with Albert J. Guerard, in his *Conrad the Novelist* (Cambridge, Mass.: Harvard University Press, 1958), pp. 275 ff. "The only genuine identification in *Victory,*" Guerard holds, "would connect Heyst's diffidence with Mr. Jones' 'horror of feminine presence' " (p. 275). It would, of course, but it is the way in which and the reasons for which it makes this connection that are interesting and that establish the paradoxical oneness-in-twoness between these men. In any case, "identification" is not the same thing as "identity"; see my discussion of this difference in Chapter 5, *infra*. Frederick R. Karl, on the other hand, goes to the opposite extreme and makes not only Mr. Jones but most other major characters in the book both "Doubles" of Heyst and "Doubles" of one another: e.g., Lena and Ricardo, and (so far as I can make out) Lena and Morrison, who never meet. Mr. Karl's general analysis of the novel seems to me excellent, but what he means by "Double" (again, it is never explained) is clearly not what I mean by the second self. See his *A Reader's Guide to Joseph Conrad* (New York: The Noonday Press, 1960), pp. 256-62.

[25] *Victory,* pp. 317-18.

[26] New York: Compass Books Edition, by arrangement with the Vanguard Press, Inc., 1956. Originally published 1947.

[27] *Ibid.,* p. 107.

[28] Cf. Chapter 6, *infra.*

Chapter 4

[1] Otto Rank, *Der Doppelgänger: Psychoanalytische Studie* (Leipzig, Wien, und Zürich: Internationaler Psychoanalytischer Verlag, 1925); Dmitri Chizevsky, "The Theme of the Double in Dostoevsky," translated by René Wellek, in *Dostoevsky: a Collection of Critical Essays,* edited by René Wellek (Englewood Cliffs, N. J.: Prentice-Hall, 1962, pp. 112-29; Eliseo Vivas, "The Two Dimensions of Reality in *The Brothers Karamazov,*" also in *Dostoevsky: a Collection of Critical Essays,* pp. 71-89; Ralph Tymms, *Doubles in Literary Psychology* (Cambridge: Bowes and Bowes, 1949), pp. 99-103.

[2] Fyodor Dostoyevsky, *The Brothers Karamazov,* translated by Constance Garnett (New York: Random House, 1943), pp. 771-96.

[3] Translated by Bayard Taylor (Boston and New York: Houghton Mifflin Company, 1870). Because of the length of this work, and the fact that the relationship between the selves is particularly evident in the earlier scenes, I shall confine my consideration to Part I.

[4] *Ibid.,* p. 54

[5] *Ibid.,* p. 68. Rendered by Taylor as "Ah, still delay — thou art so fair!" It should be noted that these words, the heart of the bargain between them, are proposed by Faust, not by Mephistopheles.

[6] *Ibid.,* p. 149.

[7] *Ibid.*

[8] *Ibid.,* pp. 148-53. Were Mephistopheles a being purely separate from Faust, the traditional tempting Devil, this is exactly what he would *not* do.

[9] *Ibid.,* p. 162.

[10] London: the Cresset Press, 1947. With an introduction by André Gide. Originally published in 1824. I do not mean that it is any longer neglected; in recent years it has received a good deal of critical attention.

[11] *Ibid.,* p. 105.

[12] *Ibid.,* p. 35. See the description of the hounding of George, pp. 36-37.

[13] Claggart also tempts Billy Budd to the disastrous act of violence, but without the intention to do so.

[14] Hogg, *op. cit.,* pp. 105-6.

[15] *Ibid.,* pp. 138-40. Claire Rosenfield, in her consideration of this work as an example of what she calls "the Double-Devil Novel," quotes this passage, but only as proof of the fact that Robert has gone mad. In the second part of the story, she feels, "demonology bows to pathology." See "The Shadow Within: The Concious and Unconscious Use of the Double," *Daedalus* 92 (Spring 1963), 335-36. The passage is certainly obsessive in tone, but the relationship between the selves, as I have pointed out, is always characterized by an obsessive quality; this is the subjective side of it, and the obsession as usual grows steadily worse as the relationship progresses. But this is not at all the same thing as to say that we are dealing simply with pathological delusion, any more than we are dealing simply with diabolical visitation in the first part. To the contrary, Hogg is very careful at all times to keep Gil-Martin the paradoxical figure, of combined subjectivity and objectivity, that he needs to be. Gil-Martin's objective existence is clearly established by the fact that he is first mentioned in the Editor's Narrative, not in Robert's own account. Cf. my discussion of the difference between *The Double* and *The Devil's Elixirs* in Chapter 3, *supra; also* Chapter 3, n. 14, *supra.*

[16] E.g., pp. 162, 170, 206.

[17] *Ibid.,* p. 207.

[18] *Ibid.,* p. 189.

[19] *The Brothers Karamazov,* pp. 78-79.

[20] *Ibid.,* p. 315.

[21] *Ibid.,* p. 317.

[22] *Ibid.,* pp. 324-25.

[23] *Ibid.,* p. 332.

[24] *Ibid.,* p. 762.

Chapter 5

[1] *Complete Works of Oscar Wilde,* edited by Robert Ross (New York: Bigelow, Brown & Co., Inc., 1905), II, 1-272.

[2] *Ibid.,* p. 190.

[3] *Ibid.,* pp. 154-55.

[4] In *Afternoon of an Author,* with an introduction and notes by Arthur Mizener (Princeton, N. J.: Princeton University Press, 1957), pp. 142-65. Originally published 1930.

[5] *Ibid.,* p. 165. This scene interestingly recalls the horrified self-encounter of two medieval couples in Rossetti's painting, *How They Met Themselves,* reproduced in H. C. Marillier's *Dante Gabriel Rossetti* (London: Geo. Bell and Sons, 1904), p. 28.

[6] *Der Tod in Venedig* (Berlin: S. Fischer, 1922). The standard translation by H. T. Lowe-Porter, in *Stories of Three Decades* (New York: Alfred A. Knopf, 1945), is a rather free one. More accurate is Kenneth Burke's, included in *Great German Short Novels and Stories* (New York: Random House, 1933), pp. 319-97.

[7] In *The Piazza Tales,* Vol. X of *The Works of Herman Melville* (London, etc.: Constable and Company Ltd., 1923), pp. 66-170.

[8] See, for instance, his reply to Amaso Delano, p. 169.

[9] In *Pale Horse, Pale Rider* (New York: Harcourt, Brace & Company, 1932), pp. 93-176.

[10] *Ibid.,* p. 94.

[11] E.g., pp. 138, 139, 142.

[12] *Collected Works of Joseph Conrad* (Garden City, N. Y.: Doubleday, Page & Company, 1925), Vol. IV.

13 In the spate of Conrad criticism during recent years, numerous critics have noticed this fact, and I make no claim to originality in pointing it out again. My interest is simply in explaining how it fits in with what I have been talking about.

14 Here again, as in the case of *Victory,* I would take issue with Frederick R. Karl, *A Reader's Guide to Joseph Conrad* (New York: The Noonday Press, 1960). Mr. Karl gives Jim a whole host of "Doubles," including not only the figures I mention here but Stein, Jewel, and the German captain of the *Patna.* But again the difficulty probably lies in the vagueness of this word that means all things to all men.

15 *Lord Jim,* pp. 386-87.

16 *Ibid.,* p. 387.

17 This Mr. Guerard makes the central point of the relationship between Brown and Jim. See *Conrad the Novelist,* pp. 150-51.

18 Translated by Constance Garnett (New York: Random House, 1956).

19 Cf. the technique of Mann in *Death in Venice.*

20 *Crime and Punishment,* pp. 25 and 452.

21 Cf. p. 52, *supra.*

22 *Ibid.,* pp. 258-59.

23 *Ibid.,* p. 261.

24 *Ibid.,* p. 420.

25 Most critics who have dealt with the relationship between Raskolnikov and Svidrigaïlov have seen the latter as the former's second self: e.g., Konstantin Mochulsky, *Dostoevsky,* translated by Michael A. Minihan (Princeton, N. J.: Princeton University Press, 1967), pp. 295, 307, 311. Philip Rahv, on the other hand, denies that there is any such "innate relationship" or "affinity of the mystical order" between the two; he holds that Svidrigaïlov's function is to provide an additional perspective on Raskolnikov, and to give the novel "the psychosexual vitality which it otherwise lacks." See "Dostoevsky in 'Crime and Punishment,'" *Partisan Review* 27 (Summer 1960), 408. Mr. Rahv is unusual in explaining what he means by "Double," apparently the same figure we are discussing, but I could not disagree more completely with the conclusion he draws. The innate relationship and mystical affinity between the two men, as I attempt to show here, are exactly what makes this one of the most remarkable and unmistakable examples of the literature of the second self. Giving us additional perspective on the first self is what the second self to a very considerable extent exists to do. So far as providing psychosexual vitality is concerned, I should say that if this is Svidrigaïlov's function he does a miserable job of it. He is preoccupied with sex in just the random and febrile and compulsive manner of one who is pathologically deficient in such a quality; he keeps knocking at all the many doors of sex (the grimy little alley doors, in the main) and getting no answer.

Chapter 6

1 Saul Bellow, *The Victim* (New York: Compass Books Edition, by arrangement with the Vanguard Press, Inc., 1956), pp. 291-94.

2 *Walden,* Vol. II of *The Writings of Henry David Thoreau* (Boston: Houghton Mifflin Company, 1893), p. 211.

3 Lawrence Kohlberg, in "Psychological Analysis and Literary Form: A Study of the Doubles in Dostoevsky," *Daedalus* 92 (Spring 1963), 345-62, includes "Christ Figures" among the six types of "Double" that his use of the "Q technique" has enabled him to find in the work of Dostoyevsky. This is the only one of Dr. Kohlberg's types, however, that resembles any of the categories used in this study, and since he includes in it such a figure as Alyosha Karamazov I rather doubt that he means by it the same thing that I mean by the Second Self as Saviour.

4 Cf. Alfred Métraux, "Twin Heroes in South American Mythology," *Journal of American Folklore* 59 (April-June 1946), 121.

5 In *The Magic Barrel* (New York: Farrar, Straus, & Cudahy, 1950), pp. 155-82.

[6] *Ibid.,* p. 182.

[7] Translated by Graham Rawson, with an Introduction by Gunnar Ollén (London: Jonathan Cape Ltd., 1939). The triology was completed in 1901.

[8] Cf. the situation in *Lord Jim,* discussed in Chapter 5, *supra.*

[9] Strindberg, *op. cit.,* p. 91.

[10] In *The Complete Works of Edgar Allan Poe* (New York: Plymouth Publishing Company, n.d.), Sec. I, Part IV, pp. 158-90.

[11] In this affectionateness Mr. Guerard, "Concepts of the Double," in *Stories of the Double* (Philadelphia and New York: J. B. Lippincott Company, 1967), p. 3, finds "homosexual, narcissistic overtones." See my discussion of this point in Chapter 1, n. 27, *supra.*

[12] For this extraordinary passage, too long to be quoted here, see *William Wilson,* pp. 173-75.

[13] Emil Lucka, apparently getting this story confused with *The Picture of Dorian Gray,* supposes that there is a real mirror, and has it fall clattering in fragments when the second self is stabbed. See *"Verdoppelungen des Ich"* in *Preussische Jahrbücher* 115 (Januar bis März 1904), 69-70.

[14] As in my opinion it is by Lucka, *op. cit.,* pp. 69-70, Tymms, *Doubles in Literary Psychology* (Cambridge: Bowes and Bowes, 1949), pp. 88-89, and Guerard, "Concepts of the Double," pp. 2-3, in all cases with resultant damage to interpretation. The second William Wilson is no bloodless abstraction or allegory; if he were, he would have no place in this study, and the story would long since have been forgotten. See my discussion of the second self as symbol (rather than allegory) in Chapter 9, *infra.*

[15] In Vol. III of *The Works of Robert Louis Stevenson,* edited by Charles Curtis Bigelow and Temple Scott (New York: The Davos Press, 1906), pp. 359-78.

[16] *Ibid.,* p. 372.

[17] *Ibid.,* p. 378.

[18] Translator's name not given (New York: Boni & Liveright, Inc., 1923).

[19] This twofold hearing of the second self is not infrequently experienced by the first. Cf. the case of Harry Haller in Hesse's *Steppenwolf,* discussed in Chapter 7, *infra.*

[20] *Ibid.,* p. 106.

[21] *Ibid.,* pp. 115-16.

[22] *Ibid.,* pp. 214-15.

[23] In *'Twixt Land and Sea,* Vol. XIII of *Collected Works of Joseph Conrad* (Garden City, N. Y.: Doubleday, Page & Company, 1925), pp. 91-143.

[24] *Ibid.,* p. 142. As Mr. Guerard has noted, the hat according to Jung has symbolic significance in dreams, suggesting the changing personality of the dreamer. In this case the captain's personality, entrusted to Leggatt to save the latter, is returned with interest to save the former. See Guerard, *Conrad the Novelist* (Cambridge, Mass.: Harvard University Press, 1958), p. 25; also Jung, *Psychology and Alchemy,* translated by R. F. C. Hull (New York: Pantheon Books, 1953), Bollingen Series XX, Vol. XII, pp. 47-48. Indeed the whole story reads like an intentional illustration of modern psychoanalytical, and especially Jungian, symbolism.

[25] "The Secret Sharer," p. 143.

[26] In *The Piazza Tales,* Vol. X of *The Works of Herman Melville* (London, etc.: Constable and Company, Ltd., 1923), 19-65.

[27] *Ibid.,* p. 40.

[28] *Ibid.,* p. 61.

[29] In other words, I would agree with Mr. Guerard's suggestion that "Bartleby perhaps exists as an image of quiet insubordinate refusal to accept the safe and prudent and methodical." "Concepts of the Double," p. 12. But simply this would give us simply a story of refusal, not in any way a story of the second self.

[30] *The Writings of Victor Hugo* (New York: Henry W. Knight, International Edition, n.d.). The same translation is published by the Chesterfield Society (London & New York, n.d.). The translator's name is not given, but the translation seems to me the most accurate of those I have examined. The volumes of this edition are not numbered, and I shall in the following references use the volume numbers of the original text.

[31] *Ibid.*, I, 149.

[32] *Ibid.*, I, 157-58. Cf. the strikingly similar vision at the end of Hermann Hesse's *Die Morgenlandfahrt,* in *Gesammelte Schriften* (Berlin und Frankfurt: Suhrkamp Verlag, 1957), VI, 9-76, where the first-self-narrator watches his own image, standing beside that of Leo, gradually being absorbed into the latter.

[33] *Les Misérables,* I, 236.

[34] *Ibid.*, I, 395. "Nothing could be so heart-rending and terrible as that face, in which was displayed all that may be called the wickedness of the good."

[35] *Ibid.*, I, 309-10.

[36] *Ibid.*, V, 90.

[37] *Ibid.*, V, 217.

Chapter 7

[1] In *The Dialogues of Plato,* translated by B. Jowett (New York: Bigelow, Brown & Company, n.d.), III, 273-358.

[2] *Ibid.*, p. 315.

[3] Actually according to Aristophanes there were originally three sexes: male, female, and androgynous. See pp. 315-17. Only the splitting of the last could result in heterosexual love.

[4] Genesis 2: 21-24.

[5] Nandor Fodor, *The Search for the Beloved* (New York: Hermitage Press, Inc., 1949), p. 277.

[6] *Ibid.*, pp. 277-78.

[7] Plato, *op. cit.,* p. 318.

[8] In *The Complete Works of Edgar Allan Poe* (New York: Plymouth Publishing Company, n.d.), Sec. III, Part I, pp. 38-62.

[9] We shall see further examples in this chapter. The contrast, which is one aspect of the universal Light-Dark contrast that runs through all literature and especially that of the second self, has of course been noticed before. Leslie Fiedler, for example, in *Love and Death in the American Novel* (New York: Stein and Day, 1966 revised), calls them the "Fair Maiden" and her "Dark Opposite" (p. 310). Robert Rogers, in *The Double in Literature* (Detroit: Wayne State University Press, 1970), follows Fiedler in calling them "Fair Maid and Femme Fatale" (pp. 126-37), and applies this contrast to the subject of the second self. Mr. Rogers, however, seems to consider the two figures of equal importance, "doubles" of each other and of the hero as well. Whatever Mr. Rogers may mean by "double," the "Fair Maiden" or "Fair Maid" (or in the case of Edgar Linton the "Fair Young Man"), in stories of this category that make use of this particular contrast, is never more than a background figure who sets off and intensifies the mystery of the true Beloved. She is never herself the Beloved, nor is she involved in the relationship between the selves, though she might dearly like to be. See my discussion of *Pierre,* later in this chapter.

[10] *Ligeia,* p. 62.

[11] Edinburgh: John Grant, 1924. With Preface by Charlotte Brontë.

[12] *Ibid.*, p. 118.

[13] Claire Rosenfield, in "The Shadow Within: The Conscious and Unconscious Use of the Double," *Daedalus* 92 (Spring 1963), 326-44, describes Cathy and Heathcliff as "themselves exact Doubles differing in sex alone." If she means by this that they are exact duplicates, I should take exception on two counts: one, that the story does not show them to be; two, that if they were there could be no relationship at all, merely coexistence. To complement is never to duplicate; it is to furnish the *other* half. Cf. my discussion of this point in Chapter 1, *supra.*

[14] In *The Day's Work* (New York: Doubleday, Page & Company, 1925), pp. 385-431. These stories were originally published between 1894 and 1905.

[15] *Ibid.*, p. 400.

[16] New York and London: Harper and Brothers, 1900. Originally published 1891.

[17] *Ibid.*, pp. 395-96.

[18] Translated by Basil Creighton (New York: Henry Holt and Company, 1929). A similar example is Ibsen's *The Master Builder.*

[19] *Ibid.*, p. 146.

[20] *Ibid.*, p. 213. In "The Treatise on the Steppenwolf" Harry has read that within a single Steppenwolf there are not merely two but innumerable souls. But it is only Hermine who is his true "looking-glass" in the sense in which she here uses the word; it is only Hermine who is sufficiently developed as a counterbalancing force to constitute a genuine second self. The other characters — Pablo, Maria, the editor of Harry's records — are at most suggestive fragments. Cf. my discussion of "multiple selves" in Chapter 1, n. 27, *supra.*

[21] *Ibid.*, p. 151.

[22] *Ibid.*, p. 177.

[23] *Ibid.*, p. 215.

[24] Pausanais: *Description of Greece,* with an English translation by W. H. S. Jones (Cambridge, Mass.: Harvard University Press; London, Wm. Heinemann Ltd., 1935), Loeb Classical Library, IV, 311. The passage in question is in Book IX, Chapter 31.

[25] J. Rendel Harris, *Boanerges* (Cambridge: Cambridge University Press, 1913), pp. 167-74. It is not so viewed by all peoples, but the idea tends to be characteristic of the more primitive, like the Malay tribes of Sumatra, and hence would seem to represent the original attitude. Cf. E. Sidney Hartland, "Twins," *Encyclopaedia of Religion and Ethics,* edited by James Hastings (Edinburgh: T. & T. Clark, 1911-58), XII (1924), 491-500.

[26] For this term see Harris, *op. cit.*, p. 67.

[27] E.g., *Steppenwolf,* pp. 175, 177, 209, 217.

[28] *The Complete Poetical Works of Percy Bysshe Shelley,* edited by Thomas Hutchinson (London: Oxford University Press, 1927), p. 407, ll. 45-52.

[29] In *Stories of Three Decades,* translated by H. T. Lowe-Porter (New York: Alfred A. Knopf, 1945), pp. 297-317.

[30] In *Complete Works,* Sec. I, Part III, pp. 152-81.

[31] *Ibid.*, p. 162.

[32] *Ibid.*, p. 171.

[33] *Ibid.*, p. 181.

[34] *Ibid.*, p. 157.

[35] *Ibid.*, p. 172.

[36] I have no wish to force this interpretation, or any other interpretation, down the reader's throat; no interpretation of literature is ever the "necessary" one. Furthermore I admit that it is unusual for Poe to depend so upon hints, rather than more clearly defining his point. But it would be far more unusual for him to waste the amount of verbiage we should have to assume he has wasted if we took all these hints, only a few of which I have had space to mention, to be simply devices to achieve "atmosphere." From the very beginning the suggestion of incest and its consequences, in the mysterious disease and doom of the "House" which is both family mansion and the family itself (p. 155), is present; see for example the long and otherwise irrelevant discussion of the inbred quality of the Usher race (pp. 154-55): the stem has put forth no enduring branch; there has never been any collateral issue; the entire family has lain always in the direct line of descent, with "consequent undeviating transmission, from sire to son, of the patrimony with the name."

I also admit that the identity of Roderick and Madeline is less clearly established than that of the twins in *The Blood of the Walsungs,* in large part because it fits Poe's purpose in this case to keep the second self so far in the background; but I should say that it was no less an example, and an infinitely more interesting one, just because the physical relationship is suggested rather than insisted upon.

Two recent studies of this story, which have also stressed the importance of the second-self theme that lies at the heart of it, are Patrick F. Quinn's "That Spectre in My Path," *The French Face of Edgar Poe* (Carbondale: Southern Illinois University Press, 1957), pp. 216-56; and Joseph J. Moldenhauer, "Poe's Aesthetics, Psychology, and Moral Vision," *PMLA* 83, No. 2 (May 1968), 284-97. Both are of special interest to us in that both recognize the prevalence of the second self throughout Poe's work as a whole; both, too, have gone into more detail regarding the symbolism of this story than I have been able to do in the brief summary-analysis given here. Mr. Moldenhauer, for example, finds six different "doublings" on the literal and symbolic planes, all centering in the relationship between the twins, "a love which culminates in a cruel *Liebestod*" (p. 295). Indeed, since the narrator is merely a sort of adjunct to Roderick, he suggests, we have a doubling between "us" (Roderick-plus-narrator) and "her" (Madeline). "That is, to exploit a pun in the hero's name, the story deals with the fall and completion of the house of 'Us-her.' And indeed the tale concludes with the merging of these complementary images and figures in the unity of death" (p. 295).

37 Vol. IX of *The Works of Herman Melville* (London: Constable and Company, Ltd., 1923).

38 *Ibid.*, p. 115. We have here, of course, an example of the kind of time-spanning relationship we shall examine in the next chapter, though not in this case between first and second selves.

39 *Ibid.*, p. 268.

40 *Ibid.*, p. 505.

41 See for example p. 265, where "her hair sideways swept over him, and half concealed him."

Chapter 8

1 *The Confessions,* translated by E. B. Pusey (New York: Dutton, 1950). Augustine's discussion of Time is in Book XI. The question has been dealt with extensively in our own century, e.g., by J. W. Dunne, *An Experiment with Time* (New York: The Macmillan Company, 1938), and by C. G. Jung, "Synchronocity: An Acausal Connecting Principle," *The Structure and Dynamics of the Psyche,* translated by R. F. C. Hull (New York: Pantheon Books, 1960), Bollingen Series XX, Vol. VIII, pp. 417-531.

2 *The Great Divorce* (New York: The Macmillan Company, 1957), p. vii of Preface, also pp. 18, 19, 23.

3 In *The Ghostly Tales of Henry James,* edited by Leon Edel (New Brunswick, N. J.: Rutgers University Press, 1948), pp. 720-62. The same idea of a "lengthwise" splitting of Time to show what might have happened is used by J. B. Priestley in "Dangerous Corner," *The Plays of J. B. Priestley* (London: Wm. Heinemann Ltd., 1948), I.

4 *The Jolly Corner,* p. 736.

5 *Ibid.*, p. 750.

6 *Ibid.*, pp. 756-57.

7 In *The Complete Works of Edgar Allan Poe* (New York: Plymouth Publishing Company, n.d.), Sec. II, Part I, p. 72-88.

8 In the report of Bedloe's death his name, by a "typographical error," is spelled "Bedlo," or "Oldeb conversed." *Ibid.*, p. 88.

9 Included in *Six Novels of the Supernatural,* edited by Edward Wagenknecht (New York: The Viking Press, 1948), pp. 157-425.

10 New York: Charles Scribner's Sons, 1917.

11 See *Ghostly Tales,* editor's note, pp. 720-25.

12 *The Sense of the Past,* pp. 87-88.

13 In *The Complete Short Stories of Nathaniel Hawthorne* (Garden City, N. J.: Doubleday and Company, 1959), pp. 90-98.

¹⁴*Der Verschwender, Sämtliche Werke,* herausgegeben von Fritz Bruckner und Eduard Castle (Wien: Verlag von Anton Schroll & Co., n.d.), II, 335-460.

¹⁵In *Sämtliche Werke,* herausgegeben von Otto F. Lachmann (Leipzig: Phillipp Reclam jun., 1887), I, 126. This poem, No. 23 of *Die Heimkehr* (1823-24), is sometimes referred to as *"Der Doppelgänger."*

¹⁶George du Maurier, *Peter Ibbetson* (New York and London: Harper and Brothers, 1900), p. 213.

¹⁷*Ibid.,* p. 380.

¹⁸In *Sämtliche Werke* (Stuttgart und Berlin: J. G. Cotta'sche Buchhandlung Nachfolger, n.d.), Vol. XXIV.

¹⁹*Ibid.,* p. 64 (my translation).

²⁰New York: Coward-McCann, Inc., 1930.

²¹*Ibid.,* pp. 103-4.

²²*Ibid.,* p. 235.

²³*Ibid.,* p. 275.

²⁴*Ibid.,* pp. 297-98.

Chapter 9

¹*Das Doppel-Ich* (Leipzig: Ernst Gunthers Verlag, 1890). Naturally I do not pretend, in any of these brief summaries, to do full justice to the writer's argument, often a very involved one.

²*Ibid.,* p. 38 (my translation).

³*Ibid.* (my translation).

⁴Emil Lucka, *"Verdoppelungen des Ich," Preussische Jahrbücher* 115 (Januar bis März 1904), 54-83.

⁵My interpretation of what Lucka says on this subject is exactly the opposite of that given by Ralph Tymms, *Doubles in Literary Psychology* (Cambridge: Bowes and Bowes, 1949), p. 95. Though making allowances for such a story as *William Wilson,* Lucka is quite specific about the usual nature of the second self; e.g., p. 60: *"In ihm* [the Double] *sind die bösen Elemente des Ich zu einer lebenden Persönlichkeit verdichtet gedacht, die nun als erschreckliche Vorstellung schon zu Lebzeiten des Mensch 'umgeht.' "*

⁶*Ibid.,* p. 65 (my translation).

⁷*Der Doppelgänger: Psychoanalytische Studie* (Leipzig, Wien, und Zürich: Internationaler Psychoanalytischer Verlag, 1925).

⁸*Ibid.,* pp. 109-10.

⁹In *Beyond Psychology* (New York: Dover Publications, Inc., 1958), pp. 62-101.

¹⁰I am using the terms "Freudian" and "Jungian" in a broad rather than strict sense. Rank, I believe, had already broken with Freud at the time of the earlier of these works, and he certainly never became a disciple of Jung.

¹¹Cf. Chapter 2, n. 2, *supra.*

¹²In large part Rank's source is Harris' *Boanerges,* already frequently cited in this study. Rank does not, however, give specific references.

¹³"The Double as Immortal Self," p. 91.

¹⁴*Ibid.,* p. 95.

¹⁵*Ibid.,* p. 76.

¹⁶Detroit: Wayne State University Press, 1970.

¹⁷Thus in Hogg's *The Private Memoirs and Confessions of a Justified Sinner,* Robert (for Mr. Rogers) is "homosexually oriented" and his matricide (if he did it) is "symbolic incest." He and Gil-Martin, doubles of each other, "function as latent doubles of George in an oedipal matrix." Thus also the statement of the narrator of *Bartleby,* that he has been not only disarmed but unmanned by Bartleby's wonderful mildness, means that he feels himself to have been castrated by Bartleby.

¹⁸*Das Doppelgängermotiv in der Romantik.* Studien zum Romantischen Idealismus: Germanische Studien, Heft 99 (Berlin: Verlag von Emil Ebering, 1930).

[19] Tymms, *Doubles in Literary Psychology,* p. 119.

[20] *Ibid.,* p. 121.

[21] "The Double in Romantic Narrative: a Preliminary Study," *The Germanic Review* 36, No. 4 (December 1961), 257-68.

[22] "The Shadow Within: the Conscious and Unconscious Use of the Double," *Daedalus* 92 (Spring 1963), 326-44.

[23] *Ibid.,* p. 344.

[24] New York: New York University Press; London: University of London Press Limited, 1969.

[25] *Ibid.,* p. ix.

[26] Among the shorter studies of the subject is A. E. Crawley's essay, "Doubles," *Encyclopaedia of Religion and Ethics,* edited by James Hastings (Edinburgh: T. & T. Clark, 1911-58), IV, 853-60. Mr. Crawley deals exclusively with what I have called the "objective second self," the physical duplicate. He includes mention of a "spiritual double," but this differs from the "material double" only in that it possesses the quality of visibility without that of tangibility. There are also numerous articles, some of which have been referred to in earlier chapters, that have studied ways in which the second self makes his appearance in the works of individual authors, but that have applied their conclusions only to these authors, and therefore are not really relevant to the present discussion. A more ambitious work in this category, Natalie Reber's *Studien zum Motiv des Doppelgängers bei Dostoevsky und E. T. A. Hoffmann* (Marburger Abhandlungen zur Geschichte und Kultur Osteuropas, Band 6; Giessen: Kommissionsverlag Wilhelm Schmitz, 1964), has not been available to me for the present study. From André von Gronicka's review, *Journal of English and Germanic Philology* 65 (July 1966), 554-57, I gather that Miss Reber takes the biographical-psychological approach, and sees the second self much as Lucka and the earlier Rank see it, as the expression of the artist's own narcissistic nature and the embodiment of his own evil conscience.

[27] This generalization is true to the extent that a clear distinction is observed (as it is by Rank and frequently is not by Miss Krauss) between the original and his *Doppelgänger,* i.e., between first self and second self.

[28] In fact the confusion goes further than this. Thus Ernest J. Simmons, *Dostoevski: the Making of a Novelist* (London: Oxford University Press, 1940), calls both Raskolnikov and Ivan Karamazov "Doubles," meaning no more than that each is a two-sided character or split personality (pp. 159, 355). In Irving Howe's "Dostoevsky: *The Politics of Salvation,*" *Politics and the Novel* (New York: Horizon Press, 1957), pp. 51-75, the fictional character Peter Verhovensky is spoken of as the "Double" of the real politician Nechayev (p. 62). I am not disputing the point with Mr. Howe; I simply have no way of knowing what he means by it. Later in this same essay Mr. Howe uses the word in a far more definite and apparently quite different sense, suggesting that all but one of the other main characters in *The Possessed* become "Doubles" of the protagonist Stavrogin, meaning that each complements a different aspect of Stravrogin's character. Though I cannot agree with Mr. Howe in this interpretation, and therefore have not included *The Possessed* in this study, an approach to something of the sort does seem to be there, as it does to a lesser extent throughout Dostoyevsky's other novels. The idea is certainly a most interesting one, similar to what I suggest at the end of this chapter as the meaning of the second self: an expression in specific form of a sense of shared identity that goes far beyond any specific case; the sense, as Mr. Howe puts it, that "he is We." Cf. Chapter 1, n. 27, *supra,* regarding the possibility of a relationship involving more than two selves.

Mr. Rogers makes similarly interesting suggestions in discussing this possibility in general terms, but his application of the idea in practice is less satisfactory. Despite his recognition of the need for "a broad, generic definition" of the double (p. 2), he never furnishes one, and gives himself no criterion by which to decide whether he is dealing with a double or not. As a result, any relationship of any sort between any two or more characters is enough to make them "doubles" of one another. Thus Macbeth has as doubles Banquo, Macduff, Malcolm, Donalbain, Duncan, the ci-devant Thane of Cawdor, Macduff's son, et. al., while Lady Macbeth's doubles include the three weird sisters, Lady Macduff, and Scotland herself. But since Macbeth and Lady Macbeth are also doubles, each possesses as doubles all the doubles of the other, and necessarily everyone in the play becomes the double of everyone else (pp. 49-51). If Mr. Rogers' meaning is that any fictional character that comes to life does so because the author has put something of himself into it, and that all the characters created by any one author are in this way related to one another, I have not the slightest doubt that he is right, though I have very grave doubt that psychoanalysis or any other system of thought understands so exactly as his work would imply all the mysteries of the creative process by which this happens. But to use the word "double" for such a relationship is to use it so broadly and loosely as to deprive it of any meaning whatever.

29 Freud has pointed out that in German the word *heimlich*, meaning "homely" in the sense of "familiar," has a meaning "which develops towards an ambivalence, until it finally coincides with its opposite, *unheimlich* ["uncanny"]." See "The 'Uncanny,' " *On Creativity and the Unconscious* (New York: Harper and Brothers, 1958), p. 131. The translation of this essay, first published in 1919, is by Alix Strachey. Mr. Guerard, in "Concepts of the Double," p. 4, makes the same point: "The experience of encountering a double is indeed uncanny: a response not merely to strangeness but to familiarity."

30 *Faust*, translated by Bayard Taylor (Boston and New York: Houghton Mifflin Company, 1870), p. 15.

31 Cf. Jung's discussion of this point in *Two Essays on Analytical Psychology* (New York: Pantheon Books, 1953), Bollingen Series XX, Vol. VII, pp. 48 ff.

32 Cf. *Ibid.*, p. 99.

33 I do not mean that such things have not been scientifically explained; I mean that such explanations, which are really descriptions, have done little to reduce the general sense of mystery about them.

34 A symbol, in Coleridge's words, "always partakes of the reality which it renders intelligible, and while it enunciates the whole, abides itself as a living part in that unity of which it is the representative." "The Statesman's Manual," in *The Complete Works of Samuel Taylor Coleridge*, edited by W. G. T. Shedd (New York: Harper & Brothers, 1884), I, 437-38. See the complete passage for his distinction, the best that I know, between symbol and allegory, "a translation of abstract ideas into a picture-language."

35 The following brief summary (and necessary simplification) of Jung's ideas is based on a study of his work as a whole. For the subject of the archetypes see especially *The Archetypes and The Collective Unconscious*, translated by R. F. C. Hull (New York: Pantheon Books, 1959), Bollingen Series XX, Vol. IX, Part I; also *Aion: the Phenomenology of the Self* (Vol. IX, Part II); also *Psychology and Alchemy* (Vol. XIII, 1953).

36 Freud, too, though not carrying the idea nearly so far as Jung, has suggested the possibility of memories going beyond individual experience. In speaking of childhood fantasies, he says that some are in his opinion "primal" in nature: in other words "a phylogenetic possession. In them the individual, wherever his own experience becomes insufficient, stretches out beyond it to the experience of past ages." Sigmund Freud, *A General Introduction to Psycho-Analysis*, translated by Joan Riviere (New York: Liveright Publishing Company, 1935), p. 324.

37 These at least are the main archetypes of the masculine unconscious, for the collective unconscious has apparently both a masculine and a feminine side. It is to the masculine side that Jung gives major attention. In the feminine unconscious the sexes, as might be expected, tend to be reversed: thus the anima becomes the animus, and the wise old man becomes the chthonic mother. Cf. *Aion*, p. 22.

38 *Aion*, p. 14.

39 *The Archetypes and the Collective Unconscious*, p. 226.

40 *Ibid.*, pp. 25, 28. Cf. also *Psychology and Alchemy*, pp. 23, 44-56, 70n.

41 See for example *Psychology and Alchemy*, pp. 30-32, 73, *et passim*.

42 *Ibid.*, pp. 40-41. Cf. also *Aion*, p. 8.

43 Most of my summary of Buber's ideas is based on his *I and Thou*, translated by Ronald Gregor Smith (Edinburgh: T. & T. Clark, 1953).

44 *Ibid.*, p. 59.

45 *Ibid.*, p. 63.

46 "Elements of the Interhuman," in *The Knowledge of Man*, translated by Maurice Friedman and Ronald Gregor Smith, edited by Maurice Friedman (New York: Harper and Row, 1965), p. 81.

47 *Ibid.*, p. 84.

48 *I and Thou*, p. 5. "Only when two say to one another with all that they are, 'It is Thou,' is the indwelling of the Present Being between them." This passage is from "Dialogue," in *Between Man and Man*, translated by Ronald Gregor Smith (Boston: Beacon Press, 1955), p. 30.

49 *I and Thou*, p. 33.

50 *Ibid.*

51 *Ibid.*, p. 51.

52 *Ibid.*, p. 59.

53 See Buber's criticism of Jung in "Guilt and Guilt Feelings," in *The Knowledge of Man*, pp. 124-25.

54 *I and Thou*, p. 63.

55 *Ibid.*

56 See for example *The Archetypes and the Collective Unconscious*, pp. 214-23, 275-89, *et passim*. For a clinical instance of the constructive, healing function of the second-self figure see Jung's account of the child Margaret and her imaginary twin Anna. C. G. Jung, *The Development of Personality*, translated by R. F. C. Hull (New York: Pantheon Books, 1954), Bollingen Series XX, Vol. XVII, pp. 129-31.

57 *I and Thou*, p. 46

58 "Dialogue," *Between Man and Man*, pp. 22-23.

59 *I and Thou*, p. 39.

60 *Ibid.*

61 "The Over-Soul," in *The Complete Works of Ralph Waldo Emerson* (Boston and New York: Houghton Mifflin Company, 1903-21), II, 269.

62 "*Der Quäler und der Gequälte sind Eines. Jener irrt, indem er sich der Quaal, dieser, indem er sich der Schuld nicht theilhaft glaubt.*" Arthur Schopenhauer, *Die Welt als Wille und Vorstellung* (Leipzig: Philipp Reclam jun., n.d.) I, 456 (my translation). Cf. Emerson's poem, *Brahma*. Schopenhauer cites as his source *Oupnek'hat*, I, 60 ff.

63 "Compensation," *Complete Works*, II, 124.

64 Schopenhauer, *op. cit.*, p. 458.

Works Cited

Andersen, Hans Christian. *The Complete Andersen.* Translated by Jean Hersholt. New York: The Heritage Press, 1942.

Augustine (Saint). *The Confessions.* Translated by E. B. Pusey. New York: Dutton, 1950.

Bellow, Saul. *The Victim.* 2nd ed. New York: Compass Books by arrangement with the Vanguard Press, Inc., 1956. [1st ed. New York: Vanguard Press, Inc., 1947.]

Bloomfield, Maurice, ed. *The Life and Stories of the Jaina Savior Parçvanatha.* Baltimore: Johns Hopkins Press, 1919.

Brontë, Emily, *Wuthering Heights.* Edinburgh: John Grant, 1924. With preface by Charlotte Brontë.

Buber, Martin. *Between Man and Man.* Translated by Ronald Gregor Smith. Boston: Beacon Press, 1955.

————. *I and Thou.* Translated by Ronald Gregor Smith. Edinburgh: T. & T. Clark, 1953.

————. *The Knowledge of Man.* Edited by Maurice Friedman. Translated by Maurice Friedman and Ronald Gregor Smith. New York: Harper and Row, 1965.

Budge, E. A. Wallis. *The Babylonian Story of the Deluge and the Epic of Gilgamish.* London: British Museum, 1920.

[229]

Chamisso, Adelbert von. *"Peter Schlemihls Wundersame Geschichte."* In *Chamissos Gesammelte Werke* II, 275-339. Herausgegeben von Max Koch. Stuttgart und Berlin: J. G. Cotta'sche Buchhandlung Nachfolger, n.d.

Chizevsky, Dmitri. "The Theme of the Double in Dostoevsky." Translated by René Wellek. In *Dostoevsky: a Collection of Critical Essays,* pp. 112-29. Edited by René Wellek. Englewood Cliffs, N.J.: Prentice-Hall, 1962.

Coleridge, Samuel Taylor. "The Stateman's Manual." In *The Complete Works of Samuel Taylor Coleridge* I, 417-84. Edited by W. G. T. Shedd. New York: Harper & Brothers, 1884.

Conrad, Joseph. *Collected Works of Joseph Conrad.* Memorial Edition. Vol. IV: *Lord Jim.* With an introduction by Sir Hugh Clifford. Vol. XIII: *'Twixt Land and Sea.* With an introduction by Christopher Morley. Vol. XVI: *Victory.* With an introduction by Bliss Perry. Garden City, New York: Doubleday, Page & Company, 1925.

Crawley, A. E. "Doubles." In *Encyclopaedia of Religion and Ethics* IV (1911), 853-60. Edited by James Hastings. Edinburgh: T. & T. Clark, 1911-58.

De la Mare, Walter. "The Return." In *Six Novels of the Supernatural,* pp. 157-425. Edited by Edward Wagenknecht. New York: The Viking Press, 1948.

Dessoir, Max. *Das Doppel-Ich.* Leipzig: Ernst Gunthers Verlag, 1890.

Dostoyevsky, Fyodor. *The Brothers Karamazov.* Translated by Constance Garnett. New York: Random House, 1943.

————. *Crime and Punishment.* Translated by Constance Garnett. New York: Random House, 1956.

————. *The Double.* Translated by George Bird. Bloomington, Indiana: Indiana University Press, 1958.

————. *Stavrogin's Confession.* Translated by Virginia Woolf and S. S. Koteliansky. New York: Lear Publishers, 1947.

du Maurier, George. *Peter Ibbetson.* New York and London: Harper and Brothers, 1900.

————. *Trilby.* New York: Harper and Brothers, 1874.

Dunne, J. W. *An Experiment with Time.* New York: The Macmillan Company, 1938.

Emerson, Ralph Waldo. *The Complete Works of Ralph Waldo Emerson.* Vol. II: *Essays: First Series.* Boston and New York: Houghton Mifflin Company, 1903-1921.

Epiphanius (Sanctus). *Panaria.* Tomus Secundus, *Corporis Haereseologici.* Edidit Franciscus Oehler. [Also translated, from Greek into Latin, by Oehler.] Berolini: Apud A. Asher et Socios., 1859.

Ewers, Hans Heinz. *Der Student von Prague.* A film scenario summarized by Otto Rank in *Der Doppelgänger: Psychoanalytische Studie* (q.v.).

Fiedler, Leslie. *Love and Death in the American Novel.* New York: Stein and Day, 1966. Revision of 1960 edition.

Fitzgerald, F. Scott. "One Trip Abroad." In *Afternoon of an Author*, pp. 142-65. With an introduction and notes by Arthur Mizener. Princeton, N.J.: Princeton University Press, 1957.

Fodor, Nandor. *The Search for the Beloved*. New York: Hermitage Press, 1949.

Frazer, Sir James George. *The Golden Bough*. Vol III: *Taboo and the Perils of the Soul*. Vol. VI: *Adonis Attis Osiris*. Vol. XI: *Balder the Beautiful*. New York: Macmillan, 1935.

Freud, Sigmund. *A General Introduction to Psycho-Analysis*. Translated by Joan Riviere. New York: Liveright Publishing Company, 1935.

————. "The 'Uncanny'." In *On Creativity and the Unconscious*, pp. 122-61. Translated by Alix Strachey. New York: Harper and Brothers, 1958.

Goethe, Johann Wolfgang von. *Sämtliche Werke*. Vol. XXIV: *Dichtung und Wahrheit*. Stuttgart und Berlin: J. G. Cotta'sche Buchhandlung Nachfolger, n.d.

————. *Faust*. Translated by Bayard Taylor. Boston and New York: Houghton Mifflin Company, 1870.

Goldsmith, Margaret. *Franz Anton Mesmer*. New York: Doubleday Doran, 1934.

Guerard, Albert J. "Concepts of the Double." In *Stories of the Double*, pp. 1-14. Edited by Albert J. Guerard. Philadelphia and New York: J. B. Lippincott Company, 1967.

————. *Conrad the Novelist*. Cambridge, Mass.: Harvard University Press, 1958.

Harris, J. Rendel. *Boanerges*. Cambridge: Cambridge University Press, 1913.

Hartland, E. Sidney. "Twins." In *Encyclopaedia of Religion and Ethics* XII (1924), 491-500. Edited by James Hastings. Edinburgh: T. & T. Clark, 1911-58.

Hawthorne, Nathaniel. "The Prophetic Pictures." In *The Complete Short Stories of Nathaniel Hawthorne*, pp. 90-98. Garden City, N.Y.: Doubleday and Company, 1959.

————. *The Scarlet Letter*. Boston and New York: Houghton Mifflin Company, 1883.

Heidel, Alexander, ed. and trans. *The Gilgamesh Epic and Old Testament Parallels*. Chicago: University of Chicago Press, 1946.

Heine, Heinrich. *"Still ist die Nacht." Sämtliche Werke* I, 126. Herausgegeben von Otto F. Lachmann. Leipzig: Philipp Reclam jun., 1887.

Hesse, Hermann. *Demian*. Translator's name not given. New York: Boni and Liveright, Inc., 1923.

————. *"Die Morgenlandfahrt."* In *Gesammelte Schriften* VI, 9-76. Berlin und Frankfurt: Suhrkamp Verlag, 1957.

————. *Steppenwolf*. Translated by Basil Creighton. New York: Henry Holt and Company, 1929.

Hoffmann, E. T. A. *The Devil's Elixirs*. Translated by Ronald Taylor. London: John Calder, 1963.

Hoffmann, E. T. A. *"Die Geschichte vom Verlornen Spiegelbilde." Dichtungen und Schriften* VI, 27-48. Weimar: bei Erich Lichtenstein, 1924.

Hogg, James. *The Private Memoirs and Confessions of a Justified Sinner.* With an introduction by André Gide. London: The Cresset Press, 1947 [First published 1824.]

Holmes, Oliver Wendell. *Elsie Venner.* Cambridge, Mass.: The Riverside Press, 1891.

Howe, Irving. "Dostoevsky: *The Politics of Salvation.*" In *Politics and the Novel,* pp. 51-75. New York: Horizon Press, 1957.

Hugo, Victor, *Les Misérables. The Writings of Victor Hugo* (volumes unnumbered). Translator's name not given. New York: Henry W. Knight, International Edition, n.d.

James, Henry. "The Jolly Corner." In *The Ghostly Tales of Henry James,* pp. 720-62. Edited by Leon Edel. New Brunswick, N.J.: Rutgers University Press, 1948.

_____. *The Sense of the Past.* New York: Charles Scribner's Sons, 1917.

James, Montagu Rhodes, ed. and trans. *The Apocryphal New Testament.* Oxford: Oxford University Press, 1924.

Jobes, Gertrude. *Dictionary of Mythology, Folklore, and Symbols.* New York: The Scarecrow Press, 1961.

Jung, Carl Gustav. *Aion: Researches into the Phenomenology of the Self.* Translated by R. F. C. Hull. Bollingen Series XX, Vol. IX, Part II. New York: Pantheon Books, 1959.

_____. *The Archetypes and the Collective Unconscious.* Translated by R.F.C. Hull. Bollingen Series XX, Vol. IX, Part I. New York: Pantheon Books, 1959.

_____. *The Development of Personality.* Translated by R. F. C. Hull. Bollingen Series XX, Vol. XVII. New York: Pantheon Books, 1954.

_____. *The Integration of the Personality.* Translated by Stanley Dell. New York and Toronto: Farrar and Rinehart, 1939.

_____. *Psychology and Alchemy.* Tranlated by R. F. C. Hull. Bollingen Series XX, Vol. XII. New York: Pantheon Books, 1953.

_____. *The Spirit Mercury.* Translated by Gladys Phelan and Hildegard Nagel. New York: The Analytical Psychology Club of New York Incorporated, 1953.

_____. "Synchronicity: an Acausal Connecting Principle.'" In *The Structure and Dynamics of the Psyche,* pp. 417-531. Translated by R. F. C. Hull. Bollingen Series XX, Vol. VIII. New York: Pantheon Books, 1960.

_____. *Two Essays on Analytical Psychology.* Translated by R. F. C. Hull. Bollingen Series XX, Vol. VII. New York: Pantheon Books, 1953.

Karl, Frederick R. *A Reader's Guide to Joseph Conrad.* New York: The Noonday Press, 1960.

Kipling, Rudyard. "The Brushwood Boy." In *The Day's Work,* pp. 385-431. New York: Doubleday, Page and Company, 1925.

Kohlberg, Lawrence. "Psychological Analysis and Literary Form: A Study of the Doubles in Dostoevsky." *Daedalus* 92 (Spring 1963), 345-62.

Krauss, Wilhelmine. *Das Doppelgängermotiv in der Romantik.* Studien zum Romantischen Idealismus. Germanische Studien, Heft 99. Berlin: Verlag von Emil Ebering, 1930.

Langdon, S. "The Epic of Gilgamish." *The Museum Journal* 8 (January 1917), 35-36.

Lewis, C. S. *The Great Divorce.* New York: The Macmillan Company, 1957.

Longfellow, Henry Wadsworth. "The Sicilian's Tale." In *Tales of a Wayside Inn,* pp. 55-68. Boston: Ticknor and Fields, 1863.

Lucka, Emil. "*Verdoppelungen des Ich.*" *Preussische Jahrbücher* 115 (Januar bis März 1904), 54-83.

Malamud, Bernard. "The Last Mohican." In *The Magic Barrel,* pp. 155-82. New York: Farrar, Straus, & Cudahy, 1950.

Mann, Thomas. "The Blood of the Walsungs." In *Stories of Three Decades,* pp. 297-317. Translated by H. T. Lowe-Porter. New York: Alfred A. Knopf, 1945.

_____. *Der Tod in Venedig.* Berlin: S. Fischer, 1922.

Marillier, H. C. *Dante Gabriel Rossetti.* London: Geo. Bell and Sons, 1904.

Maupassant, Guy de. "The Horla." In *The Life Work of Henri René Guy de Maupassant* II, 1-35. Translator's name not given. New York and London: M. Walter Dunne, 1903.

Melville, Herman. *The Works of Herman Melville.* Standard Edition. Vol. IX: *Pierre, or the Ambiguities.* Vol. X: *The Piazza Tales.* Vol. XIII: *Billy Budd and Other Pieces.* London, etc.: Constable and Company Ltd, 1923 (Vols. IX and X), 1924 (Vol. XIII).

Métraux, Alfred. "Twin Heroes in South American Mythology." *Journal of American Folklore* 59 (April-June 1946), 114-23.

Mochulsky, Konstantin. *Dostoevsky.* Translated by Michael A. Minihan. Princeton, N.J.: Princeton University Press, 1967.

Moldenhauer, Joseph J. "Poe's Aesthetics, Psychology, and Moral Vision," *PMLA* 83, No. 2 (May 1968), 284-97.

Morris, William. "The Lady of the Land." In *The Earthly Paradise,* Vol. I, Part II, pp. 164-84. New York: Longmans Green, 1900.

Myoshi, Masao. *The Divided Self.* New York: New York University Press; London: University of London Press Limited; 1969.

Pausanias. *Description of Greece.* Translated by W. H. S. Jones. Loeb Classical Library, Volume IV. Cambridge, Mass.: Harvard University Press; London: Wm. Heinemann Ltd., 1935.

Plato. "The Symposium." In *The Dialogues of Plato,* III, 273-358. Translated by B. Jowett. New York: Bigelow, Brown & Company, Inc., n.d.

Poe, Edgar Allan. *The Complete Works of Edgar Allan Poe.* New York: Plymouth Publishing Company, n.d.

Porter, Katherine Anne. "Noon Wine." In *Pale Horse, Pale Rider,* pp. 93-176. New York: Harcourt, Brace & Company, 1932.

Priestley, J. B. *The Plays of J. B. Priestley.* London: Wm. Heinemann Ltd., 1948.

Prince, Morton. *The Dissociation of a Personality.* New York: Longmans Green and Company, 1905.

Pritchard, James B., ed. *Ancient Near Eastern Texts.* Translated by John A. Wilson, E. A. Speiser, et al. Princeton, N. J.: Princeton University Press, 1950.

Quinn, Patrick F. *The French Face of Edgar Poe.* Carbondale, Ill.: Southern Illinois University Press, 1957.

Rahv, Philip. "Dostoevsky in 'Crime and Punishment,' " *Partisan Review* 27 (Summer 1960), 393-425.

Raimund, Ferdinand. *"Der Verschwender." Sämtliche Werke* II, 335-460. Herausgegeben von Fritz Bruckner und Eduard Castle. Wien: Verlag von Anton Schroll & Co., n.d.

Rank, Otto. *Der Doppelgänger: Psychoanalytische Studie.* Leipzig, Wien, und Zürich: Internationaler Psychoanalytischer Verlag, 1925. First published as *"Der Doppelgänger,"* in *Psychoanalytische Beiträge zur Mythenforschung.* Leipzig und Wien: Internationaler Psychoanalytischer Verlag, 1919, pp. 267-354.

————. "The Double as Immortal Self." In *Beyond Psychology,* pp. 62-101. New York: Dover Publications, Inc., 1958.

Reber, Natalie. *Studien zum Motiv des Doppelgängers bei Dostoevsky und E. T. A. Hoffmann.* Marburger Abhandlungen zur Geschichte und Kultur Osteuropas. Band 6. Giessen: Kommissionsverlag Wilhelm Schmitz, 1964.

Reichard, Gladys A. *Navaho Religion.* Bollingen Series XVIII, Vol. II. New York: Pantheon Books, 1950.

Richter, Jean Paul. *"Siebenkäs."* In *Werke,* II, 7-565. Herausgegeben von Gustav Lohmann. München: Carl Hanser Verlag, 1959.

Rogers, Robert. *The Double in Literature.* Detroit: Wayne State University Press, 1970.

Rosenfield, Claire. "The Shadow Within: the Conscious and Unconscious Use of the Double," *Daedalus* 92 (Spring 1963), 326-44.

Santos Otero, Aurelio de. *Los Evangelios Apocrifos.* Madrid: Biblioteca de Autores Cristianos, 1926.

Schmidtbonn, Wilhelm. *Der Doppelgänger.* Berlin: Deutsche Buch-Gemeinschaft, 1928.

Schopenhauer, Arthur. *Die Welt als Wille und Vorstellung.* Vol. I. Leipzig: Philipp Reclam jun., n.d.

Shelley, Percy Bysshe. "Epipsychidion." In *The Complete Poetical Works of Percy Bysshe Shelley,* pp. 405-19. Edited by Thomas Hutchinson. London: Oxford University Press, 1927.

Sitwell, Osbert. *The Man Who Lost Himself.* New York: Coward-McCann, Inc., 1930.

Smith, Nowell. "Coleridge and His Critics," *Fortnightly Review* 64 (July 1895), 340-54.

Stevenson, Robert Louis. *The Works of Robert Louis Stevenson.* Edited by Charles Curtis Bigelow and Temple Scott. In Vol. III, "Markheim," pp. 359-78. In Vol. V, "The Strange Case of Dr. Jekyll and Mr. Hyde," pp. 229-307. New York: The Davos Press, 1906.

Strindberg, August. *The Road to Damascus.* Translated by Graham Rawson, with Introduction by Gunnar Ollén. London: Jonathan Cape, Ltd., 1939.

Thoreau, Henry David. *The Writings of Henry David Thoreau.* Vol. II: *Walden.* Boston: Houghton Mifflin Company, 1893.

Tymms, Ralph. *Doubles in Literary Psychology.* Cambridge: Bowes and Bowes, 1949.

————. *German Romantic Literature.* London: Methuen and Company Ltd., 1955.

Vivas, Eliseo. "The Two Dimensions of Reality in *The Brothers Karamazov.*" In *Dostoevsky: a Collection of Critical Essays,* pp. 71-89. Edited by René Wellek. Englewood Cliffs, N.J.: Prentice-Hall, 1962.

Wain, Marianne. "The Double in Romantic Narrative: a Preliminary Study," *The Germanic Review* 36, No. 4 (December 1961), 258-68.

Wharton, Edith. "The Triumph of Night." In *Xingu and Other Stories,* pp. 241-80. New York: Charles Scribner's Sons, 1916.

Wilde, Oscar. "The Picture of Dorian Gray." In *The Complete Works of Oscar Wilde,* II, 1-272. Edited by Robert Ross. New York: Bigelow, Brown & Company, Inc., 1905.

Wimsatt, W. K., Jr., and Beardsley, M. C. "The Intentional Fallacy," *Sewanee Review* 59 (1946), 468-88.

Wu Ch'eng-en. *Monkey.* Translated by Arthur Waley. London: G. Allen and Unwin, Ltd., 1942.

Zabel, Morton Dauwen. Introduction to Joseph Conrad's *Lord Jim,* pp. v-xxxvii. Boston: Houghton Mifflin Company, 1958.

Zimmer, Heinrich. *Philosophies of India.* Edited by Joseph Campbell. Bollingen Series XXVI. New York: Pantheon Books, 1951.

Index

For foreign works of which no satisfactory translation
has been found, titles are given first in English
(as in the text) and then in their original form.